"There is a deep longing ....
things which Jesus promised. Len Wilson goes beyond cut-and-paste marketing methods and inspirational nuggets to provide a solid, soul stirring foundation for Christian innovation. *Greater Things* will embolden you to begin a redemptive revolution of innovation to meet the spiritual and social needs of your community."

—**REV. BLOSSOM MATTHEWS**, Pastor, Assistant Director of Congregational Vitality for the New Mexico Conference, United Methodist Church

"Sometimes a book comes along and it is clearly the book for this moment. *Greater Things* is just that book for Christian leaders today. Len Wilson, a trusted innovator and an accomplished practitioner, takes us on a journey to better understand where we are at and where the Spirit is leading. If you have felt stuck in ministry or are looking for ways to use your creativity for God's Kingdom, this is the book for you!"

—**REV. JACOB ARMSTRONG**, Pastor, Providence Church, Mt. Juliet, TN

"*Greater Things* gets to the heart of innovation from a deep, holistic biblical perspective. This is really great, theological writing. Truly a much needed reading for connecting to God's next!"

—**REV. MICHAEL SLAUGHTER**, Pastor Emeritus, Ginghamsburg Church, Founder and Chief Strategist, Passionate Churches, LLC

"Every now and then a book shoots across the sky like a bolt of lightning, cleansing the air, clarifying the subject matter, silhouetting the challenges, and lighting up the horizon for new vistas and ventures. Len Wilson's *Greater Things* is that rare, out-of-the-blue bombshell of a book that will electrify anyone concerned about innovation, creativity, and imagination in the church."

—**DR. LEONARD SWEET**, Best-selling author of over 60 books, distinguished visiting professor at five colleges and universities, and founder/president of SpiritVenture Ministries, PreachTheStory.com, and The Salish Sea Press

"In this groundbreaking new book, Len Wilson - author, innovator, entrepreneur, and follower of Jesus - takes the reader on a much-needed journey exploring Christian innovation in the church. If there has ever been a need for church leaders to think creatively and with imagination, that moment and the opportunity is now. Len helps the reader see that innovation and tradition are not at odds, but that innovation actually builds on tradition. This trailblazing book explores the promise of Jesus that if we believe in Him, we will do even greater works than he did. I highly recommend this challenging and thought-provoking book!"

—JOEL MIKELL, Consultant, Author, Senior Vice President, Horizons Stewardship

"Len Wilson's *Greater Things* offers a compelling vision and theology for Christ-centered innovation. In a sea of disruptive and evolutionary theories, Len offers a faithful perspective that embeds God's creative and redemptive character at the center of innovative work. This book is an excellent read for any Christian leader who desires to see God's kingdom on Earth as it is in heaven."

—DR. ANDY MILLER, Vice President, Innovation and Partnerships, Indiana Wesleyan University.

"This is the best book on Christian innovation I've ever read. For too long the Western church has blindly embraced the ideology of progress as our core narrative. Through faithful and penetrating Scriptural engagement, Len replaces the common adoption of 'creative destruction' with a proper theology of 'new creation.' This is not simply a book; it is a hitchhiker's guide to the future for church teams desiring to explore Christian innovation."

—REV. DR. MICHAEL ADAM BECK, Author, pastor, professor, and cultivator of movements, Director of the Fresh Expressions House of Studies at United Theological Seminary, Director of Re-missioning Fresh Expressions US, and Cultivator of Fresh Expressions for the Florida UMC

"In *Greater Things*, Len shares so much wisdom on Christian innovation and what it truly means for Christians to be the work of the new creation. Len's passion and creativity is so evident on every page, it's motivating me to continue to think outside the box, take risks, and bring my ideas into community like never before. Let's make 2021 and beyond a new era of Christian innovation and growth. Reading this is the perfect place to start."

—**REV. ADAM WEBER**, Lead Pastor, Embrace Church, author, *Love Has A Name*

"This book will give you life and inspiration for the future! Len provides not only the crucial theory, but also the tangible and practical methodology for how to innovate in your context with your people. His cultural commentary is rooted in sound biblical exegesis, and his methods are anchored in Christian history and tradition. If you want to know how to be better, how to dream better, and how to innovate more faithfully to the calling of God upon your life, then this book is a must-read (and must-own, and must-share)."

—**DR. DAVID MCDONALD**, *Founder, Fossores Chapter House and Pastor, Westwinds Church*

"For some Christians, the notion of innovation can bring anxiety, especially when compared with an 'old time religion' that feels so comfortable. We need a guide with a love for the Church and experience in Spirit-led innovation. Fortunately, Dr. Len Wilson is this person. In *Greater Things*, this pastor, entrepreneur, creative, and innovator provides a map to guide the Church in adaptation and innovation which are critical for the future. As a professor I can confidently state this book will become required reading in our degree program."

—**DR. RICK BARTLETT**, Program Director, Ministry Entrepreneurship and Innovation, Tabor College

"*Greater Things* is a riveting, thoughtful, educational, inspiring goldmine for innovational creativity. With stories from history, well-grounded and illuminating scriptural exegesis plus practical handholds for application, this new resource is loaded with everything to take your God possibilities to a whole new level. Highly recommended!"

—**REV. SUE NILSON KIBBEY**, Director, Bishop Bruce Ough Innovation Center, United Theological Seminary

"Len Wilson literally wrote the book on creativity. Now he takes on an even weightier subject: innovation. Writing with clarity and purpose about the church's clarity and purpose, Wilson ranges from Rauschenbush to Vos and from Willow Creek to Twitter. Along the way he offers this trenchant observation that I can't stop mulling over: 'Eventually, the influence of all innovations atrophy.' Oh, I don't want that to be true but I know it is. Dig in to Len Wilson's latest to feed your soul and stir your mind."

—**REV. TALBOT DAVIS**, pastor of Good Shepherd Church in Charlotte, NC, and author of six books with Abingdon Press

Also By Len Wilson

Think Like a 5-Year-Old: Reclaim Your Wonder and Create Great Things

*Taking Flight with Creativity: Worship Design Teams That Work
(with Jason Moore)*

The Wired Church 2.0 (with Jason Moore)

Design Matters: Create Powerful Imagery for Worship (with Jason Moore)

*Fresh out of the Box: Digital Worship Experiences, Volumes 1-4
(with Lumicon)*

*Digital Storytellers: The Art of Communicating the Gospel in Worship
(with Jason Moore)*

The Wired Church: Making Media Ministry

GREATER
THINGS

GREATER THINGS

The Work of the New Creation

LEN WILSON

invite
PRESS

Plano, Texas

He who was seated on the throne said, "I am making all things new." Then he said, "Write this down, for these words are trustworthy and true."
—Revelation 21:5

Contents

Introduction

How Do We Get Through the Current Cultural Crisis?

The coronavirus pandemic has served as symbol and catalyst for a long-developing sense of existentialist angst about the end of the world. If the world is truly ending, then all is moot. But we would be wise to explore the alternative: instead of the end of the world, perhaps we are merely living through the birth of a new era. The only way through our apocalyptic fervor is new thinking and innovative solutions to the major problems of our time. But not just any innovation will do. We need Christian innovation. As Christians, Jesus calls us to the work of God's New Creation with the seemingly absurd promise that we can do even greater things than he. This book is an exploration of the implications of this promise.

The Day the World Froze

Perhaps you remember what you were doing when the world froze on Friday the thirteenth of March 2020. The pandemic had begun months prior. Rumblings of personal impact had been brewing in local and national media for weeks, and then—suddenly—we were at home, "sheltering in place." Seemingly overnight, 87 percent of Americans quit traveling and 92 percent stopped gathering in public spaces.[1]

The social and economic impact was immediate. Public life shut down; unemployment shot up. Century-old businesses collapsed, and new ones sprang up.[2] An NBA player got sick and live sports abruptly ceased. The Olympics were postponed. Students were sent home from school with laptops. Live gatherings of people for worship stopped. Everyone learned how to video conference.

The 2020 triple whammy of the pandemic, economic recession, and racial reckoning will be remembered and studied beyond our lifetimes, as a year later, the consequences continue to ripple out in every sector of global culture. We are witnessing disruption to long-stable sectors of society such as business, government, education, and religion,[3] in some cases for the first time in generations.[4] In the United States, problems unleashed by this "big three" loom as large as those the country faced during a prior historic triple whammy—the Great Depression, the Dust Bowl, and World War II—in the 1930s and early 1940s.

Despite the very real struggles we face, the news is not all grim. For those who dare to think creatively, times like these are a rush of opportunity. Across the board, sectors of society engaged in innovative thinking and alternative solutions during the initial wake of the shut down in April and May of 2020:

–   Teachers created new curricula for students to engage in eLearning while teaching other students in person, and some wondered whether standardized testing might finally be on the outs.[5]

–   Car manufacturers converted factories into ventilator assemblies to keep COVID-19 patients alive.[6] Longtime retailers such as Brooks Brothers repurposed their factories from producing luxury men's suits to frontline health workers' equipment,[7] although this didn't prevent Brooks Brothers from filing for bankruptcy.[8]

–   Retail stores fully embraced digital point-of-sale systems, invented new supply chains, and installed solutions to increase sanitation and protect workers.

–   Epidemiologists began researching how to use cell phones to help track the spread of the coronavirus.[9]

–   The film industry overhauled its theatrical release model by partnering with digital streaming providers to focus on immediate release.[10]

–   One city changed its bus service from cheap to free to help low-income residents.[11]

–   Symphonies began mixing instruments as they would in a studio to perform virtual concerts.[12]

Sometimes, the innovation didn't go well. One doctor got magnets stuck in his nose while trying to invent a way to keep us from touching our faces.[13] But despite the occasional misstep, real creative change began to happen—the kind of change that, post–coronavirus, may light up the next twenty to forty years the way new technologies in the 1930s and 1940s drove economic and cultural resurgence in the 1950s and 1960s.

Of course, none of us could have predicted this at the end of 2019. The events of 2020 may be cumulatively, to use the phrase coined by cultural theorist Nassim Nicholas Taleb, the biggest "black swan" disruptor to our culture since the end of World War II.[14] It is tempting to attach cosmic significance to the events of the year, as some rushed to do in the wake of the initial shutdown. While some claim these changes are era-defining, this remains to be seen and will not be understood for years. Are changes happening right now confined to the specific problems they address? Will we solve coronavirus and go back to the way things were in 2019? Or have we left the past behind, and are we now crossing a liminal Rubicon to a new, unknown future?

Are we witnessing a cultural revolution?

Hook Me Up a New Revolution

It may be difficult to assess the magnitude of a moment as it happens. Some consider the pandemic a problem to be solved, after which we will return to "normal" life. Yet societies have weathered other, similarly lethal, pandemics with much less hoopla, which suggests that the pandemic zeitgeist is a signifier of larger cultural trends.

A common response has been to describe the events of 2020 in apocalyptic terms. Indeed, a defining theme of the millennial generation has been the imminent demise of Western civilization. The public polling firm Rasmussen has monitored weekly the question of whether America is "headed in the right direction" since 2009. In no single week of ten years of polling have a majority of Americans answered this question in the affirmative.[15] Before the 2016 presidential election, *New York Times* columnist David Brooks commented that pessimism was "just en vogue."[16] While "Obama ran on a traditional message that America is progressing,"[17] by electing Trump, American voters seemed to repudiate "progress," or at least Obama's vision of it. The threat of climate change, the rise in global population, ongoing frustrations about equality, and other seemingly intractable problems have stymied Western society. One commenter noted that the data on the state of our culture is grim, with "two diverging trend lines: one upward-sloping, for people, and one sloping downward, for everything else."[18]

Philosophical narratives have likewise provided few signs of optimism. While the Enlightenment offered a positive framework for the world based on values of science, reason, humanism, and progress, the controlling theme of postmodernism has been deconstruction and the dismantling of shared stories and belief systems. For a while, belief in science remained a shared Western cultural narrative, but now this, too, has come under attack. As a result, the public today finds it hard to believe in anything.

Nihilism and even anti natalism have emerged. A *New York Times* editorial suggested that human extinction might not be such a bad thing.[19] A curator at New York's Metropolitan Museum of Art suggested that the "human species is hurtling toward extinction," and the best we can do at this point is "design an elegant ending."[20] A movement called "Birthstrike" advocated that women not have children because of the dangers of climate change.[21] Others suggested that, not only is it preferable not to bring new humans into the world, but it is also better not even to be alive.[22] Such death wishes may seem like ravings, yet they came from United States congressional representatives.[23] When American politicians trade championing great societies to inferring the end of society within a half-century, it would seem we have removed the proverbial finger from the dike keeping culture from existential collapse.

Given the mood of the century, 2020 is a Hollywood sequel: same story, more explosions. We have a unique stagnation today of material problems and philosophical dead ends. The events of 2020 are best understood in the context of a larger cultural spirit of existential angst that has been growing for the last generation. The state of culture during the entire twenty-first century has seemed a harbinger of the apocalypse. If the world is truly ending, then all is moot. But we would be wise to explore the alternative: instead of the end of the world, perhaps we are living through the birth of a new era.

> Instead of the end of the world, perhaps we are living through the birth of a new era.

Eras have mile markers, but the events that lead to them come over time. The guns of August that started World War I were a defining moment of the twentieth century. Yet the cultural developments that led to it went off like a series of underground bombs. For example, Virginia Woolf wrote, "on or around December 1910, human character changed."[24] In her observation, there was nothing particularly spectacular about that month, just the shifting ice floes and drifts of new thinking, which had gradually taken over old, frozen foundations, subsuming habits like a rising ice tide. New thinking was on the move, overtaking the romanticism of late modern life. We reached the "tipping point," as journalist Malcolm Gladwell says, which launched the start of the modern age.[25] Soon the world was at war.

Circumstances build to obvious moments that propel us forward into new eras. In one of the famous books of the twentieth century, *The Structure of Scientific Revolutions*, philosopher of science Thomas Kuhn claimed that epochal change doesn't happen in small, incremental doses; it comes as a result of significant crises that force us to acknowledge the inadequacies of old theories and to go about the work of forming new theories. Such work is painful and disorienting and not something we enter willingly. It happens only due to circumstances that are forced upon us. As I write in August of 2020, social media memes joke about the "2020 Bingo Card." While the pandemic, racial turmoil, and economic recession take up three large squares, all sorts of other anomalies, from killer hornets to alien spaceship sightings, add unusual color to the board. Some call it a *revolution*, suggesting that old ways are gone, and the new have come.

The word *revolution*, however, is clichéd. For the past fifty years, advertising executives have used the rhetoric of revolution to sell everything from automobiles to laundry detergent, and, in the process, have melted down the idea. As the Foo Fighters sing, "Hook me up a new revolution, / 'cause this one is a lie."[26]

In its proper usage, revolution is specific. Kuhn defines the term as "non-cumulative developmental episodes in which an older paradigm is replaced in whole or in part by an incompatible new one."[27] It may also include significant political or economic change. It is often violent. Like the boy who cried wolf, our culture is finally experiencing a true revolutionary moment, but after generations of linguistic poaching in service to the acquisition of goods, we may be missing the rollout.

To consider the coronavirus as a revolutionary moment does not mean that there is no connection between the old and the new, as some innovation scholars suggest.[28] If anything, crises such as the coronavirus are accelerators for emerging cultural trends that leap forward in importance as the value of existing structures fade.

In this moment of significant cultural change, it is critical to observe culture through a spirit of innovation. Those who are already considering or implementing new ideas benefit from crises, while those traditionally resistant to new ideas find themselves at even greater odds with change.

Many continue to act as though we can just wait for a vaccine and return to life as normal, but there is no going back. Incompatibility is a key term in Kuhn's definition of revolution. The game changes, to use the idiom. Various sectors are realizing this shift. For example, the rise of video conferencing is predicted to have a permanent impact on the airline industry, as the painful but necessary corporate $1,400 next-day airfare ticket will not return.[29]

The coronavirus is a massive sign that both symbolizes and shapes the meaning of the moment. The world froze in 2020, and it is impossible to go back in time and space. The longer the pandemic stretched on, the more evident this became. The beginning of the third decade of the twenty-first century is a time of intense cultural change.

You don't often see the damage from a freeze as soon as it happens. It is only later, when things thaw out again, that cracks become visible. As the events of 2020 thaw, we will together survey the damage it did to our comfortable, late modern existence. Return will be impossible. We are crossing an ice floe. The ground on which we once stood is shattered, and we must step over into a new world. The alternative is to float away on an old, broken piece of ice. The freeze and thaw have created a crack in our foundation, which we must cross—a Rubicon from which there is no turning back.

> The ground on which we once stood is shattered, and we must step over into a new world.

In other words, every new beginning comes from some other beginning's end. The future is beginning now. We have work to do. Is it possible to ride the trajectory of culture?

Going on a Bear Hunt

When my children were little, one of our favorite bedtime stories was *We're Going on a Bear Hunt*. The book's cover shows a babysitter and three kids crossing the frame, leaning into an unseen future, seeking new adventures.[30] At each turn in the story, the group faces challenges, which grow increasingly difficult: tall grass, raging river, deep mud, dark forest, and blinding snowstorm. At each obstacle, their onward journey thwarted, they face the question: How do we proceed?

With each challenge, the group responds (and this is where my kids and I would shout for joy while reading at bedtime):

We can't go under it!

We can't go over it!

We've got to go through it!

Childlike enthusiasm for what comes next is key to how to respond to periods of significant cultural change such as the one we are experiencing. It is a joyful shout for adventure; let's go through it![31]

To change the trajectory of our stagnant culture, we need new thinking and constructive solutions. In the next several years, we will see a significant shift in our culture from a focus on the inner life (self-help and passion pursuit) to outer life (social help and public policy). We will experience rejuvenated civic energy. The time to tear down is done; now it is time to rebuild.

There is a time for everything,
    and a season for every activity under the heavens:
    ....
a time to tear down and a time to build. (Eccl 3:1,3)

As with the children's story, emerging fresh and excited from the roadblocks—in our lives, in our culture, and in the church—requires that we forge new paths, which suggests we need innovation. Through his gift of salvation and resurrection life, Jesus makes all things new. With his inspiration, we too can experience newness not only inwardly but in ways that change the way we look at life, our options, and our future. Following Jesus doesn't lead to just innovation but something more specific: *Christian* innovation.

Yet Christians do not have a sterling reputation in contemporary culture for new ideas, noteworthy solutions, and needle-moving systems. Instead, we are known for denial and resistance. Some of us pretend technology and culture are static and immutable and act as if vision is unnecessary. Others of us stick our heads in the sand. Some tend to be controlling, wanting to use new instruments and ideas to achieve theocratic visions of the future. Others rush into cultural change, blindly syncretizing every new idea. Still others of us attempt to remove ourselves from culture altogether, becoming ascetic, monastically waiting on a faraway hill.

Despite these stances, in various cultures and settings for the last two thousand years, real change that creates flourishing societies has often come through the work of Christians. Over and over, followers of Jesus have demonstrated a supernatural ability to build culture and create opportunities for human flourishing. This book will tell several stories of such flourishing. There is something about being a follower of Jesus that has empowered some groups of people to enact significant, positive social change and cultural transformation. What the world needs today is not just new ideas but Christian innovators. Christian innovation is what happens when Christ's people leverage their creative gifts and allow themselves to be used by the Holy Spirit through the work of Christ's community for the inauguration of God's future.

Jesus has a simple name for such work: *greater things*.

Greater Things

A few days before his crucifixion, Jesus gave a last lesson to his core group of disciples. During that session, he said something remarkable, as recorded in John's Gospel:

> Don't you believe that I am in the Father, and that the Father is in me? The words I say to you I do not speak on my own author-

ity. Rather, it is the Father, living in me, who is doing his work. Believe me when I say that I am in the Father and the Father is in me; or at least believe on the evidence of the works themselves. Very truly I tell you, whoever believes in me will do the works I have been doing, and they will do even greater things than these, because I am going to the Father. (John 14:10-12)

Jesus promised his disciples that they would somehow have the ability to do even greater things than he. How can this be? Jesus healed people, raised the dead, tore down the temple, and came back from the dead. Can we do more than this? The promise seems absurd, and yet Jesus said it.

> Jesus promised his disciples that they would somehow have the ability to do even greater things than he. The promise seems absurd, and yet Jesus said it.

Such a promise presupposes that we have amazing potential in us. In my book, *Think Like a 5 Year Old*, I explore a theology of creativity: each of us, having been made in the image of our Creator God, has in us a creative genius, which is obvious and clear to anyone who hangs out with a five-year-old. Tragically, as we age, this creative energy becomes marred by our sin and lost to our sight. Whereas God designed humans to create and care for one another and for the earth, we often lose our perspective on how to do this. Instead, we cast our eyes downward toward dynamics of approval, power, and control. In Christ, our eyes are bathed clean and our vision is restored. With our eyes opened, our ability to create and to care becomes visible to us.

> "If your eyes are healthy, your whole body will be full of light. But if your eyes are unhealthy, your whole body will be full of darkness." (Matt 6:22-23)

What happens after this transformation? There are two, intertwined "next acts" for a human life that has rediscovered its innate creativity: one inner, one outer. The inner act reveals how we are made more whole through a creative, collaborative relationship with

God. The outer act is about the results of this spirit "skunkworks"[32]: Christian innovation, or the in-breaking of God's New Creation over the declining, decaying spirit of the world. This book is about the latter, which is tied to the former. As we create, we are re-created.

This book is an exploration of the implications of Jesus' promise that we can do greater things. Its goal is to define and make simple the idea and process of Christian innovation. I hope to offer a means by which anyone can create positive change. Throughout the book, you will find stories of innovation and innovators in medicine, business, the church, and more. As you may or may not know, if you work in the world of the church, you already have innovation superpowers, in both the uplifting and the weary connotations of the word. The church is both an environment of superhuman strength and herculean problems. If you can innovate in church, you can probably innovate anywhere.[33] These stories are designed not to elevate innovation as a lofty ideal but to lower it to the place of accessible process. My big dream for this book is that it will help equip Christians to move to the forefront of positive social change. Thus, this is both a big-idea book and a how-to book.

This book has two parts. Part 1 is an exploration of Christian innovation, its value, and definition; and part 2 is a practical application for making Christian innovation work. Much of the secular literature on innovation emphasizes discontinuity, or the newness of the work, which contrasts with what has come before and presupposes an improvement on the past. When we as believers talk about the New Creation, we get wrapped up in an ideology of progress, as I outline in chapter 1. As chapters 2–4 describe, this ideology is problematic. In the church, we have adopted the tacit belief that we are the ones building the kingdom. But our work does not bring about the kingdom. Instead, as I outline in chapter 5, the kingdom is an entirely new and qualitatively different creation we receive from God by grace alone. But the insufficiency of our effort does not negate our need to work in the New Creation. In chapter 6, I outline a new definition of Christian innovation as something separate from the ingrained mantra of "new and improved."

Part 2 offers a practical model for Christian innovation. Like any university course, Christian innovation needs prerequisites. Christian innovation favors passion over pleasure, which I address in chapter 7; vision over maintenance (chap 8); risk over safety (chap 9); creativity over criticism (chap 10); and community over isolation (chap 11). Without these conditions, innovation cannot occur. If a community (which means its leadership and culture) responds to problems with a bias for the status quo, it cannot innovate. If a church chooses to ignore technologies emerging outside its walls, that church cannot innovate. If a community of faith is overly concerned with maintaining a specific culture or set of customs, it cannot innovate. If a community is overly concerned with failure prevention, it cannot innovate. If any community is overly concerned with ensuring everything is perfect, it cannot innovate.

In chapter 12, I look at the life cycle of innovation and offer some suggestions about how to keep it moving forward. Of course, no human effort is perfect, which is why we rarely "change the world." But that doesn't mean we can't make significant contributions to positive change. The epilogue looks at the difference between our vision and reality.

If you are without faith in Christ, this book will still be helpful. There are processes, techniques, and tips here that you can apply. But the goal of this book is bigger: to provide you with a new way of looking at the world that will fundamentally reorient your activity forward, toward the work of the New Creation. If you miss Christian innovation, you miss the opportunity to do things above and beyond your imagination.

The time to tear down is done; now it is time to rebuild.

Let's get started.

Len Wilson
Frisco, TX
December 2020

PART ONE

What Is Christian Innovation?

The work of the New Creation depends on innovation. Both culture and church have been talking about innovation for decades; however, increasing evidence of the New Creation is debatable at best. That's because not just any innovation will do; we need something different: Christian innovation. Part 1 explores the concept of Christian innovation. I look at several stories of attempts to bring about the New Creation, including both positive aspects and problems in past approaches. I conclude with a proper theology of *new* and an understanding of our relationship to the Holy Spirit in any movement of flourishing and growth.

New and Improved

What Do We Mean by Innovation?

The first step on a journey to greater things is to understand what we mean by innovation. Innovation has four defining characteristics: it is an instrument; it is an invention; it is intuitive; it is influential. Each of these characteristics shares a common value: new. In American culture, though, new isn't just a method or a strategy; it is a belief system. We believe in an ideology of progress. We assume that with new comes improved. We have developed faith in innovation and technology as the means by which we inaugurate a better future.

erhaps no image symbolizes the rise of computer technology in American culture as well as Steven Spielberg's T-Rex in *Jurassic Park,* released in 1994. More than twenty-five years after its debut, our first glimpse of the hungry, angry dinosaur still feels realistic enough to make us fear for the kids stuck in the sport utility vehicle.

In the early 1990s—pre-*Jurassic Park* days—I was a graduate student at the Annenberg School of Communication, the University of Pennsylvania. While there, I had a job rendering digital tanks on Silicon Graphics machines for the U.S. Department of Defense. These graphics were no T-Rex; they were quite crude. No one at that time considered computer graphics an endeavor worthy of the emotional drama of a world-class feature film.

The rise of computer technology is exhibit number one for any study of innovation, and no example served better to demonstrate the advancements in computing than the big machine that sat idle down the hall from where I worked. As I toyed on Silicon Graphics machines, a dusty 10'x20' room housed one of the paeans of twentieth-century American innovation: the first modern computer.

Although it was a museum piece by the time I was a student, it was still impressive. Engineers John Mauchly and Presper Eckert started construction on it in June 1943. They called it the Electronic Numerical Integrator and Computer, or ENIAC. (Their creativity was in engineering, not branding.) It was operational in November 1945 and employed the processing power of a small alarm clock.[1]

In its original form, not everyone saw the need for a room-sized machine that could compute a fraction of the work of a single human. There's an apocryphal quotation attributed to IBM chairman Thomas J. Watson, who, on hearing of the ENIAC, declined the opportunity to invest, saying that there was a world market for maybe five computers.[2] Many people miss opportunities because they see what something is, not what it may become.

The ENIAC functioned for ten years. Mauchly and Eckert were not the only inventors of the computer though. Before the ENIAC, a *computer* was a person, usually a woman—à la butcher, baker, or candlestick maker—a data-entry employee who punched keys and cranked handles on desktop adding machines. As humans are prone to error and fatigue, many had seen the need for a more consistent and efficient way to compute mathematical equations. The first sketches for mechanizing mathematical operations date to 1820. But nothing stuck. What made Mauchly and Eckert's machine the original computer?

In his study of the history of computing, biographer Walter Isaacson suggests three defining reasons, which also serve as characteristics of innovation:

- Fully functioning and in constant use.
- Working for a long period of time. (The ENIAC worked for ten years.)
- The basis for subsequent innovations (aka the alpha dog).[3]

Our first step on a journey to greater things is to understand what we mean by innovation. Isaacson's example offers a good starting point. I'll expand it into four components.

A Definition of Innovation

Instrument

Innovation is, first, a working *instrument* that serves as an agent for "significant, positive change."[4] It is a solution to a problem. In his classic, *The Innovator's Dilemma*, Harvard business scholar Clayton Christensen defines innovation as a change in technology, with technology as the process by which organizations transform "capital, materials, and information into products and services of greater value."[5]

Christensen's word value is important here. A more common Christian synonym for value is worth. But innovation is not just a material change in technology in which "greater value" is nearly synonymous with more capital. It may also be understood as a new, working idea in service to social good. Ideas can be social, political, or even theological: new processes or forms of organizational management, new ways of social organization, or even new forms of meaning. For example, before Dr. Martin Luther King Jr. introduced nonviolent resistance, African Americans in the Jim Crow South had two options: violence or painful acquiescence. King modeled a third way, beginning with a specific action in response to a specific social problem: the Montgomery Bus Boycott of 1955.[6]

> Innovation is an instrument that solves a problem and leads to positive change through the introduction of greater value.

In either case, whether material or conceptual, innovation is, first, an instrument that solves a problem and leads to positive change through the introduction of greater value.

Invention

Whether material (like a physical product) or conceptual (like a service or a mobilized idea), to innovate is to activate new, creative solutions. This is our second definition of innovation: the instrument in question must be an *invention*.

King had a creative idea. This is where innovation begins. Education advocate Sir Ken Robinson says that creativity is the process of having original ideas with value.[7] My preferred definition for creativity is one offered by my youngest son at five years old: having fun and making stuff. As innovation precedes entrepreneurship, creativity precedes innovation.

Creativity is more than an instrument; creativity is an ontological reality. As people made in the image of a Creator God, we are made as creative beings. Innovation flows out of this universal human trait, but creativity and innovation are distinct: we all are creative, and some of us innovate. This is because creativity calls for context. Innovation is applied creativity that helps people. It is community-centered and outcomes-based.[8] We may celebrate creativity as its own intrinsic good while also recognizing that innovation is the work of turning creative ideas into solutions that work, help others, scale up, and influence subsequent thinking. Innovation is creativity that does something specific. It meets a need. As Steve Jobs supposedly said to his original Macintosh team after another delay, real artists ship.[9] Applied creativity that impacts the work and leisure of others for good becomes innovation.

Intuitive

Third, innovation is *intuitive*. It is often simple, shockingly ordinary, light on design, and more concerned with function than form, at least initially. It does a job; it just works. It is less concerned with reaching for greatness than with fixing the problem at hand. This is crucial. Greatness comes later. This one is hard for the visionary and the aesthete. We want the working solution to be as fully formed as the initial vision in our mind, but our perfectionist tendency only slows us down. Working beats perfect every time. The goal isn't perfection or even changing the world. That is what the 2.0 version is for.

Influential

Last, innovation is *influential*. Isaacson notes that, of his three definitions for innovation, the basis for subsequent innovation is the distinguishing factor.[10] We celebrate the story of Walt Disney, not just because he made a neat theme park and some great cartoon characters, but because his vision has been the basis for cartoon characters and theme parks to come. Innovations are trendsetters. Your idea doesn't have to affect an entire industry, but it can't be a one-off. It has to be something on which others build. In other words, while creativity is an essential part of life, sometimes we need more than just a good idea. We need an idea that delivers new ways of thinking and acting.

Thus, innovation is specific, not mystical or even necessarily grand. Whether material or immaterial, all innovations begin as ideas, and there's a life cycle to them. As ideas lead to innovations, they build and combine with other ideas, and this web of activity creates positive change in culture over time. Culture may be understood as the layering of innovations, material and immaterial, leveraged by a group of people in shared time and space. The computing industry, which originated in East Coast labs and migrated to northern California, is perhaps the most prominent example of innovation in culture today and is a fitting place for Isaacson's exploration of innovation. Some even claim it is the only true example of sustained innovation in American culture today.[11]

Each of these four characteristics of innovation (instrument, invention, intuitive, influential) shares a common value: the creation of something new. Many innovation scholars name new as the essential trait of innovative activity. To understand innovation, we need to look at this word *new* in more detail.

An Ideology of Progress

The other day, my teenagers and I were listening to the radio and an announcer described her station as "the new Air One." One of my kids laughed and said, "How long are they going to be new?"

New is a powerful word, especially in America. We love *new* and its implicit promise of a better future. It has proven to be one of the most powerful words copywriters can use in advertising.[12] It is part of our identity as a nation, a "new world," which reflects an eschatological fervor among early American pilgrims that has never fully abated. New is part of the American origin story.

Part of the appeal of innovation in America is the ethos of new. Economist Joseph Schumpeter described innovation with the paradoxical phrase "creative destruction," which he said is an ongoing process of destroying the old and creating the new.[13] This, he said, is the essence of the free market. His association of destruction and creation has had a significant influence on thinking about market economics and creative entrepreneurship. From Christensen's focus on new technology to Sawhney, Wolcott, and Arroniz's description of innovation as "new value"[14] to Birkinshaw's term "discontinuous," innovation scholars often assume that innovation signifies not just incremental change and improvement but a profound shift that can come only from disruptive change: the unexpected arrival of something completely new.[15] Eric Schmidt of Google describes innovation as "the production and implementation of novel and useful ideas."[16] Much of the copious literature on innovation shares the assumption that innovation is a necessarily revolutionary overturning of the old to make way for the new.

> Much of the literature on innovation shares the assumption that innovation is a necessarily revolutionary overturning of the old to make way for the new.

In the use of new in advertising copy, of course, the other word we often see is *improved*. New suggests, not just something different, but something better. There is a strong sense of material progress about innovation, in that what we are creating supersedes what has come before. This assumption of material progress as a common good, in which what is new is better than what already exists, reflects a larger ideology of progress. It is part of the modern experiment.

To understand our obsession with new things, we must consider the origins of the modern age. Consider the first president of the United States, who died because of bad medicine. Political scientist Philip Tetlock writes,

> When George Washington fell ill in 1799, his esteemed physicians bled him relentlessly, dosed him with mercury to cause diarrhea, induced vomiting, and raised blood-filled blisters by applying hot cups to the old man's skin. A physician in Aristotle's Athens, or Nero's Rome, or medieval Paris, or Elizabethan London would have nodded at much of that hideous regimen. Washington died.[17]

We read of Washington's treatment plan and shudder. Of course he died! But his treatment plan was quite normal for late-eighteenth-century physicians. Washington lived in an era in which knowledge was still largely artisanal: the practice of medicine was understood to be an art, which meant that physicians relied on personal techniques over shared knowledge, which was fine in the arts, but often deadly in the sciences. For example, the use of leeches to bleed patients such as Washington dated to antiquity, despite its failure as a practice.

This is because, before the rise of Enlightenment thought, assumptions about authoritative knowledge lay in the past. Perhaps without understanding it, Washington's doctors were still heavily influenced by an ancient view of knowledge, which relied on an eternal balance of four fundamental "humors": earth, fire, water, and air. All knowledge was rooted in sensory experience, as art historian Jack Hartnell writes about medieval medicine:

> So revered were these texts that they often took precedence over observation of the actual medieval body itself. This goes some way toward explaining why anyone might have kept going with cow dung, boar's bile or bleeding. Consistency in implementing the medicine of their learned forebears was the paradigm of this medicinal movement, not innovation. Even if a particular method seemed questionable or ineffective—and at times they must have—to find a new route through medieval bodies would have required the overturning of centuries of thought.[18]

Of course, this overturning eventually happened. An increased emphasis on empirical thinking, as well as other concurrent changes, provided the foundation for an intellectual revolution. Practical observation rather than tradition led to an enlightenment of the Western mind, which introduced a fundamental shift in the acquisition of knowledge from a past orientation toward a future orientation defined by "principles of experiment and trial and error."[19] The Enlightenment replaced the four ancient pillars of earth, water, fire, and air with four new, modern pillars: science, reason, humanism, and progress.[20] Oxford literary scholar Iain McGilchrist notes that proponents of this Enlightenment believe "that all genuine questions can be answered, that if a question cannot be answered it is not a question, that all answers are knowable, and that all the answers must be compatible with one another."[21] Discovery via the scientific method replaced tradition as the basis for shared, applied human knowledge.

The method of this new empiricism was inquiry and testing, through which scientists and scientific thinkers began to solve long-standing human problems in a variety of fields. Over time, people began to realize tangible change and improvement in problems that had once seemed intractable and unsolvable. These improvements, particularly in medicine and engineering, were measurable, widespread, and visible, leading to growth in social knowledge, standards of living, and longevity. Improvements were so rapid and ubiquitous that an entire philosophy of history began to emerge, which suggested that, because of science, improvement in the human condition itself was, over time, incremental and inexorable. What was happening in science seemed possible in society, politics, and even religion.[22] Shared knowledge gained through inquiry incrementally improved many facets of society, and humans gradually avoided making the same mistakes over and over. Doctors (eventually) stopped sticking leeches on people to heal them.[23]

The application of scientific thinking and subsequent improvements to the human condition made its value self-evident. To the eighteenth-century European citizen, improvements to society driven by Enlightenment values were obvious and life-changing, a proverbial cultural light being turned on after centuries of endless dusk. Industrial culture yielded massive improvements to standards of living, and people began to assume that history was on a linear march toward a progressively better future.

Science was so successful that it began to take on a philosophical dimension. Out of its success in the hard disciplines, the notion of incremental improvement began to permeate theology, the humanities, philosophy, and the realm of knowing and epistemology, eventually creating a meta-narrative of progress, the idea that things will continue to get better over time. To many Christians, the discovery of powerful new technologies offered a natural eschatological explanation, in which heaven will eventually arrive on earth via social improvement created by a scientific method. The romanticism of nineteenth-century literature, particularly in the wake of Marx, combined to create an image of history as rising or arching upward, suggesting a steady move through time toward a utopian or perfect ending.[24]

The view of a perfect ending to history achieved through scientific discovery challenged and changed a centuries-old epistemology rooted in the Christian faith. Progress became not just a result of empiricism or even an ideal but an ideology, a belief in social, political, and economic improvement achieved through technological innovation by human—not divine—means that is incremental, inexorable, and increasingly immediate.

Nowhere has progress become more embedded in culture than in the United States. Founded at the height of the Enlightenment, the United States is the ultimate manifestation of the modern experiment. American intellectual Stephen Pinker's four pillars of Enlightenment thought—reason, science, humanism, and progress[25]—are evident in the founding constitutional papers of the American experiment, which not only wove progress into the fabric of the United States Constitution but imbued the culture with a mandate to make a better future.[26]

The ideology of progress emerged in the Enlightenment, was articulated in the British empire, was made manifest in the early American pioneer spirit, and reached its peak in the technological innovations that achieved Allied victory in the Second World War. Political historian Matthew Slaboch observes, "There is no alternative tradition to optimism in America. It is a country founded at the height of the Enlightenment and imbued with a faith in progress."[27] In American culture, new isn't just a method or a strategy, it is a belief system. We believe in an ideology of progress.

Tomorrowland

One of the foremost American prophets of progress[28] was "Imagineer" Walt Disney. After a half-century, the number one family vacation destination in the United States remains Walt Disney World,[29] a sanctuary of family-friendly Enlightenment ideals. One of its signature attractions, and one that Walt supposedly loved the most,[30] is called The Carousel of Progress, which resides in the middle of a themed area titled Tomorrowland. While Tomorrowland has been a staple of Walt Disney World since its opening in 1971, the ride itself premiered several years earlier in the 1964 New York World's Fair. By the early 1960s, Disney's work had become synonymous in culture to art and as an ode to technology and scientific progress. Over the previous century, a series of World's Fairs in Europe and the United States had been the commercial showcases for human scientific advancement.[31] Thus Walt Disney and the World's Fair were a fitting marriage. Chief architect Robert Moses called the New York World's Fair the greatest single event in human history.[32]

Mid-twentieth-century America was a time and space in which such exaggeration seemed reasonable, and 1964 was a highwater mark. The nation had survived the Great Depression and won the war, and the power of new technology was at its peak. Modern technology was the engine of Enlightenment progress, beginning with mechanization in the English textile industry in the eighteenth century. The seemingly inexorable Industrial Revolution was based on two simple, scientific concepts: every endeavor could be broken down into simple tasks, and those tasks could be accomplished on assembly lines. This practice gave rise to machines that could replace human labor.[33] As people innovated new, more efficient machinery, productivity went up, and everyone benefited.

"Everyone," of course, excluded those whose livelihoods were wrapped up in ancient, artisan hand-weaving processes. If you have ever been called a "Luddite" for resisting new technology, you are in the company of Ned Ludd, the nineteenth-century English weaver who was put out of a job by a machine, then broke it in a fit of rage. Despite some resistance, though, use of the machines eventually took over. The vast majority of jobs available in the early 1800s no longer exist, a phenomenon that is now known as "technological unemployment."

But innovators have little time for those who don't get on board, and technology found a good fit in the new world. The forty-year period before World War I was a time of intense technological innovation and social disruption, much like the one American culture is experiencing now. Conventional references to the *modern* world begin here, with such culturally disruptive advancements as home electrical power, indoor plumbing, the automobile, the telephone, and film and radio, to name a few.

These new technologies broadened people's view of the world, such as one young man in the first decade of the twentieth century who, while messing with his new radio, could not believe it when he picked up the signal from a doctor in a neighboring town, broadcasting, "Can anyone hear me west of Steubenville?"[34] Reflecting on the power of radio, broadcaster Peter Jennings writes, "radio was to the air as the automobile was to the earth, an agent of transport to a world as wide open as the imagination."[35]

In early- to mid-twentieth-century America, the human imagination seemed to be the only limit to what was possible. While critics such as Orwell and Huxley, among others, argued that not only does progress not happen, "it ought not to happen,"[36] the popular view tended toward optimism for a streamlined, leisurely future of convenience. Public fascination with futurology and the benefits of technological advancement outran literati pessimism. As Beatle Paul McCartney seemingly summarized for all of Western popular culture in the 1960s, "It's getting better all the time."[37]

Indeed, there exists a mountain of evidence on the benefits to society that advancements in technology have provided, in areas such as food, sanitation, life expectancy, the reduction of violence, improvements in literacy, freedom, and equality.[38] And while "large-scale narratives about how we supposedly came to be" have become uncoupled in recent historical reconstructions from "rosy evaluations of an onward-and-upward, progressive view of Western history,"[39] assurance of the potential of new technology, particularly American technology, to usher in a better future has never fully diminished in society. While we wait for flying Jetson cars, we still click articles about them, curious about the power of technology to inaugurate a better future.

Perhaps the reason we assume *improved* comes with *new* is because our love of innovation, like a belief in progress, has many of us assuming that innovation will solve our problems. We have developed a faith in technology and in the study and practice of innovation as the means to accomplish our scientifically promised better future. An entire industry has formed around it. Just search the TED talk database to get a feel for our fascination with progress.

> Perhaps the reason we assume improved comes with new is because our love of innovation, like a belief in progress, has many of us assuming that innovation will solve our problems.

The ideology of progress has had a profound influence on the American understanding of technological innovation (which due to Americanization, has, in turn, influenced the entire world) and on Christian theology and the practice of Christian faith. In the church, innovation has become the unspoken subtext of our understanding of the kingdom of God. It is to the correlation between innovation and our role in the kingdom of God that we will turn next.

Kingdom Building 2

Does Our Work Build God's Kingdom?

At the height of an era of innovation, Baptist minister Walter Rauschenbusch sought to solve social ills in the streets of New York City by combining evangelical faith with social reform. He joined Jesus' promise of the New Creation with an ideology of progress and refashioned the kingdom of God as a product of social reform. His vision of the inauguration of God's kingdom was based on social improvement through progress. The problem was that it led to an elevation of the power of human hands at the expense of the movement of God's Spirit. History has proved that humans are not equipped to inaugurate God's kingdom.

Walter Rauschenbusch was sent to work in Hell's Kitchen—the center of "the worst neighborhood on the American continent."[1] The neighborhood housed some of the first tenement buildings in New York City. After the Civil War, European immigrants to the United States, mostly Irish and German, filled a set of newly erected housing high rises on the west side of Manhattan. Tenements were a relatively inexpensive means for cities such as New York to house a large number of people in a small, contained space.[2] But, as urban planners would learn, packing low-income families into small spaces together only aggravated conditions of poverty and resulting social ills. With few job prospects, crime and street gangs soon emerged. By the 1880s, the neighborhood was run by gangs that numbered up to five hundred people. Imagine the flashback scenes from *The Godfather II*, with Robert De Niro playing a young Italian immigrant in turn-of-the-century New York City who chooses crime for his livelihood. An apocryphal story from the era tells of one police officer who says to another, commenting on the neighborhood, "Hell's a mild climate. This is hell's kitchen."[3]

Rauschenbusch was a 24-year-old graduate of Rochester Theological Seminary.[4] He arrived at Second German Baptist Church in 1886 and was instantly disturbed by the poverty, disease, and suffering he witnessed: rampant crime, despairing men unable to find employment or improve their households' conditions, dozens of brothels, and children recruited at a young age by gangs. Among the myriad of difficult circumstances, the children's suffering was the worst. Later in life, describing his feelings at the time, he recalled, "Oh the children's funerals! . . . Why did the children have to die?"[5]

Rauschenbusch had gone to Hell's Kitchen as a pietist, a preacher concerned with saving souls and improving personal virtue. However, as he witnessed suffering, he began to consider how to help his 125 working-class German immigrant parishioners improve their situation in life. Frequently asked to financially intercede on behalf of his congregation, he developed a conviction that unearned income was inherently parasitic and needed to be "benevolently overseen by the state."[6] Within one year, he wrote to a friend that he had become "obsessed with two questions: the spiritual care of his congregation and the social conditions of the city that separated the rich and the poor."[7] He began to search for ways to integrate his evangelical faith with social reform.

His combination of piety and reform was radical and new for its time—a theological innovation.[8] Amid his daily ministry, he began to ask theological questions. One central topic came to dominate his intellectual life: the kingdom of God. Is God's kingdom only a future destination? Or is it also a present reality? If a present reality, then what is the Christian's responsibility to it?

The results of his work and intellectual ruminations were both practical and theological. His first major church project was the construction of a new church building, funded in part by a relationship he developed with millionaire businessman John D. Rockefeller (the recipient of much unearned income). The building he had inherited was in squalor, and without it, the congregation had difficulty meeting.[9] He reasoned that a new building would lift both their lives and their morale. As he worked on a new building using Rockefeller's funds, he began to articulate a new series of ideas: the kingdom of God is a just society, the "quest for the kingdom of God was the primary purpose for living as a disciple,"[10] and the Christian's work in the public square is to imitate Jesus' ethic of sacrifice, even unto death.[11]

In sermons and papers, he argued that the goal of Christianity was to create a society in which all persons were equal. Significantly, how this should happen was not the church, which he saw as a "necessary evil,"[12] but through modeling God's kingdom in the home and engaging in political activism for the abolition of class privilege.[13] Further, Rauschenbusch believed this work was one of the few things that could keep humanity from descending into the destructive, downward spiral of sin.[14]

Through the early 1890s, a cultural period rife with technological innovation, Rauschenbusch continued to develop these ideas while ministering to his congregation, which had grown. He instituted several innovative programs, including a home for impoverished young women, a local seminary to train laity, and a daycare center for working mothers. Despite these programs, though, his ideas were met with significant resistance in his church, and by 1895, the church found itself on the verge of a major conflict. Many of the parishioners distrusted his new, socially focused gospel message.[15]

In 1897, he returned to his alma mater at Rochester and eventually settled into the chair of church history. The position allowed him to write and speak more, and his profile grew. His work *Christianity and the Social Crisis*, published in 1907, took off immediately because it provided a theological foundation for an emerging social concern: why Christianity must address social questions. He became a sought-after speaker and lecturer and found himself the leader of a new "social gospel" movement. In 1918, when he died from cancer, he was perhaps the most well-known minister in America.[16]

One hundred years later, Walter Rauschenbusch is generally considered to be one of the great American theologians.[17] His work reminded American Christianity that the incarnation is evidence that God is a God of history, and to follow Christ is not just an exercise in personal piety but a concern for justice in the present time. Arguably, he is the most influential theologian behind America's current sociopolitical environment. The entire Protestant landscape, from the most fundamental to the most liberal, is obsessed with Rauschenbusch's question about the kingdom of God. Rauschenbusch's work gave language to the emerging tension and later split between conservative and progressive groups in Protestantism. His work influenced the liberation theology of Gustavo Gutiérrez and the nonviolence of Martin Luther King Jr. One can even define the social unrest of 2020 according to the same question, whether the parties involved are Christian or not: What is the kingdom of God, and what is our responsibility toward making it come to pass?

Rauschenbusch's influence was not without significant problems, even in his lifetime. By the end of his short life, the social-gospel movement was already moving away from the orthodox faith he saw as central. As it developed, the progressive Christian movement he helped spawn largely abandoned classic orthodox Christianity in favor of social activism. His last book, *A Theology for the Social Gospel*, which he wrote a year before his death, attempted to bring the social-gospel movement back to orthodox Christianity.[18] As University of Rochester historian Christopher Lasch describes, "He sensed that orthodox theology, notwithstanding its puzzling habit of holding individuals accountable for sins that were nevertheless in some sense collective, provided a better understanding of sin than a liberal theology that attributed it to ignorance or 'cultural lag.' "[19]

Lasch hints at an assumption behind the theological innovation of Walter Rauschenbusch. To understand his influential theology of God's kingdom, and the relationship of the kingdom of God to Christian innovation, let us briefly return to the Enlightenment, specifically to its philosophical roots. From here we will find that Rauschenbusch's theology was heavily influenced by the philosophy of Descartes and filtered through the ideas of Karl Marx and Charles Darwin.

Advancing the Kingdom

In the 1600s, the philosopher René Descartes created an innovative research methodology that "revolutionized the developing field of science and changed the way mankind thinks in the world."[20] Descartes was a devout Catholic who was obsessed with certainty. His obsession culminated in *The Discourse on Method*, which ended with the simple observation that all might be doubted except one thing; namely, that he, the doubter, existed because he doubted. His famous statement *cogito ergo sum*, "I think therefore I am," includes a lesser-known margin note that says, "we cannot doubt of our existence while we doubt."[21] This has been summarized as *dubito ergo sum*, or "I doubt; therefore I am." The Cartesian *raison d'être* is doubt—not faith. In his obsession with knowledge, Descartes created a divide between science and religion that lasts to this day. While the epistemological basis for religion is faith, the epistemological basis for science is doubt.[22]

Cartesian doubt works through falsification. We test ideas by making proofs. If we cannot prove them to be false, then we declare them to be scientifically verified. Empiricism, introduced by natural philosopher and Reformed Protestant Francis Bacon, expanded Descartes' ideas by promising to answer questions through the systematic use of human sense and experience, which Bacon championed not outside the church but as an "instauration" or restoration of humanity's dominion over creation lost in Adam's fall.[23]

The application of this scientific thinking resulted in new technological advancement and the assumption that technology is how societies progressively improve. Therefore, according to Enlightenment thought, doubt improves the world with the unintended side effect of reducing the need for faith. The meta-proposition of empiricism became that doubt drives meaning. Cartesian doubt provided a basis for a cultural leap from scientific verification to truth, or from research to philosophy.[24] In this way, science came to be known by many as a counter to and cure for religion.

> According to Enlightenment thought,
> doubt improves the world.

In response to this existential threat, theologians and pastors in Europe and America searched for new ways to reconcile orthodox Christianity and Enlightenment ideals. It was in this environment, when the word *evolution* was being applied in all sorts of ways,[25] that Rauschenbusch participated in a vibrant theological conversation on the kingdom of God. From his chair at the seminary, he taught about reframing the Christian narrative around a new, social interpretation[26] of the gospel.

Fighting against an asceticism that ignored the suffering of people, he advocated for the ethical nature of the Christian life. He argued for justice and mercy, joined Jesus' promise of the New Creation to an ideology of progress, and refashioned the kingdom of God as a product of social reform. As discussed, an essential feature of the ideology of progress is humanism, or faith in the prime importance of human beings. Humanism believes in the essential goodness of people, seeks to identify human needs, and solves them by (rational) human means. Mirroring the technological optimism of the era and writing before the full horror of the first World War was realized, Rauschenbusch described a vision for the "advancement" of God's kingdom.[27]

His theology fundamentally challenged orthodox Christianity. For example, he defined sin essentially as selfishness, not pride,[28] and saw it not as an individual problem but as an institutional problem of "suprapersonal entities." Building on Marxist philosophy, he defined sin as "systemic," which reoriented sin from a question of the human heart to a question of class struggle. He defined the cross in purely human terms as the consequence of the expression of these sins on Jesus' life. He denied that baptism was a response to metanoia or personal conviction of sin, claiming instead that John the Baptist understood baptism as "not a ritual act of individual salvation but an act of dedication to a religious and social movement."[29]

Countering what he saw as an increasingly privatized religion that refused to engage the massive societal needs of industrialized society, Rauschenbusch repurposed orthodox Christian theology under a banner of social reform. Along with others, he taught the radical idea that the kingdom of God was not just a future, spiritual concern, but a present, human concern. As with all knowledge in the modern worldview, God's kingdom was not something to be progressively revealed but to be discovered.

Thus, to Rauschenbusch, the kingdom of God is something to be manufactured by humans.

He wrote,

> Ascetic Christianity called the world evil and left it. Humanity is waiting on a revolutionary Christianity which will call the world evil and change it. We do not want to blow all of our existing institutions to atoms, but we do want to remold every one of them. . . . We need a combination between the faith of Jesus in the need and the possibility of the kingdom of God, and the modern comprehension of the organic development of human society.[30]

Note that his orientation is toward human agency, or intervention. While faith plays some vague part, our calling is to develop society. By refashioning the kingdom of God as a product of social reform, Rauschenbusch suggests a kind of Christianity in which humans have an authority that differs from that practiced by the ancients. He encouraged Christians to engage culture through social reform and, through this engagement, to "build" or "advance" the kingdom of God:

> The essential purpose of Christianity was to transform human society into the kingdom of God by regenerating all human relations and reconstituting them in accordance with the will of God.[31]

His use of the past tense "was" is notable; he also defines the church as "the organized expression of the religious life of the past."[32] Instead of using the authority of the church, he encouraged his parishioners to direct political engagement. As support for this position, he noted that leaders of the Constantinian church gradually learned to be courtiers to further their interests, because a church supported by the state is beholden to the interests of the state.[33]

The squalor he witnessed at Second German Baptist Church did not dissuade Rauschenbusch from his faith in human nature. If anything, it reinforced his claim that Christians can build God's kingdom through the good works we do for our fellow humans. In hubris characteristic of his time, he wrote, "The religious, political, and intellectual revolutions of the past five centuries, which together created the modern world, necessarily had to culminate in an economic and social revolution such as is now upon us."[34] Comparative literature scholar A. Owen Aldridge writes,

> Following the lead of such nineteenth-century theologians as Samuel Harris and Horace Bushnell, who believed that America had a special destiny and mission in realizing the kingdom of Christ on earth, the advocates of the social gospel undertook the application of the "social principles of Jesus" to American urban and industrial society, de-emphasizing personal justification and religious experience of a traditional kind.[35]

The optimism of the age is clear in Rauschenbusch's writing. Repurposing Darwinian language, the social gospel took "social evolution" as gospel and re applied it to the work of the church.

Rauschenbusch's solution to reclusive nineteenth-century Christian practice was to syncretize orthodox Christian faith with Enlightenment values of humanism and progress.

Faith as a Tool

Perhaps to you, the reader, Rauschenbusch's desire to champion the potential of human ingenuity through political means sounds quite normal. If so, this is evidence of his influence. He spawned a century of Christian social and political engagement, with its myriad causes, which continues to this day, on both the political left and right.

The theology of Walter Rauschenbusch was a key part of a larger battle in the Protestant church through the late nineteenth and early twentieth centuries, which divided progressives, who sought to make the kingdom of God immanent through Enlightenment values, and fundamentalists, who sought to keep the kingdom of God transcendent.

Rauschenbusch was not the only church leader advocating for social reform. Early American evangelicals pursued the same ends, although with a higher view of Christ and the work of the church. Journalist Michael Gerson observes that some evangelicals "were an optimistic lot who thought that human effort could help hasten the arrival of God's kingdom. . . . Evangelicals generally regarded almost any sort of progress as evidence of the advance of the kingdom."[36] Rauschenbusch considered himself an "evangelical liberal."

Evangelism and social justice have been two sides of the same human-centered coin. Rauschenbusch's social gospel, while a needed corrective to an other worldly faith that failed to meet people in their need, led to an elevation of the power of human hands at the expense of the movement of God's Spirit. This is the through line that leads to our current situation, in which the pursuit of public policy supersedes character, and there is no discernible difference between the behavior of politicians and public church figures on both sides of the aisle. Rauschenbusch envisioned a church that could keep the instrumental nature of power without the corrupting influence of state power: thus, a church that could wield political advocacy for the sake of the kingdom of God.

Now, whether it is positive or negative, Christianity is known for activism, and churchgoers are known for wielding faith as a tool and manipulating outcomes for righteous ends. Mainline Protestantism has long been strongly linked to activism, with the cause du jour draped as a banner over the cross. But the same is true on the right: Rauschenbusch's social gospel activism has recently reemerged in the evangelical world. For example, Richard Stearns, CEO of the nonprofit mission agency World Vision, claims that God's kingdom lies unfinished and will remain that way until we do "that thing that Jesus left us to accomplish . . . [which is] establishing and building the kingdom of God on earth."[37] Religion sociologist James Davison Hunter writes, "It is not an exaggeration to say that the dominant public witness of the Christian churches in America since the early 1980s has been a political witness."[38] Andy Crouch, the former editor of the evangelical flagship *Christianity Today*, advocates for our ability to "change the world" while acknowledging the common, unspoken assumption among Christians that we are changing it "for the better."[39]

2020 = 1968

In this context, we return to innovation and the power of "new and improved." If millions of Americans claim Christ, if progress is how we build Christ's kingdom, if progress comes through technological innovation, and if innovation has both an established history and current interest in America, why is culture so stagnant and hardened? Why are divisions between groups and threats to stability not abating, and, if anything, increasing? If the underlying assumptions of progress within Christian theology are right, shouldn't every generation be more like God's kingdom than the last?

As you look back on the year 2020, consider: peaceful protests turned violent. Political strife peaked. American astronauts floated above the atmosphere. A pandemic that originated in China killed millions of people globally. As more than one commenter observed with anguish in 2020, are we reliving 1968?[40] History repeats, albeit with a twist.

Both the political left and right now assume that advancement of a more just society is the calling and responsibility of the good Christian, and of the humanist. Our current polarization is just a question of tactics. We have been swept up in the assumption that we are responsible (and capable) of creating a perfect future. Our cultural deathmatch is an argument over strategy based on the false assumption that the peace and human flourishing we seek is up to us.

> Our cultural deathmatch is an argument over strategy based on the false assumption that the peace and human flourishing we seek is up to us.

What we call Christianity today is often a syncretized form of Christian naturalism. By relying on sight, we have stripped our faith of its power and made the orthodox faith handed down by the saints indistinguishable from an ethical civic sensibility that seeks a common good. Rauschenbusch was right to bring the historic faith back from a pietism that abandoned God's created world, but he was also a product of his age in believing science was the revelation of the mind of God and in finding empiricism synonymous with truth.

Science is part of truth but not the whole truth. As followers of Jesus, we worship in Spirit *and* truth (John 4:24). What we need is not an abandonment of science but a recovery of the Holy Spirit that is more than the sum of scientific thinking. For, as Paul writes, we live by faith not by sight (2 Cor 5:7). While the modern naturalist lives by sight alone, the Christian lives by believing, not by seeing. If we claim to believe in Jesus, we need to relearn what it means to live as we claim.

Perhaps our cultural deathmatch has covered up a dawning realization that the perfect future we seek may not be possible through our own effort. The bloodiest century in human history has demonstrated that the social-gospel movement has failed. Historian and theologian Leonard Sweet characterizes the social-gospel movement this way: "To a church that was operating on the principle 'change hearts, change world,' the social gospel countered 'change world, change hearts.' "[41] Indeed, activism was not the default position of the church before the Roman emperor Constantine. Before Constantine, the church was not acquainted with power; as historian Alan Krieder writes, the dominant ethic of the church was patience. Constantine's decision to bring the Christian faith into the palace changed everything. Constantine called his approach a sort of "righteous manipulation,"[42] an activism in which he, as emperor, encouraged the church to use the tools of power to righteous ends and replace the traditional patient stance toward culture with urgency and speed.[43] Constantine's position sounds a lot like Rauschenbusch's.

As I outlined in the introduction, our efforts to improve society have not worked, and history has proved that, so far, humans are not inaugurating God's kingdom. The result for 2020 is that the church keeps replaying the same failed solutions over and over. The decline of Christian witness is related to the hubris and naiveté of a reduced, material gospel that has attempted to marry the Christian story with the power structures of political institutions. The relationship of the church to power changes the church. The problem is that we tend to believe what we can see and act out of our strength—the "inclination of the human heart" (Gen 6:5)—which cannot be improved, only surrendered to Jesus. We have placed ourselves in authority as the arbiters of change, but as Jesus reminds Peter, he is the one who builds the church (Matt 16:18).

The irony of the social-gospel vision is that it has become an *Inception*-like folding of reality back on itself in a near-identical match but without the Christ-center. While Rauschenbusch mixed what we now define as differing views of personal and systemic sin in his writing, many progressives now ignore sin altogether in favor of a progressively improving society; when pressed, they downplay sin in favor of the "sacred worth" in every person. As Sweet writes, "[The social gospel's] naive view of sin and optimistic outlook on the betterment of human nature failed to look up close and see that evil is real and personal. Evil is not just impersonal systemic forces but hurting people hurting people."[44]

Reducing the Christian faith to an instrument of social reform has diminished its witness. The potential of social improvement to realize the kingdom of God is debatable at best because the benefits of human power are limited at best. English baron John Emerich Edward Dalberg-Acton famously wrote, "Power tends to corrupt, and absolute power corrupts absolutely."[45] The result is that, despite one hundred years of concentrated human effort, culture does not appear to more closely resemble God's kingdom. While we extol technology and new solutions for our problems, our current social and political zeitgeist is anything but utopian. Today we are more known for polarization, stalemates, and resistance than we are for flourishing. Progress is oversold.

Do the theological ruins of the twentieth century evidence an inability of innovation to reveal the New Creation and solve the problems of church and society? Or is it not innovation, per se, but how we conflate the work of innovation with the promise of progress: incremental, inexorable improvement?

To understand the limitations of our obsession with progress and begin to separate it from true Christian innovation, we need to look more closely at two major reasons innovation has failed to improve society. The first is that it never lasts, and the second is that it benefits some people while harming others. The first begins with a story of innovation in ministry.

Inevitable Change

3

If Innovation Is Key to Improving the World, Why Isn't It Working? (Part 1)

There are two major problems with innovation. The first is that it does not last. The second is that it seems to apply only to a specific group of people for a limited time. I analyze the second problem in chapter 4. Here, I examine what happens within us after a period of innovation, using a personal story of ministry. While exciting in the moment, innovation devolves into stasis as new challenges and problems emerge. Our gospel of "new and improved" gives us a false sense of completion and prevents us from continuing to move forward with new innovations during periods of plateau. As the resonance of our methods fade, we struggle to adapt. Like Jesus' disciples, we end up adopting attitudes of retreat, rule, and self-reliance. The problem is that we have a limited, material view of the world—a gospel of "new and improved."

magine leading a congregation that tripled in size to more than four thousand people a weekend within two years. It is the dream of most pastors, church staffs, and local church lay leadership committees. I lived it, and the results were not what you might think.

When I joined the staff of a large congregation in Ohio as a young associate minister after graduating from seminary in 1995, the "church growth" movement was in full swing. The movement believed that growing churches was the means of revealing the New Creation and solving society's problems. The church I served, Ginghamsburg United Methodist Church, was becoming one of the foremost examples of church growth in the latter part of the twentieth century.

A postwar phenomenon in American Protestantism, the church growth movement is generally accredited to missiologist Donald McGavran,[1] whose primary interest was in evangelism. Unlike Rauschenbusch, who saw the church as a necessary evil to the work of advancing the kingdom of God through personal and social transformation, the church growth movement assumed that the local congregation was central. Church growth became an innovative strategy and then a missiological assumption to maximize the efficiency of the work of salvation.[2] By the 1960s, many Protestant denominations had begun to build theoretical models of congregational growth as a social science. The assumption was that, since larger churches were synonymous with kingdom-building, it was possible through careful planning and engineering to discover just the right set of variables that would result in church growth, just as a CEO would engineer company growth or a mayor would engineer city growth.

These twin perspectives, church growth as evangelism and church growth as social science, co existed through the latter decades of the twentieth century, likely due to a confluence of favorable factors, including: professional career interests of local pastors, goal-setting by lay business leaders in local congregations, judicatory bureaucratic pressure, and the contextual explanations of researchers and practitioners responding to the first statistical reports of congregational decline in the early 1970s.[3]

My volunteer and staff colleagues and I did not pay too much attention to these larger social contexts, however. We were just trying to hang on in response to the questions of thousands of people coming to our church, seeking an experience of God. Instead of the "sheep swapping" that characterized much of church growth (existing members transferring from church to church), we were having conversations with people who had no previous church experience or understanding of what it meant to follow Jesus.

The impetus for our attendance explosion was innovation in worship. The church had already experienced growth through the application of innovative methods of ministry in music and education, but the catalyst for the most explosive growth was a new worship venue. While many churches built new sanctuaries, ours was unique. Though I have no way of making this definitive claim, we may have been the first church in our denomination tradition of United Methodism to install a permanent large screen with video projection technology in our primary worship venue. It was sixteen feet tall and dominated the back wall behind the stage (chancel) space.

The church had installed the screen and video projector during construction in the fall of 1994 and held a grand opening for the venue in December. I was hired six months later to "get the screen in focus," as we joked, and then to develop and create content that would go on the screen each week in worship. I took on the title of "Media Minister" and worked with a staff team and a volunteer crew of more than one hundred people to help design and develop weekly worship using this new technology.[4]

Our new venue increased those we could seat in worship at one time from four hundred fifty to approximately fourteen hundred. Before the transition to the new facility, Ginghamsburg averaged about twelve hundred a weekend in worship. After a brief period of decline following the transition (an observation of church growth theory is that big changes often lead to small decreases before big increases, just like an "s" curve in the cycle of business development[5]), we began to see dozens of new faces each week. Building on the more measured growth of the previous fifteen years, from late 1995 through early 1998 we began to fill five worship services a weekend and tripled from approximately one thousand in live worship on an average weekend to more than thirty-three hundred, not including students, children, or infants.[6]

To some degree, I thought what happened in my first three years of professional ministry life was normal. Curiously, by the age of 26, I was teaching pastors from around the globe about innovation and strategy in worship and technology. As our Senior Pastor Mike Slaughter liked to point out, we were a small church hidden in a cornfield twenty miles north of the dying rust belt city of Dayton, Ohio. By any conventional analytics-based insight, Ginghamsburg should not have grown.

The daily experience was exhilarating and daunting. Our growth was so remarkable that we began to attract thousands of pastors per year from across the United States, Canada, Australia, and western Europe to the numerous conferences we held onsite and at various remote locations. United Methodism was, at this time, the second-largest Protestant denomination in America, and Ginghamsburg may have been the most explosive, organic, onsite growth of a church in that tradition in the last fifty years. Understanding that growth and its relationship to innovation have been topics of fascination since.[7] The most interesting topic is that it did not last.

The More Things Change

The core innovation of Ginghamsburg was simple: worship as experience. Let us review what happened there using my four-part definition of innovation.

One, it was an instrument. Ginghamsburg solved the problem of people who were disengaged from their faith by allowing a new expression of faith that resonated with people's experience in that time and space. What has become a commonplace observation among pastors and lay Christians, that we are now in a post-Christian public context, was just emerging at that time. This cultural shift happened in the American North about ten years before it happened in the American South. We looked to postmodern thinkers such as Douglas Coupland and pastors such as Erwin McManus to understand these cultural shifts and realized that we could no longer assume people had heard the story of Jesus. This meant we had to learn to quit making assumptions. During one sermon, Slaughter spoke of Mary, the mother of Jesus. After the service, as we stood in the front of the congregation chatting, someone approached us with questions; they had never heard that Jesus had a mother. Such religious ignorance was shocking in America in 1995; it is a default assumption for most ministry contexts today. The worship as experience model was innovative because it shed the assumption that the congregation understood the traditions of the church. Instead, it saw worship as a means to teach people the historic faith using contemporary methods.

Two, invention. Of course, worship has existed for thousands of years and will continue to exist. Innovation can occur within the context of ongoing behaviors and habits. At Ginghamsburg, our worship team experimented with a new model that invited a "whole person" experience of God using the five senses of taste, touch, smell, sight, and sound. Before the mid-1990s, worship at Ginghamsburg already reflected trends at the time, including the introduction of drums and electric instruments. The move into a bigger venue, the large-screen installation in the center of the sanctuary and subsequent use of video and graphic imagery, the use of dramatic and humorous theatrical sketches to teach, and the coordination of all the worship elements into a single thematic experience were catalysts that fostered invention. Later studies, such as brain researcher Iain McGilchrist's seminal work *The Master and His Emissary*, provided the scientific rationale for what we discovered firsthand, that people first learn with their immediate five senses and then develop abstract concepts to categorize their experience.

Three, intuitive. Once in place, the process just worked. As the church staff, we invented a system by which a new "worship experience" (as we called it, as opposed to the "worship service") could be produced each week. It was not dependent on one or two specialists to operate but could plug in any number of talented people. More important to the parishioners of the church, the worship experience made sense without further context or explanation.

Four, influential. While the study of who was "first to market" on worship as experience is worthy of more research, the influence of the Ginghamsburg worship model is undeniable, as evidenced by the books and resources the church generated, the level of national and international interest, and the dozens of sold-out conferences we held from 1996 to 2001. Anecdotally, I have experienced the influence of this period in the years following and to this day as I have had conversations with pastors and church staff across America. More often than not, when I meet pastors over 45 years old, I hear a story about the time they and their staffs made the trip to western Ohio to witness worship or a conference on the campus of the church.

As influential as Ginghamsburg was, however, this model did not last. The power of the innovation faded. Why did this happen, and why does it seem to happen to every story of innovation?

While Ginghamsburg was perhaps extreme, such stories of growth and decline are certainly not atypical in church life. What, for a time, seemed to make Ginghamsburg different was the innovative use of new technology, which, if not causing the growth, certainly had a high correlation to growth. The effect was powerful for a period and helped launch what became known as the "seeker-sensitive" movement. Yet, despite innovative worship practices and success as measured by weekend worship attendance, we recognized our congregational faith practices were missing something. While we marveled at what was happening and did our best to keep up, we were also discovering the challenges of helping that many people work through deep and personal spiritual questions. While we focused on the live worship event, telling the story of Jesus and welcoming new attendees, we struggled to adequately disciple those who were now claiming the church as their home. Unable to find a friend to help them navigate personal and profound questions of life, some people quit trying and left or went to another church. Typical problems and dysfunctions of congregational life emerged, or rather never left but were briefly covered up by the shared excitement of growth, and we struggled to close a back door that rivaled the size of our front door.

At Ginghamsburg, the seeming inability of worship as experience to change hearts and lives resulted in a shift in the early 2000s to mission work in Sudan. In 2008, another large church with whom Ginghamsburg shared ideas and staff, Willow Creek Community Church in Barrington, Illinois, published a widely distributed study that questioned whether their worship and technology outreach efforts were succeeding at their named ministry goal, "making disciples of Jesus Christ." The study, called REVEAL, made a distinction between onsite weekly worship attendance and the "Great Commission" Jesus gave the earliest disciples, as recorded in Matthew 28:18-20.[8] While screens have not disappeared from most sanctuaries, it is fair to say that early expectations for their influence on the work of ministry have faded.

Eventually, the influence of all innovations atrophy. New generations rise, not knowing the limitations that led to the new thing, and they push against the limitations of the new thing's imperfections. All congregations with history experience waxing and waning; in fact, it seems a natural consequence of communities that grow up and grow old together. This inevitable regression to the mean, to use a statistical term, is the first of two major problems with innovation. All innovation is rooted in specific time and space; therefore, as the temporal and spatial context changes, its effectiveness fades. In other words, innovation applies to only a specific group of people for a limited time. As the resonance of our methods fade, we struggle to adapt.

> Innovation applies to only a specific group of people for a limited time.

The contemporary American church has been obsessed with growth strategies. Some church leaders constantly seek new, innovative practices. On one hand, this makes theological sense. One of the strongest themes of the New Testament is the New Creation, which began with the resurrection and will culminate at the eschaton, or the final destiny of humankind.[9] The church is fundamentally about new things. Yet, in an age and culture obsessed with new things, the church has declined precipitously in the past two generations.[10] Our attempts as Christians to innovate and make new things happen has had a spotty record, at best. Yet we retain Rauschenbusch's assumption that Christians, whether in or out of the church, are responsible (and capable) of creating a perfect future. We remain obsessed with a worldview of "new and improved," and yet, we do not know how to proceed.

Some even wonder whether the idea of Christian innovation is an oxymoron.[11] If the church is about *new*, and the culture has been about *new*, then why has the church struggled as much as it has? Is innovation worth the work when it seems things eventually atrophy?[12]

We need a different way of understanding Christian innovation beyond "new and improved." One of the core themes of this book, and one that must be addressed for Christians to innovate, is that our theological definition of *new* is problematic. As we learned in the previous chapter, the American obsession with "new and improved" has harmed a Christian understanding of innovation. The way we understand it today, *new* is informed more by modernity than by scripture. In a culture of "new and improved," in which innovation rejects what came before and elevates the new thing as superior, we do not know how to deal with atrophy.

> In a culture of "new and improved," in which innovation rejects what came before and elevates the new thing as superior, we do not know how to deal with atrophy.

To get past the culture of "new and improved" and discover a better definition of Christian innovation, we need a biblically grounded, theologically robust understanding of what we mean by *new*. This means we first need to answer the question of *change* adequately. To do this, let us look at the story of the poor way Jesus' disciples acted after Jesus' resurrection.

Christians Don't Handle Change Well

My first boss at Ginghamsburg had a poster on the wall behind his desk that said "change is everything" and showed a picture of some crumpled up tighty-whitey underwear. While crude, it got the point across that change can be good, though we tend to resist it. Psychological studies have established that people are naturally averse to change.[13] Change is hard because it places stress on comfortable existing behaviors, which creates a biological "fight versus flight" response.[14]

Any book that talks about Christian innovation needs to name the elephant in the room: Christians don't handle change well. Change that challenges existing behavior is difficult in any circumstance, but it is worse in the church, where we mix our status quos with a healthy dose of holiness. When my wife was a music director at a church, she once came home crying because, while trying to introduce a new song at a choir rehearsal, one of the choir members crumpled up the sheet music, threw it in her face, and called her the devil. Sadly, if you have tried to innovate in any capacity as church leader, there is a good chance you have experienced or heard of similar stories. When it comes to religious expression, people get attached to specific customs, tastes, and preferences and fear anything that might challenge them. Some turn the way they experience God into a god, which, of course, is a tendency addressed by the third commandment. In the church, change is often labeled not different but evil.

Sadly, such a culture of fear among Christians is commonplace,[15] and no place is this more obvious than in the way the church today is missing from frontline news. Just search Twitter (and avert your eyes). As problems in culture mount, the church is known to the larger public not by solutions that promote human flourishing but by a debilitating fear of change.

Yet this is not new. Such fear appears from the very beginning of the church in a story of the first disciples. In the story, the disciples had a problem; they were bound by fear. Let us briefly consider each

of three symptoms of fear, and through them establish three prerequisites for us to be better able to deal with change.

Retreat

The first response to the fear of change is retreat. The classic
caricature of Christian retreat is the sandwich-board, street-corner,
fundamentalist preacher, predicting the end of the world on a specific date derived from a literalist reading of the Bible. This image is
a cartoon of fundamentalism, which formed as an ostensible rejection of modern, Enlightenment ideals of science, humanism, and
progress. It famously solidified with the 1925 Scopes Monkey Trial,
in which the arrest of Tennessee teacher John Scopes for teaching
"an evolutionary view of human origins"[16] became a pretense for a
long-standing cultural showdown between scientific and Christian
worldviews.[17] Fundamentalism holds to a theology of the kingdom
of heaven that is separate from culture and in another realm. It believes knowledge is fixed and revealed, not growing and discovered,
and that the work of the church is to proclaim the arrival of God's
kingdom and invite people to reject the world to direct their attention to the spiritual realm. Its view of the kingdom of God is
premillennial, meaning Christ will come before humans succeed in
making the world a better place. Implicit in this view is a belief that
culture is declining, that the state of humankind is irreparable, and
humanity's task is to preserve what is left while waiting for Jesus'
return.

The dominant characteristic of Christians who retreat from culture is fear. Lacking sufficient faith in God's power to work in a sinful world, some cower, unable to process what is happening in the
world. Rather than leaning into the adventure of what comes next,
the locked-room Christian retreats from society, opts for safety, and
looks for leaders to save them from beasts that lurk.

Fear is what the disciples felt on the day of Jesus' resurrection.
The eleven remaining disciples, who would shortly become the lead-

ers of the church, initially responded to news of Christ's resurrection not with bold leadership but by cowering behind a locked door.

> On the evening of that first day of the week, . . . the disciples were together, with the doors locked for fear of the Jewish leaders. (John 20:19a)

After hearing the news from Mary Magdalene that Jesus' body was missing, their leader Peter ran to the empty tomb to examine the evidence. At this point, having not yet seen Jesus walking around, Peter (naturally) considered the body stolen, not risen, and he returned to the other disciples. Then Jesus appeared to Mary, and Mary shared the incident with Peter and the group. As evening came, however, the disciples sat in a locked room, unable to process what was happening.

Having heard the good news that Jesus was alive, why was Peter still sitting in a locked room? Such an easy question for us today, isn't it? How would any sane person react to news of a dead body come to life? Peter was paralyzed. Fear is a natural response when the world shakes everything we think is true. Then, this happened:

> Jesus came and stood among them and said, "Peace be with you!" After he said this, he showed them his hands and side. The disciples were overjoyed when they saw the Lord.
>
> Again Jesus said, "Peace be with you! As the Father has sent me, I am sending you." And with that he breathed on them and said, "Receive the Holy Spirit." (John 20:19b-22)

Even after Peter heard the good news of Jesus' resurrection from the women at the tomb, he was still consumed by his fear. What was he afraid of? Was it the Roman authorities? The Jewish leaders? Or was it the realization that his rabbi had supernatural power over death?

His fear didn't dissipate until the living Jesus showed up. Thus, the first prerequisite to change a culture of fear is the presence of Jesus. This can happen only when we find ourselves, by no doing of our own, in the presence of the risen Christ. It is then that our retreat turns to advance, and we become equipped to do good work.

Rule

As the story of Rauschenbusch's social-gospel movement illustrates, the language of *advance* has a downside, which manifests in a
second temptation for the Christ follower when faced with moments
of significant cultural change. This response is to opt for strength and
a desire to fix things ourselves: the *fight* in the "fight versus flight"
response.

Whether characterized by the political left or right, the temptation to rule is based on a virtuous impulse, as we seek to build or
establish God's kingdom on earth. In this view, the role of Christians
is to take matters into our own hands and advance the kingdom
of God on Earth. Such a view is deeply ingrained in the Western
church, going backward from the social-gospel movement to the Enlightenment and perhaps even to the cultural position the church
has held since Constantine brought Christianity into the palace in
the fourth century.[18] The question is one of power. Whose worldview
dominates? Who is controlling the advancement of society?

The irony, of course, is that for the church to do anything based
on a worldview of power is to undermine the way of living that Jesus modeled. One pastor posted on social media that God's grace is
enough only if we "name our sins, repent of them, *and build God's
kindom [sic]*".[19] Such a response is dangerously close to the attitude of
the disciples who assumed Jesus' mission was political (the overthrow
of the corrupt Roman government), an ideology that Jesus rejected.

Consider Thomas. When Jesus appeared to the disciples, throwing open their locked door to let in the fresh wind of the Holy Spirit,
Thomas was the only one of the twelve not present. Thomas was no
shrinking violet. Earlier in John's Gospel, Jesus is faced with a moment of real danger when he hears of his friend Lazarus' sickness.
He decides to return to Judea to see him. The disciples are worried
because Jewish people there had already tried to stone him once. But
Thomas steps forward, leading the others, saying, "Let us also go,
that we may die with him" (John 11:16). Thomas was willing—perhaps even eager—to fight.

The problem with a strength of spirit such as Thomas' is the temptation to sufficiency. Thomas had leadership qualities; he trusted his own experience. Thus, when he heard the news that Jesus was alive, he responded with doubt:

> Now Thomas (also known as Didymus), one of the Twelve, was not with the disciples when Jesus came. So the other disciples told him, "We have seen the Lord!"
>
> But he said to them, "Unless I see the nail marks in his hands and put my finger where the nails were, and put my hand into his side, I will not believe." (John 20:24-25)

In Thomas' strength, he was not willing to simply accept such an incredulous claim. Like a modern humanist, he trusted his own five senses. He needed to experience firsthand news of the resurrection of a human being.

This same spirit is present in the politics of the church today, which is indistinguishable from the culture at large. Behind both the political left and the political right is a good desire to inaugurate God's kingdom, which, when unrealized, leads to frustration and then force. We cannot abide waiting and trusting other people's experience, particularly as it seems things worsen. We seek to take matters into our own hands. Both sides assume the necessity of the exercise of human power.

> We must learn to rely on the supernatural power of Christ, who appears with us and goes before us.

Thus, the second prerequisite to change the culture of fear is that we must learn to rely, not on our material reality and personal experience, but on the supernatural power of Christ, who appears with us and goes before us. When we let Jesus lead, our frustrated desire to solve problems with our strength turns into a joyous accompaniment as we follow the risen Christ.

Self-Reliance

While these first two responses maintain a sense of community in which decisions are made together, the third common response to change is to abandon any obligation to others and instead focus on self. America has a long history of combining Christian faith with stoic self-reliance, sacrifice, and a boot-straps work ethic. While traditional cultural values of sufficiency and responsibility have served society in some capacities, individualism has its limitations. Indeed, Jesus didn't appear to Thomas individually; he waited a week until they were again all gathered in one place:

> A week later his disciples were in the house again, and Thomas was with them. Though the doors were locked, Jesus came and stood among them and said, "Peace be with you!" Then he said to Thomas, "Put your finger here; see my hands. Reach out your hand and put it into my side. Stop doubting and believe."
>
> Thomas said to him, "My Lord and my God!"
>
> Then Jesus told him, "Because you have seen me, you have believed; blessed are those who have not seen and yet have believed." (John 20:26-29)

This seems unbelievable: a week after being in Christ's presence and receiving commissioning to go out and do the work, where were the disciples? Still in the same locked room! For Peter and the others, even the presence of Christ was not enough to persuade them to open their doors and take action. They were still trapped by fear.

Why? Perhaps this is because one of the eleven was still not on board. Until they had a consensus that Jesus was risen, they could not proceed. It was only when Jesus appeared to Thomas that the eleven were freed to move. We cannot go alone, or even without some. We need one another, and indeed Christ's kingdom is predicated on a shared life.[20] It was not until this point that the disciples became all "of one accord." In other words, we cannot do God's mission in the world single-handedly. We cannot create and innovate all on our own. True Christian innovation comes only through and for the community.

The Gospel of New and Improved

Retreat, rule, and self-reliance have each proven insufficient to improve the world. What the political left and right have shared is a common understanding of human agency, or their perceived need for people to actively intervene in history to improve the human condition. In this false view, humans must manage the emergence of God's kingdom, which requires power; thus, it is necessary to maintain the influence the church has held over Western culture since the time of Constantine in the early fourth century. This means the church must reconcile itself to the interests of the state and the production of new technology. In contemporary times, the religious left has focused on humanism and the social good while the religious right has attempted to re frame improvement according to divinely appointed theocratic impulses. The result is that we conflate new technology with belief in the eschaton, the coming kingdom of God, and with the United States of America's unique role in this emergence.

The result is a paradox. Although our fearful reactions to change stifle continued innovation, still the political left and right continue to support a theology of human agency. I call this a "gospel of new and improved." Instead of Jesus' gospel of new life, we continue to choose our own gospel of human agency and progress.

> The problem with the gospel of new and improved is that it conflates material progress with spiritual progress and inevitably lifts humankind to the role of chief architect of the New Creation.

The problem with the gospel of new and improved is that it conflates material progress with spiritual progress and inevitably lifts humankind to the role of chief architect of the New Creation. We have taken a good desire for *new*, properly understood as an active, persistent hope, and fetishized it as an ideology of progress. We believe in what we can see and act out of our strength, which we assume is good. Yet scripture repeatedly questions the "inclination of the thoughts of the human heart" (Gen 6:5), which cannot be improved but only be surrendered to Jesus. Jesus warns, and the early church understood, that material gain may be dangerous to the well-being of one's soul. As he reminds Peter, Jesus is the one who builds the church (see Matt 16:18).

Any cultural observer today must acknowledge that the promise of a "new and improved" gospel eventually leading to the final perfection of the world at the end of time does not seem to be coming to pass. Likewise, as the disciples huddled behind a locked door, their own visions of a more perfect world, free of Roman oppression, were falling apart.

The problem, as it turns out, was that their view of *new* was limited to their own experience. When our end-goal becomes our imagined vision instead of God's transcendent vision, we can create a false sense of reality about innovation. When innovation fades, instead of continuing to innovate, our false reality crashes, and we become discouraged. Or when it appears that our innovations have not effected lasting and eternal change, we can continue desperately to hold onto the old vision. In either scenario, we stop innovating. We don't understand why our theology of *new* has failed us.

While the first problem with innovation is that it does not last, the second problem of innovation is that it tends to benefit some people while harming others. To understand this let us turn to the story of Saigō Takamori: the last samurai.

Better and Worse

4

If Innovation Is Key to Improving the World, Why Isn't It
Working? (Part 2)

The rapid modernization of Japan and the samurai resistance offer a distilled commentary of the entire modern experiment—and for our purposes—both the promise and the peril of innovation. We have been obsessing over innovation and progress for hundreds of years and are both better and worse for it because change creates winners and losers. In the church, we have syncretized orthodox Christian faith with a secular worldview of scientific progress through human agency. But innovation defined as new solutions that disrupt the status quo and lead to change is not all good. Rather, it is a contronym: it creates both good and bad meaning. The problem is that innovation reflects human nature.

Saigō Takamori died on a hillside at dawn by *seppuku*, more commonly known as hara-kiri or ritual suicide by disembowelment with a sword. By 6:00 a.m. on the last day of the battle in September 1877, only forty of Saigō's rebel samurai remained, impossible odds against the twenty-thousand-plus troops of the Imperial Japanese Army that surrounded their mountain hideout.[1]

Though Imperial Commander General Yamagata Aritomo called for Takamori to surrender, he knew his request would be rebuffed. Both men had been trained in *bushido*, the way of the warrior, which considered surrender as without honor. Mortally wounded, Takamori asked his faithful lieutenant Beppu Shinsuke to ensure he died as a samurai. Once the act was completed, Beppu and the remaining samurai emerged from their hideout and ran straight into the final onslaught of mechanized artillery from the newest American-made technology, the Gatling gun.

The story of the last samurai captivated a Japanese nation whose leadership had chosen rapid modernization to survive the perceived existential threat of Western power. For two and a half centuries, from the time the Tokugawa shogunate expelled all foreigners and outlawed Christianity, the island nation of Japan remained aggressively isolated, ruled by feudal lords and enforced by a samurai warrior class. In 1853, American Commodore Matthew C. Perry approached Japan on orders from President Millard Fillmore to obtain a treaty. Perry saw Japan not as a sovereign nation but as a means by which America might continue to progress toward its "manifest destiny."[2] Japan made for a crucial way station between America and far-reaching Asian destinations. Over the next several years, Western powers, including America, Britain, France, Russia, and the Netherlands, all presented a show of superior technological force, which humiliated the Japanese and led them to engage in one-sided treaties. The subsequent internal conflict led to the overthrow of the feudal Tokugawa.[3]

As the new emperor Meiji took the throne in 1871, an era of cultural innovation began that is unparalleled in history. The Japanese nation aggressively embraced the latest technology in a variety of disciplines. A group of Japanese oligarchs set out on a world tour of Western power, known as the Iwakura Mission. Historian Maria Christensen writes, "They spent several months each in the United States, England and Europe . . . [and] brought home anything which might be useful to Japan, in one form or another, including a police system modeled somewhat on the French system, an educational system influenced by both America and Prussia, and new forms of agriculture."[4]

Already versed in the samurai way, one of the innovations the Japanese adopted from the West was the use of technology as a means of military progression. Seventy years later, in the International Military Tribunal for the Far East, which convened to try the leaders of Japan for joint conspiracy to start and wage what became the Second World War, General Ishiwara Kanji testified, speaking to American generals:

> Haven't you ever heard of Perry? . . . he aimed his big guns at Japan and warned that "If you don't deal with us, look out for these" . . . and so for its defense it took your own country as its teacher and set about learning how to be aggressive. You might say we became your disciples.[5]

As the new ruling class of Japan blended samurai culture with Western technology, the last samurai came to symbolize the final destruction (and sacralization) of an ancient philosophy and way of life. The rapid modernization of Japan and the samurai resistance offers a distilled commentary of the entire modern experiment, and—for our purposes—both the promise and the peril of innovation.

Winners and Losers

From the last samurai, Saigō Takamori, to Ned Ludd, the nineteenth-century English weaver who was put out of a job by a machine, there have always been people for whom technological innovation does not lead to "greater value." In chapter 1, I described a tacit assumption about innovation, first proposed by economist Joseph Schumpeter, as "creative destruction," that innovation is understood not just as incremental change and improvement but as a disruption to the status quo that leads to positive change.

The gospel of new and improved tends to adopt a utilitarian ethic about change. In other words, it assumes that as long as innovation helps society *as a whole*, it is good, even when evidence is clear that it may be harming specific groups of people. In fact, some argue that disruptive change is not only justified but also may be a necessary part of growth. It is like the journalist Peter Arnett's infamous Vietnam dispatch to the Associated Press, "It became necessary to destroy the town to save it."[6] Or, as the idiom says, history is written by the winners.

If you have wondered how the coronavirus and racial protests are related, consider that the street marches of 2020 may be understood as a repudiation of the breezy ideal that technological improvements benefit all or even most and are, therefore, justified. Sociologist Sherry Tuckle, who has written extensively about technology and human vulnerability, states that technology is more than "just a tool." It is a means of making meaning, and innovation brings both positive and negative consequences. We err as a society when we ignore systems we disrupt and people we diminish with our innovation.[7]

> We err as a society when we ignore systems we disrupt and people we diminish with our innovation.

In 2008, as the economy of the United States was about to collapse, a sermon by Rev. Jeremiah Wright of Trinity United Church of Christ damaged the candidacy of Barack Obama by its willingness to question the "American Dream," a Depression-era phrase that sought to hold on to the ideal of progress despite the worst economic circumstances in American history. As a pastor and an African American scholar, Wright protégé Frank Thomas observes that the American Dream has largely been "a ritual of benefit for a certain class of people,"[8] a class that has excluded people of color.

Wright's prophetic sermon generated controversy for not only its polemical rhetoric but also the realization from both the political left and right that segments of the population dared to question the idea of progress. While many like to correlate the Enlightenment with abolitionism and a rise in the autonomy of all persons, the majority of African slaves shipped to the New World were transported during the period now recognized as the height of the Enlightenment.[9] As cultural historian David Brion Davis writes, "Enslavement has usually been seen by the enslavers as a form of human progress."[10]

This has created deep ambivalence for people of color. Some reappropriated technological progress through the lens of biblical justice. Martin Luther King Jr. famously paraphrased nineteenth-century abolitionist Theodore Parker, who had preached that the long arc of the moral universe "bends towards justice."[11] While Obama followed King's lead, his pastor Jeremiah Wright did not share his optimism. Neither does next-generation Democratic congressperson Alexandria Ocasio-Cortez, who "depicts American history less as an arc of progress than as a circle, in which America repeats—rather than rises above—its past."[12] This shift is significant, as it serves as an indicator of what may be a generational rejection of the ideology of progress, though it is ironic that it comes from progressives.

While the rhetoric of innovation begs the question of "greater value," to use the phrase from innovation scholar Clayton Christensen's definition, the question remains: what do we mean by *value*? Value according to whom? The problem with innovation is that it benefits only specific people in specific time and space. It creates winners, but, in zero-sum fashion, it also creates losers. As Lenin famously summarized (and prophesied) regarding the progressive political ideal, "who? whom?"[13] In other words, who overtakes whom to achieve "equality for all"? Oriented toward power, society has typically defined value according to the winners. As we justify innovation by pointing to aggregate benefit, the reality is that there is also a dark side in which history is lost, people are displaced or eliminated, and entire cultures eradicated.

While corporate America buzzes over creativity and innovation, our current social and political culture is more known for polarization, stalemate, and stagnation than it is for flourishing. From personal computing to the internet, to mobile devices, and to social media, innovations in computer technology have had far and away the most disruptive influence on our lives in the last generation. But other sectors of society are repetitive and derivative. Cultural sourpuss Ross Douthat rightly observes that "from the academic heights to popular bestsellers, from Christian theology to secular fashion, from political theory to pop music, a range of cultural forms and intellectual pursuits have been stuck for decades in a pattern of recurrence."[14] The difference is observed in starkest relief when we compare our current culture to the period before the First World War. Such inventions as household electricity, the automobile, and the telephone utterly transformed the way people lived and even thought within a single generation and led to a period of expectation of actual, utopian realization. Now, while digital technology has led the way in modeling innovation over the past generation, some make the case that innovation today does not lead to cultural flourishing but may instead be a cause of cultural stagnation.[15]

In the practice of innovation, there are winners and losers. The dual nature of innovation as disruptive change sheds new light on John Wesley's famous three ethical rules for the Christian life to do no harm, do good, and attend upon all the ordinances of God.[16] Innovation may do good for society as a whole, but does it pass the test of doing no harm?

Equal and Opposite

The last samurai is a good story for illustrating the limitations of innovation because we are mostly removed from the time and space in which the story happened. Current examples get politicized in both the church and the culture at large. Arguments about any change—whether something as simple as minutes in a meeting or something as profound as the definition of marriage—become conflated with our assumptions about the future and the past. Most arguments about innovation boil down to this: is the new change inaugurating a better future or diminishing a more sacred past?

In the streamlined, modern telling of *new*, there is only "new and improved." There is no samurai or any group of people for whom technological improvement leads to suffering. In the hallowed, conservationist telling of *new*, the opposite is true. Every story of disruptive technology has both winners and losers, at least in the immediate term. While the mechanized loom that displaced Ned Ludd may have led to more efficiency and greater production, it also led to the end of livelihoods for many.

What both change advocates and change adversaries share is a fundamentally material view of the world. In the gospel of new and improved, the belief that things are getting better is married to an Enlightenment ideology of progress. Historian Diarmaid Mac-Culloch writes that Descartes, the philosopher most responsible for what became Enlightenment thought, "was the decisive influence in encouraging his contemporaries and successors to think of a human being as dual in nature: material and immaterial. The problem which has haunted Cartesian views of personality thereafter has been to show how in any sense the two natures might be united."[17]

Raised a devoted French Catholic, Descartes certainly would have understood orthodox theology on the dual nature of Christ, divine and human, as well as arguments about the human soul. Yet, "while Chalcedonian Christianity has sought to settle that difficulty, . . . [he] tended to resolve the difficulty by privileging the material over the spiritual."[18] Science's focus on observable experience encouraged the continuing emphasis of a material world over an immaterial world. After all, observable phenomena are easier to deal with.

But not every form of material progress is evidence of God's kingdom, and history has shown that a focus on innovation yields mixed results. Consider the state of education in America, both public and private. Mobile devices are easily one of the most invasive new technological innovations of twenty-first-century Western culture.[19] The predominant age when children receive a smartphone with a service plan is now age 10,[20] which is old news to anyone with school-aged children. The result has been mixed at best. On one hand, personal devices have been an aid to teaching through a pandemic; on the other hand, teachers are constantly waging an attention battle in the classroom, and they are losing. The connected world is living out a real-time experiment, and the returns are not looking favorable, as a growing body of research suggests that "smartphones are causing real damage to our minds and relationships."[21] Concern, which began in the 1990s, over the rise of a "digital divide" giving privileged groups unfair access to the internet has inverted:

> The real digital divide in this country is not between children who have access to the internet and those who don't. It's between children whose parents know that they have to restrict screen time and those whose parents have been sold a bill of goods by schools and politicians that more screens are a key to success.[22]

Or consider this anecdotal chart, compiled by two of my teen-aged children, on their perceptions of things that are better and things that are worse, on aggregate, in the past one hundred years:

SINCE 100 YEARS AGO	
BETTER	WORSE
Education	Environment
Medicine	Civility
Safety	Culture
Life Expectancy	Language
Standards of Living	Quality of Life

Of course, one could argue some of these choices, but the point remains. Some things improve; others worsen. Christians should be cautious about breezy support of progressive, utilitarian approaches to societal advancement, in which benefits to the majority outweigh losses to minorities, or an approach in which we use the levers of politics to remove power from some and give it to others in a zero-sum attempt to engineer a more humane, "kingdom" society. Political scientist James C. Scott critiques "the imperialism of high modernist, planned social order,"[23] which seeks to organize society according to scientific principles and ignores local, contextualized knowledge and relationships. Centrally managed social planning fails, Scott argues, when it imposes inadequate schematic visions that do violence to complex local and relational dependencies that cannot be fully understood.[24]

Or as French political philosopher Margaret Majumdar writes, "Even those who believed in the generally progressive march of history, such as Karl Marx, had been forced to concede that there could be losers as well as winners in the actual processes involved in economic and social change."[25] The case studies of twentieth-century geopolitics have demonstrated that the ability to engineer a more perfect solution, as we are still prone to do in society and church, is vastly overstated. Technological innovation is dangerous when we conflate it too closely with Enlightenment thought. As sociologist Robert Wright notes about Stephen Pinker's defense of Enlightenment values:

> Pinker attributes too much of our past progress to Enlightenment thought (giving short shrift, for example, to the role of Christian thinkers and activists in ending slavery); his faith in science and reason is naive, given how often they've been misused; his assumption that scientifically powered progress will bring happiness betrays a misunderstanding of our deepest needs; his apparent belief that secular humanism can fill the spiritual void left by rationalism's erosion of religion only underscores that misunderstanding.[26]

Leaning on the promises of progress seems naive at best and more likely dangerous when it ignores history, displaces people, engenders violence, and endangers children. Progress increases knowledge with little thought of wisdom. It empowers individuals with little thought to community. Or, as philosopher John Gray writes, "Nothing is more commonplace than to lament that moral progress has failed to keep pace with scientific knowledge."[27]

Even medicine, which improved radically through the application of empiricism, is not immune to this phenomenon of unintended consequences. In our sanitizer culture, increases in standards of living through a decline in bacterial disease[28] are offset with an alarming rise in new, infectious diseases.[29] A global pandemic was predicted by some, including billionaire technologist Bill Gates.[30]

The same is true for all disruptive technology. The Western obsession with "new and improved" assumes the phrase is a redundancy, that *new* is always better. Progress, of course, does not suggest just technological advancement but also an associated humanism, or increasing individual autonomy. But policies and ethics that celebrate individual autonomy sometimes create unexpected collisions, for example in the tension between sexual freedom and rape culture.

New is never just improved; it makes some things better, and others worse. *New* is a contronym, meaning it is a word with two opposite meanings at the same time, one positive, one negative. In the church, we have syncretized orthodox Christian faith with a secular worldview of scientific progress through human agency. In our eagerness to expand the umbrella of progress, we forget Newton's Third Law, that for every action there is an equal and opposite reaction. We strive for "equal" but get "equal and opposite." Contrary to the ideal of progress, if technology has done anything for us, it has magnified human tendencies to do good and cause harm. As Ronald Wright observes, we become victims of our success, and every time history repeats itself, the cost increases.[31] Innovation as disruption helps only some people, only some of the time.

> If technology has done anything for us, it has magnified human tendencies to do good and cause harm.

If only we were more intelligent or more moral, we might use technology for purely benign ends. When it comes to technological advancement, the fault is not in our tools but in ourselves. The paradox of progress and the reason innovation has failed to work is because its resulting technology reflects us—in all our glory and all our depravity. Progress leaves only one problem unsolved: the frailty of human nature. Unfortunately, this problem appears to be scientifically intractable.

A New Theology of *New*

My career has, to a large degree, been about innovation in ministry. In this work, I often find myself in discussions on the topic of whether "technology" (usually meaning the latest digital advancement) is good or bad for the church. The most common argument I hear from people is that it is neutral. But the question is a red herring. When it comes to technology, *new* is never just neutral because it is not passive. As social media has proved beyond a doubt, new technology actively reshapes its culture. Yet new technology is neither solely good nor solely bad. New technology, and the innovation that leads to it, is both utopian and dystopian. The ultimate example is the splitting of the atom, which ushered in a new phase of scientific understanding. This technology with its "as of yet unrealized" potential for abundant energy also introduced a bomb with destructive power previously unknown in human history. New is *agathokakological*, meaning it contains both good and evil, just like the humans who do the work.

So, for the Christ follower, if creativity reflects who we are as image bearers of God, new technology is capable of improving the common good. Innovation remains an urgent need in our culture, yet innovation may also lead to suffering. Where does this leave us? As Christians, we cannot accept a world that creates suffering for any.

The next place to look is our definition of the word *new*. While the secular field of innovation emphasizes innovation as disruptive and fundamentally novel, the limitations of our obsession with *new* should now be obvious to anyone paying attention to culture. Defining *new* as "disruptive" is not sufficient as a definition of Christian innovation. We need a better theology of *new*. It is to this we turn next.

New Creation

5

What Is Unique about Christian Innovation?

The story of Norman Borlaug illustrates the power of some people to do global, life-changing things that benefit humankind. We marvel at such works, but to compare our work to people such as Borlaug is to misunderstand Jesus' intent. *Greater* is an adjective to describe the presence of God's Spirit in us, not the scale or relative influence of our work. To work as if we can incrementally progress toward a new kingdom of God through our effort reflects an ideology of progress (and usually a false dichotomy between personal piety and social reform). The New Creation is a qualitatively different reality, happening in our present time. Christian innovation is what happens when, in faith, we participate in God's ongoing work of the New Creation.

Norman Borlaug saved more lives than any other human in the history of the world.[1] Borlaug's story is a story of Christian innovation.

Borlaug's story begins in Minneapolis. While riots there after the death of George Floyd were a hot spot for the events of 2020, they were not the first in the city's history. Another riot happened in 1933, in the depths of the Great Depression, when striking truckers dumped the city's inventory of milk onto the streets. While the 2020 riots focused on race, the 1933 riots focused on hunger.

Witness to this event was a young Norman Borlaug, an incoming freshman at the University of Minnesota. Seeing the effects of hunger had a profound effect on Borlaug, who grew up a Lutheran farm boy in rural Iowa. He witnessed "huge numbers of desperate, hungry people huddled in the streets, begging for food, sleeping on newspapers spread over the sidewalks."[2]

His faith, along with the problem of human hunger, would motivate Borlaug for his entire life.[3] By his death in 2009, he was widely credited with launching a "Green Revolution" and saving over a billion lives.[4] Magicians and self-described atheists Penn and Teller describe Borlaug as the "greatest human who ever existed."[5] His page-one, 2200-word obituary in the *New York Times* credits him with breeding high-yield varieties of crops that "helped to avert mass famines that were widely predicted in the 1960s, altering the course of history."[6] Writer Gregg Easterbrook observes, "Perhaps more than anyone else, Borlaug is responsible for the fact that throughout the postwar era, except in sub-Saharan Africa, global food production has expanded faster than the human population, averting the mass starvations that were widely predicted."[7]

The problem Borlaug saw was the rapid expansion of the world population, which had exploded since the beginning of the twentieth century, rising from two billion when Borlaug was a youth in the 1920s to almost eight billion today (due, in no small part, to innovations in medicine, thus proving that one solution may lead to another problem).[8] By the late 1960s, famine had become a primary concern. Could agriculture keep up with such insatiable demand? Stanford biologist Paul Ehrlich was a representative doomsayer, predicting the inevitable starvation of hundreds of millions of people, particularly in India, in his 1968 bestseller *The Population Bomb*.[9]

While Ehrlich critiqued, Borlaug was out working in the fields, building on and refining techniques he had cultivated since boyhood. In Mexico following World War II, he discovered high-yield agricultural methods. Next, Borlaug turned his attention to the Asia subcontinent. His growth system, which led to exponentially higher yields in Pakistan and India, is widely credited with averting famine and was the basis for his Nobel Prize award in 1970.

At his acceptance speech, Borlaug was still talking about the issue of human hunger. He quoted a line from the charter of the previous year's winner, the International Labor Organization, which said, "Universal and lasting peace can be established only if it is based upon social justice. If you desire peace, cultivate justice." Borlaug added:

> Almost certainly, however, the first essential component of social justice is adequate food for all mankind. Food is the moral right of all who are born into this world. Yet today fifty percent of the world's population goes hungry. Without food, man can live at most but a few weeks; without it, all other components of social justice are meaningless. Therefore I feel that the aforementioned guiding principle must be modified to read: If you desire peace, cultivate justice, but at the same time cultivate the fields to produce more bread; otherwise there will be no peace.[10]

Borlaug then cited Isaiah 8:21: "Distressed and hungry, they will roam through the land; when they are famished, they will become enraged and, looking upward, will curse their king and their God." Borlaug understood the destructive power of human hunger both because of scriptural witness and because he had witnessed it firsthand. He devoted his life to the everyday, practical work of agricultural innovation and was successful beyond his wildest dreams.

The story of Norman Borlaug illustrates the power of a single human life to do global, life-changing things that benefit humankind. Is this what Jesus had in mind when he told his disciples they will do greater things? Borlaug improved the lives of an untold number of people. His work wasn't just innovative; it was an incredible example of Christian innovation.

Greater is not a description of comparison
but a statement of being.

We marvel at such works, yet to call Borlaug's work *greater* based on its scope or the number of people he touched, or to compare his work to our own, is to misunderstand Jesus' intent. Borlaug's work does not necessarily embody Jesus' idea of "greater things" because of the millions of people he helped. *Greater* is not an adjective about scale or size, though it may lead to it. What does it mean, then? *Greater* is not a description of comparison but a statement of being.

The Greater Could

Let us return to Jesus' promise. On the night of his betrayal, he told his disciples,

> Very truly I tell you, whoever believes in me will do the works I have been doing, and they will do even greater things than these, because I am going to the Father. (John 14:12)

In the introduction, I asked the question: How can we, as Jesus' disciples, somehow have the ability to do even greater things than he? Jesus answers this question with the phrase "whoever believes in me," which begs the question: What about believing in Jesus influences our ability to do great things?

While modernism has encouraged us to think of belief empirically, as intellectual assent, the disciples experienced Jesus in a more holistic and transforming way. Earlier, we visited the eleven disciples as they sat in a locked room. Jesus had died. Two days later, they heard through Mary that he was alive. Then, as they huddled up in a locked room, they saw him alive, firsthand. But what happened next?

> Again Jesus said, "Peace be with you! As the Father has sent me, I am sending you." And with that he breathed on them and said, "Receive the Holy Spirit." (John 20:21-22)

Though the disciples had followed Jesus for three years, this was something new. In this moment, they received a "holy spirit." Consider the name "Holy Spirit" not as a proper noun—one of the three Persons of the Trinity in Christian theology—but as an adjective and noun phrase. The Scriptures define *spirit* as *ruach* (Hebrew) and *pneuma* (Greek). Both words connote a breath or a wind, a fresh breeze. The later Latin translation *spirare,* to breathe, gives us our contemporary word *inspiration.* So the breath they received was a spirit of holiness. A breath of fresh air. To receive the Holy Spirit is to intake the breath of God.

As God is good, this holy spirit gave the disciples an infusion of all that is good, an infusion of relaxation and release followed by an aha of inspiration, which is the elixir that animates our very best work. Breathing is central to our entire being. Breathing is life. God's breath filled the disciples with life. It inspired them, wiping out their fear and replacing it with life and purpose. By breathing on them, the risen Jesus offered them a new kind of reality: life with God's Spirit within their being.

Jesus had portended this moment in his teaching to the rabbi Nicodemus earlier, when he said,

> "Very truly I tell you, no one can enter the kingdom of God unless they are born of water and the Spirit. Flesh gives birth to flesh, but *the Spirit gives birth to spirit.* You should not be surprised at my saying, 'You must be born again.' The wind blows wherever it pleases. You hear its sound, but you cannot tell where it comes from or where it is going. So it is with everyone born of the Spirit." (John 3:5-8, emphasis added)

The Spirit gives birth to spirit! Here we find what Jesus means by *greater.* God is great, as Jesus describes when he says, "My Father, who has given them to me, is greater than all" (John 10:29). Since

God is great, and, through the Holy Spirit, God abides in us, we become great when we receive God's Spirit. Greatness is defined not by scale or influence, or by being the winner instead of the loser. *Greatness* is a word to describe God's presence in our lives. It is a description of our personage, who we become as followers of the risen Lord.

> *Greatness* is a word to describe God's presence in our lives. It is a description of our personage, who we become as followers of the risen Lord.

Consider John the Baptist, the prophet who proclaimed the coming of the Messiah. The Gospels tell the story of his imprisonment. Though he had been thrown into prison, he was still getting word of Jesus' deeds. So John sent his disciples to inquire: Are you the Messiah? They arrive as Jesus is instructing the teachers of the law. In front of everyone, he answers them. But rather than make a claim or defend himself, Jesus tells John's disciples to use their senses: what do they hear and see? Do the deaf hear? The lame walk? The blind see? (See Matt 11:1-10.)

John's disciples leave the scene, and then Jesus turns to the crowd that witnessed the exchange and begins to talk about John. He says,

> "Truly I tell you, among those born of women there has not risen anyone greater than John the Baptist; yet whoever is least in the kingdom of heaven is greater than he." (Matt 11:11)

The prophets were the greatest of all figures in ancient Israel because they spoke for God, and Jesus describes John as the greatest prophet. Yet, while John the Baptist was the greatest prophet—no less than the greatest human, according to Israel's understanding—he was still less than the least person in the kingdom of heaven, because, like everyone else, he had not received God's Spirit. This means greatness is understood first in Holy Spirit terms not in human terms. It is defined first according to our spiritual lineage. While John the Baptist was among the greatest of all people born of nature and of flesh, above John is an entirely new category of humankind.

The very least person who receives God's Spirit is greater than the greatest person who does not—not because they are "better" or "more accomplished," for these are categories the world uses to determine status and power—but greater because that person has status as a child of God. Anyone who is part of this new reality, which Jesus describes as a "kingdom," has importance and gifts that surpass even the greatest of those who are marred and bound by a sin-dimmed world.

If this is a little confusing, imagine how those who heard his teaching felt. They did not have the benefit of orthodox Christian theological teaching. Jesus had not yet been crucified. He was describing a new kind of kingdom that did not yet exist. As Jesus died, he claimed, "It is finished" (John 19:30). Later, after Jesus' resurrection, when he breathed the breath of the Holy Spirit on the disciples in their locked room, Jesus began an entirely new category of human being: those persons who are part of God's kingdom because they have been born of spirit and truth. Instead of breathing in old, diseased aerosols of fear and debilitation, the disciples caught a new kind of wind. When the disciples believed, they received the Holy Spirit, and as recipients of God's Spirit, they were transformed, their fear becoming courage to do new, greater things.

Thus, the word *greater* is not a word of comparison, or a description of one person's abilities or achievements. The resurrection created a new category of human. Greatness is defined by the presence of God's Spirit in us. This is lofty and theological—they were experiencing a new kind of reality—yet it leads to practical ends. As recipients of God's Spirit, the disciples had a new, energized, and very clear purpose in life. For the first time, God's Spirit abided in the spirits of the disciples.

When my middle-school-aged-son gets excited about something, he says it is "juicy." Jesus was giving them the juice to move. With such power in them, how could they not get out and begin to share with others what Jesus had done for them? So we do likewise. As Christians, we get out and create new things, alive with the possibilities and "could bes" of true inspiration.

Yet we immediately encounter problems. As we have established, reasons for innovation's fundamental limitations are that new improvements don't last, that they are never universal, and that they cause suffering to some. While our culture desperately needs new ideas that lead to "significant, positive change," if we, as followers of Christ, continue with conventional understandings of innovation, we will continue to see the same limited results, regardless of the people involved or the goals pursued. The best of what we call innovation merely produces tiny empires, built on things of the world, which inevitably fade.

To solve these limitations, we need a better understanding of *new*, defined not by a utilitarian ethic of "greater good" but based on the promises of Jesus. To understand this, let's take a look at Jesus' use of the word *new*.

A New Thing

While Christians today are known for retreat, rule, and self-reliance, historically one of the greatest assets to culture has been the church—the body of believers—who, having heard Christ's call to go, responds to the needs of the world with brilliant new ideas that save lives. Consider for example that health insurance came from a group of church people.[11] While in challenging times such as we face now, the temptation may be to go backward, God calls us forward. Christian innovation is about being Spirit-mended and solution-minded.

Christian innovation is about being
Spirit-mended and solution-minded.

Christian innovation is in many ways just like secular innovation. As I described earlier, innovation is an instrument, an invention, intuitive, and influential. But we cannot stop here. In addition to these characteristics, Christian innovation is something greater: Christian innovation is how we participate in the emergence of God's New Creation. Dean of Duke Divinity School Greg Jones describes "Christian social innovation" as activity that helps reveal a transformed creation.[12] But how do we avoid falling into the trap of the social gospel? Let us look at this word *new* in more depth.

The New Testament contains two Greek words commonly translated into the English as *new: neos* and *kainos*. The first is about time; the second is about substance. *Neos* connotes change: something recently created, not previously known or used. It is closer to our current understanding of innovation as "new and improved." This has a strong implication of time; it is a comparison of something new to something old. *Kainos*, however, is more than a question of time. It is a type of *new* defined by a quality. Both definitions are critical to understanding Christ's New Creation.

There is the one story in the Gospels in which Jesus uses both definitions. Here it is (I've inserted which Greek word for *new* Jesus uses throughout):

> They said to him, "John's disciples often fast and pray, and so do the disciples of the Pharisees, but yours go on eating and drinking."
>
> Jesus answered, "Can you make the friends of the bridegroom fast while he is with them? But the time will come when the bridegroom will be taken from them; in those days they will fast."
>
> He told them this parable: "No one tears a piece out of a new [*neos*] garment to patch an old one. Otherwise, they will have torn the new [*neos*] garment, and the patch from the new [*neos*] will not match the old. And no one pours new [*neos*] wine into old wineskins. Otherwise, the new [*neos*] wine will burst the skins; the wine will run out and the wineskins will be ruined. No, new [*neos*] wine must be poured into new [*kainos*] wineskins. And no one after drinking old wine wants the new [*neos*], for they say, 'The old is better.' " (Luke 5:33-39)

The question posed to Jesus compared his disciples to the disciples of his cousin, John the Baptist. As I wrote earlier, Jesus declared John to be the greatest prophet. John's disciples ask Jesus about John's methods. Shouldn't people fast and pray, like John did? It would make sense to follow in John's footsteps, right?

No, Jesus says. John obeyed the rules of the Law, which is the old wine, but Jesus himself is the new wine. (The first public image he uses for himself is wine, at Cana; and the last image he uses for himself is wine, in the Upper Room.) The key is the phrase "new wineskins," which is the only use of *kainos* in his parable. The new wineskins are not just newer in age, but a qualitatively different kind of material. *Kainos* means unprecedented, both fresh and superior to that which came before. In other words, Jesus is not just another teacher in a line of teachers or prophets, including his cousin John. Jesus is new wine; when we believe in him, we become part of a New Creation. While the promised kingdom of God exists in time, it refers not just to the future but points us toward a substantially different, greater reality—one in which we already participate because of our faith. The New Testament refers to this reality as the New Creation. The New Creation is a qualitatively different reality, happening in our present time.

If Jesus is the new wine, what is the wineskin? Old wineskins are practices and habits, such as fasting, which become ways of thinking and being that made sense to those who once obeyed the Law and waited for the Messiah to come. Now that the Messiah has come, though, those who seek God no longer need those practices; in fact, they may inhibit us from knowing God. When Jesus says new wine must be poured into new wineskins, he means that believing in him introduces an entirely new reality, and with it, entirely different ways of living. If you try to follow Jesus using the practices of the old covenant, everything bursts. Jesus is telling John's disciples that to follow him means to no longer worry about ascetic living or about the Roman occupation.

Thus, the word *kainos* is synonymous with innovation: the old religious practices that preceded Jesus are not going to work for following Jesus. *Christian* and *innovation* are redundant, according to Jesus. While we seek fresh solutions for the problems we face, as Christian innovators, our best new innovations will not work if they are built into the same old contexts—systems of communication, turns of phrase, ideas and activities—the sum of exchanges that compose the seamless web of our culture.

> The New Creation is synonymous with innovation: the old religious practices that preceded Jesus are not going to work for following Jesus. According to Jesus, *Christian* and *innovation* are redundant.

As all innovators and change agents know, when confronted with the old world, our efforts to create new solutions often burst, atrophy, and encounter rejection. Many creative, talented people have tried to bring fresh thinking to the church, only to give up in frustration at the forces of stasis and resistance that prevent new growth from happening. Lasting innovation needs qualitatively different contexts to thrive. This may happen only with the fresh wind of the Holy Spirit, which introduces the *kainos* kingdom.

The apostle Paul describes this in my favorite Bible verse when he writes, "Therefore, if anyone is in Christ—new creation! The old has gone, the new is come" (2 Cor 5:17, my translation). The Greek for this verse is tricky and belies simple English translation. A direct, word-for-word translation reveals a present tense emphasis on not just a new person in time but a qualitatively different person. Paul is describing a sense of time that is beyond one tense—to be a *kainos* creation is both present reality and future hope.

Another way of saying this is that Christian innovation is both rooted in time (*neos*) and out of time (*kainos*). Or, to use innovation scholar Clayton Christensen's term *value*, innovation becomes Christian when *new* includes both incarnate value and eternal value. Our work is of the Spirit; it is Christian innovation when it includes both these attributes.

> Christian innovation includes both incarnate value and eternal value.

What does this mean for the work of Christian innovation? It means our work is relevant to the present and is oriented toward the future. This has proven to be rather difficult to do, as we noted earlier. We can find a solution in the Christian doctrine of the incarnation.

Flesh and Blood

As God is a God of history, and God's kingdom is rooted in time, *new* necessitates an understanding of time. The Christian witness tells of a changed world that began with Christ in the beginning (past), is coming in the fulfillment of all time (future), and is come (now). Therefore, the New Creation is *neos*. But the New Creation is also *kainos*: qualitatively different, a whole different realm. It is both a present reality and a different entity.

Perhaps this is best understood with a theology of incarnation. As Leonard Sweet observes, "Incarnation is not something that happened once and for all time. It is something that happened once, in all time, and for all time."[13] To be in all time means that God is in the past, present, and the future—all three tenses at once.

So how do we live in all three tenses? One way is to learn to think concurrently, not consecutively; simultaneously, not sequentially. As followers of the risen Lord, we are invited to participate in the revelation of his kingdom. This is a calling to remember the past, activate the future, and live in the present.

To incarnate is to put flesh (*carne*) on spirit. God modeled this very thing with God's scandalous choice to take on flesh in the form of the human Jesus. One sure mark of Christian innovation is that it is "flesh and blood": it meets real needs happening this very day—not twenty years ago or some possible future situation—but real needs.

> One sure mark of Christian innovation is that it is flesh and blood: it meets real needs happening this very day—not twenty years ago or some possible future situation—but real needs.

Staying present in a quickly changing culture is no easy task. I am reminded of the insurance commercial that shows a father pushing his boy on a swing. The boy disappears from the frame for a moment. When he comes back, he has become a grown man, and his weight knocks the father over. The tagline: Life moves at you fast. As the father of four, I can relate. Since life moves at us fast, the challenge is to maintain a constant presence with others in community. As we stay sensitive to rising generations with changing needs, the need to update our methods becomes obvious.

This is also how to understand Christian innovations that cease to be as effective as they once were. The Ginghamsburg worship story was Christian innovation because it was not just *neos* new, it was *kainos* new. It made a qualitative difference in people's lives, such as the story of Mike Sandlin, a Dayton, Ohio, drug addict. He had spent twenty years drifting through life, wishing for death, until he came into our congregation one morning in August 1998. In one of our "worship experiences," he had an encounter with God that instantly changed him and healed him of his desire to get high. The rest of his life, Mike told the story of what Jesus had done for him. I thought of Mike as a living, breathing, 1990s Ohio embodiment of the demon-possessed man healed by Jesus as told in the Gospel according to Mark, chapter 5.

Stories such as Sandlin's actually happened. Yet, on the larger scale of church life, the methods we used began to fade in popularity. We were part of a larger, "seeker sensitive" movement that sought to reimagine Christian worship as evangelism and adopt methods that make sense to a culture no longer familiar with Christian ritual. Eventually, the movement ran out of steam. Critics emerged. Does this make what we did a failure? No; it was helpful for the time and space in which it was designed. Now we need new innovations for a different time and space. Even Norman Borlaug has his critics.

As followers of Jesus, we are constantly called to be about the business of learning new ways to put flesh on the presence of Jesus in our current time. We must constantly be about changing with the signs of the times. Christian innovation scholar Scott Cormode offers a definition of *innovation* as making "spiritual meaning." Though this definition is problematic in that it suggests "meaning" is an invention of the one making the meaning,[14] his definition is helpful in understanding the idea of ministry as incarnation, or—as members of a congregation will sometimes say to one another—how to "be the hands and feet of Jesus."

The problem with the cultural legacy of the Enlightenment and its ideology of progress is that Christians have read *new* as only *neos* and not *kainos*. Confusion about the two has led to a rejection of the past. Rauschenbusch made this mistake when he defined Christianity in evolutionary terms and described the church as "the organized expression of the religious life of the past." Jesus promises to make all things new (Rev 21:5), yet Jesus is the same yesterday, today, and forever (Heb 13:8). We need both new and the old in order to be rejuvenated and tied to something greater than ourselves.

Rauschenbusch's contemporary, Princeton theologian Geerhardus Vos, clarified this misunderstanding when he wrote what is the seminal understanding of the kingdom of God as a paradoxical "already/not yet" reality. Vos argues that the kingdom and the church are one and the same.[15] Peter's confession forms the foundation, Jesus builds the house, and, at the end of his ministry, Jesus hands over the keys to Peter to receive and occupy.[16] Thus, any view that separates God's kingdom and the church does not reflect Jesus' teaching on the subject.[17] Since the church is the New Creation, the church is also Christ's bride, and the church is made up of disciples (us), the question of the New Creation is actually a question about us and our willingness to fully believe in Jesus and receive the Holy Spirit. As Christians, our promise is for a future that doesn't fade and for a world built on the words of Jesus, which will never pass away (Matt 24:35).

Our efforts to innovate haven't worked because we have limited our understanding of our work to *neos* and have worked as if we can incrementally progress toward and eventually realize Jesus' promised New Creation. Our *neos*-exclusive understanding of innovation is a half-truth. There is actually nothing new under the sun, to quote Ecclesiastes 1:9. This attitude toward work reflects an ideology of progress and has led to a false dichotomy between personal piety and social reform. We cannot *make* the New Creation. Instead, we *receive* the *kainos* New Creation as a gift.

Whereas secular innovation is temporal—rooted in time—Christian innovation is eternal. But, you may say, churches close too. Yes, but the hearts that they touch while in motion are changed forever, and their effect lasts for generations. Secular innovation will pass away, but the kingdom will not pass away. Christian innovation comes from a new way of looking at the world, is fueled by God's Spirit, and results in new solutions of eternal value. It is different from other forms of innovation by virtue of its focus on eternal value—value according to what is true, good, and beautiful by standards of God's kingdom.

Christian innovation is what happens when, in faith, we participate in God's ongoing work of the New Creation. Thus, the answer is to seek after Christ, to incarnate Christ. The work of Christian innovation isn't just a matter of making something better. It is to give flesh and blood to Christ in our current culture. As culture changes, every generation is called to do this work. To be Christian innovators and create something that is both fully present and fully eternal, is to be used by the Holy Spirit through the work of Christ's community for the inauguration of God's future. As Christians, we need to learn what is happening, how technology develops, the role of creativity, where God is moving, and our role in joining. God wants us to live without fear, knowing that the future is not only okay but that God is already there, and that taking steps toward a better future is an act of faith.

Borlaug met such a need on a grand scale. By answering the problem of hunger, Borlaug became the hands and feet of Jesus, meeting current needs and healing over a billion people from the threat of starvation. Quite literally, by giving a significant percentage of the people of this planet food to eat, he made Jesus incarnate to them.

Given this understanding of Christian innovation, let us finally look at what this means for our work.

6
Spirit Work
Is It Actually Possible to Change the World?

Florence Nightingale saved untold lives and founded modern nursing, not for ambition or wealth but because she could accept no less than a life fully integrated with her faith and her gifts. When we let God's Spirit fill our spirits, we become empowered as priests of God; our work becomes our ministry, no matter the calling; and we pursue lives that seek to integrate the spiritual and the material. Because of this we don't have to worry about such grand results as "changing the world." Instead, we simply join in the work God is already doing. Christian innovation is work that is revealed by the Holy Spirit, relates to the current time, and results in a whole and complete life of flourishing. But this work is never done; because of sin, every generation is called to incarnate God's Spirit anew.

The entire hospital smelled like a sewer. When Florence Nightingale arrived at the British camp near Constantinople, Turkey, on November 5, 1854, with a group of trained nurses, what she saw was horrifying. A slurry of feces and water covered the floor, up to an inch thick. A dead horse floated in the water supply.[1] Rats ran about, supplies were practically nonexistent, and the death rate of the patients in the beds was an appalling 42.7 percent.[2]

A major engagement of the Crimean War, the Battle of Inkerman, was raging on the day of her arrival. Soldiers were coming into the hospital at an alarming rate, but the hospital was ill-equipped to help them. As the *London Times* reported after another victory a few weeks prior, "sick and wounded British soldiers were being left to die without medical attention. Not only were there too few surgeons and not even linen to make bandages but also there was not a single qualified nurse in the British military hospital at Scutari."[3]

On reading the newspaper article, Nightingale wrote her friend, Sidney Herbert, the Secretary of War, offering to help. But he had already dispatched a letter to her, asking her to recruit a group of nurses and travel to Turkey to intervene in the hospital. When they arrived three weeks later, Nightingale and her new team immediately set about cleaning up the environment, despite hostility from military authorities and doctors who were administering aid in much the same way as ancient physicians had, using long-established, artisanal medical practices.

Using private funds from multiple sources and working under the authority of Herbert, independent of the local military, Nightingale began by having crews scrub down the walls and floors. She set up a boiler room for hot water and a laundry for sanitizing linens. She had extra kitchens installed for proper nutrition. Hostility from local military authorities ran so high that her nurses were initially even barred from walking the wards. Nevertheless, she persisted; eventually, she and her nurses began to make rounds, treating wounds properly and caring for the soldiers' needs. At night, Nightingale would send her team to bed and walk alone among the prostrate, sick men, holding a lamp, checking on their comfort and morale. The poet Longfellow captured this image and reported it back to London, where she appeared in the *Times* with a new nickname: The Lady with the Lamp. The image of the solitary Nightingale holding up a light in the darkness of the physically mortifying hospital wards was not lost on the British people. Conditions immediately improved, and within six months the mortality rate at the British military hospital in Scutari, Turkey, had dropped from 47 percent to 2 percent. Eight months after she left, she returned home to London a world-famous heroine and the founder of modern nursing.

But her work was far from done. Using notes from the eight months in the field, she began to analyze larger trends. She soon realized that sixteen thousand of the eighteen-thousand deaths were not caused by battle wounds but by preventable, unsanitary hospital conditions. Knowing that a simple table may not help communicate this truth to British authorities and the public, she invented a new form of data visualization using what was dubbed the "Nightingale Rose Diagram" (and has since become known as a polar-area chart). The data was so easy to understand that it created a significant swell of public attention to the issue of hospital sanitation and led to a new national sanitary science, an army medical division, and even statistics departments.

Prior to her work, nurses were considered low class and had a reputation for "promiscuity and drunkenness." While Nightingale saved an untold number of lives and almost single-handedly formed the modern understanding of nursing, her work is more impressive considering her ability to overcome the social restraints on women in nineteenth-century England. The daughter of a wealthy landowner, the expectation for Florence was to marry and raise children; women in her social circles did not pursue degrees or careers. Yet she rejected suitors and offers of marriage to pursue a mission to serve others through the prevention of needless illness and death. As journalist Bernard Cohen writes, "Much of what now seems basic in modern health care can be traced to pitched battles fought by Nightingale in the 19th century. Less well known . . . is her equally pioneering use of the new advanced techniques of statistical analysis in those battles."[4]

Why would a wealthy young woman, with access to the highest levels of British society, reject the comforts of her environment to wade in feces and kill rats, all while fighting hostile resistance from her medical colleagues at every step? Simply, her Christian faith compelled her. After a conversion experience at the age of sixteen, her faith became a driving force in her life. But unlike many in nineteenth-century England, her faith was not only an inward force for personal edification but an outward force for social reform. As Cohen writes, "Her religious feelings, however, centered on the conviction that the best way to serve God was through service to mankind."[5]

Nightingale lived a life in which her faith and her daily actions needed to align. When she rejected a marriage proposal despite her own romantic feelings, she told her suitor that her "moral" and "active" nature could never be satisfied "making society."[6] Her theology, if you will, was the same we find in many stories of Christian innovators. From an early age, she adhered to a holistic understanding of the Christian life. She used every gift and resource at her disposal in pursuit of a calling that was greater than herself. At age thirty, she wrote in her journal about her work with a maturity that eschewed personal reputation for a desire to "regenerate the world."[7] But the fame she shunned came to her anyway, because the fruit of her work was so dramatic. She saved untold lives and founded modern nursing because she could accept no less than a life fully integrated with her faith.

> Florence Nightingale used every gift and resource at her disposal in pursuit of a calling that was greater than herself.

The story of Florence Nightingale raises questions of control: Under whose agency does the end of history—whether initially characterized in Christian terms as God's kingdom or, in more recent secular terms, as a "great society"[8]—emerge? Does it emerge as the result of the work of a sovereign deity, a king given god-like power, or the work of human agency, also known as "the people"? As Victor Dias writes, "One of the differences between the idea of progress and Augustine's view of providence ultimately depends on whether or not the psychical and social elements of humanity are the sovereign factors in history."[9]

In other words, if the Holy Spirit is the architect of the *kainos* kingdom, yet the Holy Spirit works through people, how are we to understand who is doing the work? To fully understand Christian innovation, we need to understand our place in the *kainos* kingdom, which leads to the question of work.

A Life of Flourishing

My son's current favorite movie is *Rudy*. It is (perhaps loosely) based on the true story of Rudy Ruttinger, a young Catholic man from the 1970s industrial Midwest who, in part due to his factory-worker father's fandom, had one passion above all others in life: to play football at the University of Notre Dame. The only problem, as he is told in the film, is that he is "five foot nothing, a hundred and nothing," with hardly a "speck of athletic ability." Yet, his lack of natural giftedness is no deterrent, and he pursues his dream.

In one scene, as high-schooler Rudy tries to board a bus to visit Notre Dame, he is stopped by his instructor. His grades are not up to the entrance standards of the university, and the priest, knowing this, tells Rudy, "The secret to happiness in this life is to be grateful for the gifts the good Lord has bestowed on us. Rudy, not everyone is meant to go to college."[10]

The father's advice reflects a long-established theology of vocation, articulated by Martin Luther and largely unchanged since the age of the Reformation. In Luther's view, every human has a vocation in life, and any kind of work can be a vocation. (He wrote to counter the idea, then prevalent, that only monks had a calling.) Yale theologian Miroslav Volf describes Luther's theology as a "double vocation": a spiritual call to enter God's kingdom and an external call to serve God and others in the world. The external call "comes to a person through her station in life or profession. This call, too, is addressed to all Christians, but to each one in a different way, depending on his particular station or profession."[11]

While helpful at the time in extending human participation in God's kingdom from a certain class of people to all people, Luther's theology of vocation has led to several problematic consequences, which are visible in the theology of the film. First, it was indifferent to alienation. People have passions and dreams in life, which we call *gifts* (because they are not from our own making but come from outside ourselves), and we want to use them in life. To separate the spiritual call and the vocational call creates separation in our spiritual and material existence. The result is that many people feel alienated from their life circumstances, yearn for a life calling or pursuit that fully aligns with their passions, but lack the means (whether abilities, resources, or fortitude) of someone like Florence Nightingale to make them come together. In the film, Rudy's older brother had joined their father at the factory, and, while only in his twenties, was already drowning the sorrows of his limited future options in a bottle.

Second, by integrating calling with vocation and vocation with job, Luther's theology of work led to a professional clergy class that divorces any sort of integration between faith and work for anyone who does not pursue professional ministry by ordination.

> Many people practice sincere, devoted faith in Jesus Christ at church and at home, and innovate at work, but do not see these activities as connected. They hold a privatized view of faith.

Many people practice sincere, devoted faith in Jesus Christ at church and at home, and innovate at work, but do not see these activities as connected. They hold a privatized view of faith. Luther's doctrine taught that the New Creation applies only to the heart and not to our hands and our minds. It separated the "inner man" from the "outer man" and believed the Spirit renewed the inner man but left the outer man unchanged in this life.[12] Because a spiritual calling renews the "inner man," leaving the "outer man" unchanged, Luther's theology functionally equates to a limited form of salvation that does not apply to the daily life of work. The result is that we tend to bifurcate the material and spiritual. We privatize and separate faith from work and leave ministry up to the professionals, namely, the ordained clergy. Theologian Howard Snyder says,

> The clergy-laity dichotomy . . . is one of the principal obstacles to the church effectively being God's agent of the Kingdom today because it creates a false idea that "holy men," namely, ordained ministers, are really qualified and responsible for leadership and significant ministry. In the New Testament there are functional distinctions between various kinds of ministries but no hierarchical division between clergy and laity.[13]

Perhaps more damaging, because we have privatized faith, we have come to see faith as irrelevant to the public square. We have replaced God with humankind as the main driving force of social and political activity. Humanism has become the dominant understanding of work, and innovation has become divorced from the life of faith. We carry around a humanistic understanding of work.

> We carry around a humanistic understanding of work.

Third, and perhaps most critical to our exploration of Christian innovation, Luther's theology of work limited a person's vocational life to a single job. Just as there is one spiritual calling, to Luther there was one external calling; to change one's employment was to fail to remain faithful to God's commandment.[14] His theology reflected a fixed understanding of human development and a separation of the spirit from the body and the mind.

Over and again in the Gospels, Jesus describes a faith that leads to the fullness of a whole life. When we receive God's Spirit, we gain an entirely new life. We are born a second time, to a completely *kainos*-new existence. We start over, not simply spiritually but materially as well. We become participants in the greater kingdom in which there is no bifurcation of spirit and flesh. This realm includes our entire person, which is the definition of soul.[15] Further, Jesus' ministry was about healing as a whole-body experience. His healings are proof that we cannot separate the spiritual and the material.

Thus, we need a new way of understanding work that integrates the whole person. Christian innovation participates in ministry to the whole person by creating a virtuous cycle of healing. This happens when, to paraphrase theologian Frederick Buechner, our passions and world's problems align.[16] We are made more whole as we participate in making the world more whole.

One reason the disciples sat in fear behind a locked door was that Jesus' death messed up everything they thought they knew about the coming of the Messiah. For centuries, God's people had understood God's presence spatially. The Promised Land was a geography of salvation. God appeared in the Temple or proxy synagogues. On special moments, when God appeared in unusual places, the people of God quickly erected shrines to mark the occasion. This is why the destruction of the Temple was so devastating. God's people thought, "How can we worship God when our enemies have destroyed God's home?" As they followed Jesus, the disciples dreamed of overthrowing Roman oppressors and reestablishing a physical kingdom.

When the resurrected Jesus appeared to the disciples in the locked room, and breathed God's Spirit on them, they discovered something completely new: God's Spirit does not just reside in a specific sanctuary or holy space, but in us—in people. God is everywhere that Jesus' followers are. This was a massive shift for his disciples. Afterward, as evidenced throughout the New Testament, Jesus' disciples spoke of a New Creation, one that is no longer confined to a single location. When we try to reduce God to a specific room, we make a false distinction between sacred space and secular space. To bifurcate all of life between holy and profane settings is to deny the work of the Holy Spirit. As if it is possible to contain God anyway! Jesus says, "the Spirit blows wherever it pleases" (John 3:8). Paul teaches, "Now the Lord is the Spirit, and where the Spirit of the Lord is, there is freedom"(2 Cor 3:17).

A theology that leads to a fixed understanding of vocation leaves no room for Christian innovation. Yet we know God is doing new things, and the kingdom is the inbreaking of a new reality into the world. We know Jesus sends us out with God's Spirit to join in this work. We need a theology of work that allows for new things. By giving us God's Spirit, Jesus encourages us and challenges us to tear down our barriers of sacred and secular time and space and to discover a God who seeks to be part of our whole lives. The curtain that kept God's Spirit in a room tore from top to bottom at the crucifixion, and God's Spirit emerged for all of creation. Because of Christ, we may find God not only in our sanctuaries but in our automobiles and living rooms, in our kitchens and gardens, and in our activities, such as our work. The New Testament doctrine of ministry is a work for all people, not a special class of priests. We are all priests and all equipped to do great things, that is, the things of God.

> We are all priests and all equipped
> to do great things, that is, the things of God.

So how does God's Spirit move and work? Through the hearts and minds of God's followers. This means our faith is by nature public, not just private. We are part of a new community of humankind. Our civic relationships are inexorably a reflection of our privately held beliefs. We cannot have one without the other. This is why character affects policy. Christian innovation is activity that marries spirit and flesh, the spiritual with the material.

> Our civic relationships are inexorably a
> reflection of our privately held beliefs. We
> cannot have one without the other.

When we let God's Spirit fill our spirits, we become empowered as priests of God. Work is more than a means to an end, which is a self-oriented way of thinking of work; it is a gift from God.[17] Our work becomes our ministry, no matter the calling, and we pursue lives that seek to integrate the spiritual and the material. And this work is fun! The Spirit invites us back to the joy of the garden where we are given the ability to create with God.

We've Got Spirit

The implications of this change from self-empowerment to God-empowerment are transformational and include our very way of understanding how the world works. Because we see reality differently, we see both problems and solutions differently. We create based on a material understanding of the world, which is formed from our five senses, but the Holy Spirit introduces a new form of understanding, which leads to three changes: (1) what we know to be true, (2) what matters and is worthy of our time and energy, and (3) how we go about doing the work.

Spirit and Truth

First, the Holy Spirit changes what we know to be true. As people made in God's image, we are given five material senses at birth by which we understand the world: taste, touch, smell, sight, and hearing. Immediate, preconceptual-sense experience provides the data by which we form meaning, as brain researcher Iain McGilchrist affirms.[18] The apostle Thomas, who missed Jesus' first appearance, demonstrated this when he spoke of the reliability of his own five senses: "Unless I see the nail marks in his hands and put my finger where the nails were, and put my hand into his side, I will not believe" (John 20:25).

Enlightenment empiricism gave rise to a philosophy or worldview that affirmed sensory knowledge, a natural way of understanding the world in which our five senses are the total means by which we discover knowledge. I once heard a professional football coach say, "I know what I see." This is the default human state: a material world, understandable through our senses. To be clear, this is good. It is part of what it means to be made in God's image; full understanding of our sensory experience has been the basis for scientific advancement.

However, the breath of God, as Jesus gave to the disciples, introduces another source of understanding, one that doesn't use our senses. When we believe, as Thomas acquiesced (John 20:28), God's Spirit animates our spirits. We are initially made in God's image, which is visible from the outside in; when we receive God's Spirit, we are remade from the inside out, which is invisible.

The presence of God's Spirit in our lives begins a new journey of growth in which we no longer rely solely on our five senses. Greater than these is the presence of God's Spirit in us, which, over time, reveals to us the full measure of truth. By faith we understand, as the writer of Hebrews wrote (Heb 11:1). In other words, as much as we can glean about the world from our five senses, we cannot gain full understanding only through what we experience. There is an immaterial world, a spiritual reality, that we can begin to understand only by faith. The Holy Spirit gives us access to an entirely different level of understanding. As Jesus said to the woman at the well,

> Yet a time is coming and has now come when the true worshipers will worship the Father in the Spirit and in truth, for they are the kind of worshipers the Father seeks. God is spirit, and his worshipers must worship in the Spirit and in truth. (John 4:23-24)

Spirit and Creativity

Second, the Holy Spirit changes our understanding of what matters. Greatness is a word that describes a life lived to its fullest (see John 10:10). To receive a new kind of understanding is not fuzzy or mystical. It extends to the work we do, which is a product of our creativity. When Jesus promises that we will do greater things than even what he had been doing, he is telling us that we will have the power of God in us to create. To fully understand this, we need a theology of creativity, which I will try to briefly describe here.

Perhaps you say you are not a creative person. Many people claim that self-assessment. Yet somewhere in you is creative power. This is because God is the Creator, and we are made in God's image (Gen 1:27). Therefore, we have the image of God's creativity in us. As humans, we have in us—just as we are—the ability to create. We have a natural creative spirit, given to us by God.

This creative spirit was given to us for a purpose. In God's garden, the first story of Adam, before Eve, is a creativity story. God gave Adam a purpose and a project. The purpose was to "work [the garden] and take care of it" (Gen 2:15). The project was a collaboration with God to name the animals as God made them (Gen 2:19-20). This was no menial task, as biblical naming is significant. A person's name is indistinguishable from his or her being and character. Thus, in God's original design, humankind is given not only creative purpose but also power to care for and name creation into being.

The fall damaged this beautiful creative design. We remain creative people, caring for what has been made, tilling new ground, and naming our creations into being. But our creativity is marred by sin. Thus, our innovation and our technology—our creative work—reflects us as both good and evil. We are saints and sinners. We make amazing things, and we mess things up.

> The presence of the Holy Spirit is the way we participate in the work of a new, holy kingdom.

This is why Jesus' act of breathing a new, Holy Spirit into the disciples is a hinge point in the entire biblical story. God's Spirit reanimates our being, restores our purpose, and reinvites us to collaborate with God. The presence of the Holy Spirit is the way we participate in the work of a new, holy kingdom. It is not our natural state, but the Holy Spirit in us, which is the activating agent that enables us to do greater things.

Ora et Labora

Third, the Holy Spirit changes how we go about doing the work. The problem with the creative spark is that we humans can't help but take credit for the work. The sin of pride (the chief and progenitor of all sins) rears its ugly head, and we beat our chest and say, "I'm the one!"

The entire modern experiment has been driven by such human agency. Enlightenment humanism begat a naturalistic, "kingdom building" mentality, which put an impossible burden on humankind. We are not equipped to inaugurate the kingdom. When we elevate our own abilities, we demote God. Yet God is the Creator who has power we cannot fathom. As French philosopher and theologian Etienne Gilson wrote, "God added nothing to Himself by the creation of the world, nor would anything be taken away from Him by its annihilation."[19] The paradox of faith is that we come to know a God who is both infinitely powerful and immanently personal.

This means a better world is achievable, not by human improvement over time but only through the movement of the Holy Spirit.

When Jesus breathes the Holy Spirit into us, we join a kingdom already in place; our invitation is to participate in the work God is doing. As cultural theologian Leonard Sweet writes,

> Productivity has to do with giving and giving and giving until you end up with some product outside of yourself to which you can look and say, "I made that." Bearing fruit has to do with receiving and receiving and receiving until the fruit of the spirit begins to ripen inside of you. God then looks at it and says, "I made that!"[20]

This does not mean we have no role, but it does place proper authority on Jesus, not on humankind. We are relieved of the impossible obligation to "build the kingdom" and freed to live our lives as God's people, which results in solutions that help others to flourish. As the physician Luke wrote, Christ will restore. Our job is to be witnesses, those who declare it to be true (Acts 1:6-8). Human pride always wants to take credit. We need to let Christ lead. This leads to more questions of creativity and work, which I address later in a discussion of *ex materia* versus *ex nihilo*.

The Spirit of God is critical to our work. Most of Protestant theology limits the Holy Spirit's activity to salvation and the human spirit's activity to the present, compartmentalizing the Holy Spirit into a redeeming force. But the Holy Spirit is also a creating force. In the creation of all things, who was there? "The Spirit of God was hovering over the waters" (Gen 1:2). In Jesus, the Spirit of God comes "that which was his own" (John 1:11). Though it has been invaded by evil forces, the earth is God's, and the Holy Spirit comes not just to save us but to collaborate with us in the work of ridding the world of evil and restoring the home.[21] Thus, the presence of the Spirit is the critical issue. Our work is temporal, but the presence of the Spirit is eternal.

God's Spirit is always moving, and when it enters us, it sets us moving. This movement is life. We are no longer fixed in a single station, charged with staffing it for a lifetime through our faithful work, dreary though it may be. We are free to set out on an adventure of growth and learning, in which God's Spirit moves in us and equips us for whatever comes next. Perhaps we should focus less on the power of Caesar and more on the power of the Holy Spirit.

> Perhaps we should focus less on the power of Caesar and more on the power of the Holy Spirit.

Yet, though God is restoring the kingdom, and we are recipients of this gift (which we call grace), we are not passive. Though God is in charge of *new*, God is with us and within us through the Holy Spirit. When we receive the Holy Spirit, we join in the work of *new*. The result is that we become Christian innovators. We join in the emergence of God's kingdom and begin doing greater things. And is this supernatural difference mystical or like a form of magic? Not at all. This happens in two ways: through vision to see God's future and through the gifts to help make it happen.

The first, *spirare*, is the source for our word *inspiration*. The Holy Spirit gives us a passion or vision to create. The second manifests itself through what Scripture calls *charisms* or gifts. The Spirit gives us the gifts or charisms to do the work. With the power of God's Spirit, we are equipped to do the work of God's kingdom. Christian innovation is the harnessing of the supernatural power of our gifts. God's Spirit unleashes our spirits.

This "doing greater things" is a working out of revealed truth and working through our Spirit-led gifts. Thus, "doing greater things" is doing things from out of this revealed truth. Work in the Spirit reveals this spiritual reality. We call it God's kingdom. The results of this work are not just new and improved, or different than what has come before, but qualitatively distinct. Further, the results then are both spiritual and material; they involve the whole self, biblically known as the soul. The work of God's Spirit in us and through us is holistic. We are made whole as we participate in making the world whole.

Greater things happen not when we create something literally big but when we collaborate with the work of God's Spirit. We do this through prayer and work, or as the monks say, *ora et labora*. Labor is an extension of prayer. This is the theological and spiritual heart of this book: prayer and work together are ways we nurture the vision and gift of God's Spirit in us.

> Ora et labora. We begin with prayer, and then we work. Labor is an extension of prayer.

The phrase *ora et labora* comes originally from Saint Benedict. Benedict lived in the late fifth and early sixth centuries. He had a twin sister named Scholastica, from whom we have the concept of being a scholar. Benedict wrote a set of rules for living in Christian community. It became a set of rules for monks in the Benedictine order, but there's no evidence to suggest that he was trying to start a new community. He just saw order and the resulting spiritual growth as requirements for the fulfillment of human vocation. Each of us has vocational work to do, according to Paul's letter to the church at Ephesus (Eph 2:10). Benedict extolled a life of contemplation combined with action:

> Benedict envisioned a life ordered and made rich by both work and prayer. You should get your job done, he said, but not be consumed by it. You should pray, but not the exclusion of daily responsibilities. As with everything else, work should be given its due, but not more.[22]

I work with a colleague who once exclaimed to me about ministry, "I get to pray at work!" That was Benedict's intent. It is a spirit that sees work as not just tasks to be accomplished but as spiritual discipline. Before Jesus sent his disciples to preach, he first called them to be with him (Mark 3:14). We both begin and ground our work in relationship with Christ.

Because of God's Spirit, we don't have to worry about such grand results as "changing the world." We just need to look for ways to help the whole soul, both ours and others, material and spiritual. This means material solutions (cures) with eternal worth. When we work for others, we join with God's Spirit in incarnating the kingdom of God for people in time and space. We simultaneously help them to live better lives in the here and now while showing them a new, eternal view.

Got to Go Through It

Now, let us return to the problems I outlined in the introduction. How do we begin to think about fixing the cultural mess we are in? If all that I have outlined so far is true, then why do things atrophy? To understand this, consider the story of the restoration of the Sistine Chapel. Prior to its recent restoration, art critics had claimed that the masterful ceiling of the chapel was intentionally painted dark by Michelangelo as a commentary on the brutish, short nature of medieval life. Then workers restored it—to much controversy—and the world discovered that the artist had originally designed a world of light and life, which had over time become dark because of soot from the candles below, burned as an offering to God in worship.

Because of our imperfect nature, our best offerings to God and one another inevitably add soot and muck to the world. As long as sin remains, this is inevitable. Like Florence Nightingale, the Lady with the Lamp, Jesus says we are a light to the world, but alas, we have not yet been made perfect. Our imperfections come off of us as soot from candlelight, which gradually obscures and dims even the best of creations. This is why Christian innovations are not permanent, and we cannot progress toward a utopian, perfect future. As long as there is sin in the world and sin in us, then our works both reveal God's kingdom and gradually cover it up again. Thus, the Holy Spirit calls every generation, in every time and space, to do the work anew of incarnating Jesus in the world and, in doing so, elevating people toward the transcendence of the kingdom of heaven.

When we innovate through the work of the Holy Spirit, we restore God's creation. Our work helps us to see life as it is supposed to be—not the grimy, dim, soot-filled lives we often lead, but the beautiful image of creation God intended. Christian innovation is a means for us to live out an ethic of love by introducing significant, positive change into the world. It is about human flourishing. The key difference is that, whereas secular innovation brings temporal value, Christian innovation also brings eternal value: new expressions of what is true, good, and beautiful by the standards of God's kingdom.

God wants us to live without fear, knowing that the future is not only okay but that God is already there, and that taking steps toward a better future is an act of faith. To share God's vision for the world is to groan with all of creation for release from our bondage to decay and for life as we know it to be made perfect. Concern for this in Christian theology is known as *teleology*, or the end purpose (as opposed to *eschatology*, which is a focus on the final days that lead up to the end). Whereas secular innovation is temporal—rooted in time—Christian innovation is eternal. Secular innovation will pass away, but Christ's kingdom does not pass away. Simply, when we innovate as a reflection of Christian faith, we seek to make the world more like heaven. Christian innovation comes from a new way of looking at the world, is fueled by God's Spirit, and results in new solutions of eternal value.

> When we innovate as a reflection of Christian faith, we seek to make the world more like heaven.

Recall the story of the babysitter and the kids who went on a bear hunt. At each obstacle, what do the children and their guardian say? Before recognizing that they must go through it, there is another verse. In it, they declare their bold fearlessness, exclaiming:

We're going on a bear hunt.

We're going to catch a big one.

What a beautiful day!

We're not scared.[23]

As the bear-hunt group exclaims, we must go through it, but how? This is the lesson of the story of the disciples in John 20. As I outlined, Christian innovation needs these three prerequisites: (1) the presence of Christ among us, which turns our retreating fear to joy; (2) the presence of Christ leading us, which turns our propensity for ruling authority to followership; and (3) the presence of Christ binding us, which turns our tendency to go it alone into a shared life in community. These are three unique characteristics of Christian innovation.

As Christians, we follow a God who is not only powerful but good. God's great I AM is God saying, I will be who I will be. In other words, God's character doesn't change. Jesus is that same good God, and Jesus gives his followers God's Spirit. When we allow God's Spirit to move in us and through us, we experience God in us. We take on the character of God. The result is that we become good. We replace fear with love. As 1 John 4:18 says, love drives out fear. When you love people, you look for ways to help people. It drives you to step out of your locked room and create, solve problems, invent solutions, and find answers. As Gregory Jones writes, "Love made me an inventor."[24]

Okay, so Jesus sends us. But where do we go? Part 2 describes how to join the Holy Spirit in the work of making all things new.

PART TWO

The Work of the New Creation

Doing the work of the New Creation is not a matter of executing a plan of best practices, and any "how to" guide for Christian innovation is bound to be incomplete and to frustrate. While stories of Christian innovation may differ in specifics, they all share a set of basic characteristics, shared in the following chapters. Consider these six characteristics the starting points or signposts for the work of the Holy Spirit in contextualized settings specific to local communities such as yours.

7

Personal Problems

How Does Significant, Positive Change Begin?

All Christian innovation—social or technological, conceptual or material—begins with genuine need, such as Florence Nightingale's suffering soldiers or Norman Borlaug's hungry populations. People in places of need are typically "down and out"; they lack power and resources and cannot easily change their own circumstances. They need the collaboration of people in comfortably "up and in" places. The problem is that people in up-and-in places are typically unmotivated to change circumstances, either their own or others. The catalyst for change is, thus, not just need but moments when problems become personal. This happens through powerful stories that motivate the "up and in" to innovate for the benefit of the "down and out."

In any process of change, we ignore most of what happens and focus instead on a few key moments.[1] One of the significant stories in the history of human rights is the story of the slave ship *Zong*. The ownership of slaves was once such a regular part of society that anyone who questioned it fought a serious uphill battle. That began to change at the 1783 trial of the slave ship *Zong* in London.

Eighteen months earlier, while sailing the Atlantic Ocean, someone had given the order to throw one hundred thirty-two of the surviving slaves on the *Zong* overboard into shark-filled waters. The responsible party was unclear at the trial. It probably was not the captain, who lay deathly ill in his bed. He had passed command, not to his first mate, but to the lone passenger on the slave ship, Robert Stubbs, a shadowy, former slave-ship captain himself.[2]

Whoever was in charge was facing a life-or-death crisis. The year was 1781, and the *Zong*, which ironically means "care" in Dutch, had been carrying African slaves to the newly formed American republic. In the Doldrums, a portion of the Middle Atlantic Passage of the journey characterized by low winds and still waters, sickness took the lives of seven crew members and fifty of the four hundred forty slaves.[3] Captain Luke Collingwood had become ill. As he lay in his bed, the ship passed by its destination in the West Indies, and the journey went long. Compounded by the problem of leaking water barrels, the ship faced a severe water shortage for the hundreds of people left on board.

For fear that they would run out of supplies, the crew, which now numbered only eleven, were assembled and asked what they thought of the idea that "part of the Slaves should be destroyed."[4] The decision was unanimous, and the crew began work immediately to jettison the "cargo." They threw one hundred thirty-two human beings into the sea, with shackles and irons still on, "heaved, bound, off the boat, some jumping to their fate."[5] Humans do not go lightly to their death, and later testimony described the shrieks of terror that filled the night sky.

The captain's moral calculus was purely financial: on his return to London, his ship's owners could file an insurance claim and get their money back. Killing slaves aboard a ship was not a new practice. That area of the ocean in the West Indies was known for its heavy shark infestation because of the availability of human flesh.[6]

Though the violence on slave ships was an open secret back home in European cities such as Liverpool, something about this particular event was worse. The story of the *Zong*, told at the subsequent insurance trial, became a sensation.[7] The trial transfixed the public and laid bare a variety of attitudes about the slave trade and slavery as an institution. At one point, the judge compared the murdered people to horses, saying they were alike from a financial perspective. Although the captain was not held liable for the insurance claim, much less murder, the *Zong* trial had a significant consequence: a new, rising public awareness of the horror of the slave trade, which began to chip away at public support.

Among the transfixed public was Olaudah Equiano, a Christian person of color and former slave who lived in London as a freedman and spoke of the evils of slavery. He took news of the *Zong* trial to fellow Christian, theologian, and longtime abolitionist Granville Sharp.[8] Outraged, Sharp wrote the Lord's Commissioners of the Admiralty and demanded that they bring separate murder charges against the crew of the *Zong*.[9]

Slavery had already become a highly personal issue for Sharp, dating back to an experience he had when he was young, in which he helped free Jonathan Strong, a young, enslaved man who had been severely beaten. Sharp's relationship with Strong had set a course for his life. Though he did not have any formal legal training, Sharp was studying the law in order to convince one man, Lord Chief Justice Mansfield, to outlaw slavery in the British Empire. Abolition was his all-consuming passion, and the *Zong* was the moment he had been waiting for.

The event ended in mistrial and no compensation was distributed to the ship's owners, but that mattered little to Equiano and

Sharp. The tide of public opinion had turned. Prior to this trial, slavery was mostly an economic issue, not a moral issue, not just for England but throughout human history. In the ancient world, as well as for much of the medieval world, slavery was simply the bottom rung of the social and economic ladder. It took the full telling of the horrors of the slave trade and the wonton killing of human beings for its moral relevance to become visible to society.

Sharp used the moment well. He engaged in a flurry of activity, drawing on twenty years of contacts and relationships on the issue of slavery to keep awareness of the event high. He was one of many clergy and theologians whose witness led to the establishment of the Abolition Society in 1787, which Sharp chaired.[10] The Abolition Society became ground zero for a movement that spurred on the end of legally and socially sanctioned slavery in England.

The *Zong* trial was a hinge point in history. It offers a clue to the question, How does significant, positive change begin? To understand how Christian innovation works, we must understand more about the social and economic stratification of societies and our role within them.

Down and Out

Christian innovation begins "down and out," on the fringes. By this I mean down the economic strati of society and out away from the centers of social and networked power. Behind every story of innovation are real human needs, people seeking new solutions to problems of their material condition and the social order. These "down and out" groups pursue positive change for themselves, their family and friends, and others in a similar situation. However, people in places of need typically lack power and resources and cannot easily change their own circumstances. They need the collaboration of people in "up and in" places. While change originates from the bottom, it grows only with influence from the top.[11]

The relationship is correlational, not causal. In other words, to say that innovation begins "down and out" is not a declaration that people who enjoy the benefits of social or economic influence cannot innovate, because—as this book aims to show—anyone can innovate. Rather, it is a question of motivation. People at the upper echelons of society are more motivated by the maintenance of order and institutions that benefit them than they are by change.

The paradox of innovation, and the reason change is difficult, is that while the "down and out" need the cooperation of the "up and in," the "up and in" do not desire an altered social order. The "up and in" are motivated by stasis, not change. In fact, keepers of the "up and in" often consider what they do to be sacred, and those "below" them to be profane.

If the work of innovation is successful, it generates fruit, a biblical metaphor for positive outcomes, be it matters of individual character, social equality, technological advancement, financial equity, and so on (see John 15). In free societies (those not bound by class systems based on familial structure), as those associated with or in proximity to successful innovation enjoy its fruits, they move up, over time and across space, from the fringes to the center of society. Innovation is the way people move "up and in."

At first, the "up and in" accept something for utilitarian purposes. Gradually, change happens. Some beneficiaries of innovation, including followers of Jesus, become elite—if not the proverbial one percent, at least elite relative to their context. For example, employees become employers or owners, players become coaches, students become teachers and then administrators. Innovation facilitates access to leadership and the power to make decisions about money and people. Not everyone, of course, rises to elite status because of innovation. Some innovate and fail to enjoy the fruits of their work. Likewise, some people in positions of power did not achieve privilege because of innovation but through networks, personal charisma, or loyal drudgery up the ladder. Nevertheless, the fruit of successful innovation is improved social and economic status, and this is true for Christian innovation as well.

With this improvement comes access to decision making. Innovators find themselves, sometimes after lifetimes of effort, in a position to change the world, perhaps to invent new technologies or to enact new policies. The means and methods of the "down and out" become, if not sacred, at least normalized. Thus, the path of a successful new idea is this: rejection, fear, limited acceptance, normalization, and finally sacralization.

The irony of the journey from "down and out" to "up and in" is that it often changes our motivations. The closer a person—including a Christian—gets to a position that actually enables her to change the world, the less concerned she may become with changing anything, and the more concerned she may be with preserving the world that has emerged around her. With the fruits of innovation come protection and the desire to maintain gains earned. But the shift from change to conservation does not always do us good, and sometimes we turn away from the very activity that gave rise to our flourishing. We trade our passion for glory, to quote a famous song. A healthy sense of stewardship sometimes swells to an unhealthy sense of stasis. Fruitful, innovative activity creates growth, which necessitates structure, which leads to systems, which leads to the establishment of rules, which chokes off innovation. The good desire for order leads to a bad tendency to close others off. Rebels become loyalists, and in many cases, fruit turns to rot.

> The irony of innovation is that the closer a person—including a Christian—gets to a position that actually enables her to change the world, the less concerned she may become with changing anything, and the more concerned she may be with preserving the world that has emerged around her.

Meanwhile, as the center corrupts, new generations arise on the fringes—the children of those who did not participate in the fruit of the previous era of innovation. Since they do not benefit from the existing system, they seek to change it. This is why dismissing the concerns of those who protest as invalid is ignorant to the way social change occurs. The fringe protests for one reason only: those in the streets do not benefit from the current system. They are "down and out."

Thus innovation is cyclical, and the keepers of existing technologies are usually unable to see the new thing coming. Self-proclaimed "Apple evangelist" Guy Kawasaki tells the story of the history of ice manufacturing, which had three stages: ice harvesting from rivers, ice making in factories, and personal ice in homes. None of the ice harvesters became ice manufacturers, and none of the ice manufacturers became refrigerator makers.[12] The business leaders of each stage did not see the next change coming. Change doesn't occur from the top but from the bottom, and new solutions rarely blossom under the control of those invested in the status quo. This is why it is so hard to create positive change and why forces array against those who try.[13]

Such was the case with abolitionism, why the trial of the *Zong* was so influential, and why it is important to tell the story. While not innovation per se, the trial of the *Zong* was the inciting incident that led to social innovation, a catalyzing moment for the rise of the abolitionist movement. Stories such as the *Zong* trial serve as a form of personization, binding us to the needs of others. Perhaps this is one reason Jesus taught in stories: they are an innovating force.

Dissatisfaction with the Status Quo

Among the outraged clergy over the *Zong* trial was Anglican clergyman John Wesley, perhaps the most influential moral voice of the day, and his followers, the Methodists. A decade prior, the sixty-nine-year-old had published his first public tract on the topic, *Thoughts Upon Slavery*. Wesley's tract and the *Zong* trial were significant influences on a rising young British Parliamentarian named William Wilberforce.

The year after the much-publicized *Zong* trial, Wilberforce reconnected with childhood friend and Wesley acolyte Isaac Milner on a long train ride.[14] In a long, intense conversation, Milner's influence catalyzed a spiritual crisis that had been brewing in Wilberforce, which led him to Christian faith.

Wilberforce's high social status had given him access to the most famous names in European and American society, such as King Louis XVI, Marie Antoinette, Marquis de Lafayette, Benjamin Franklin, and others. He had been elected to Parliament at the earliest possible age of twenty-one. Along with his best friend William Pitt, he was a rising star. Pitt would go on to become prime minister at the age of twenty-four.[15] Wilberforce was the definition of "up and in," and assuredly in line for a future of significant political power. However, his status had, to date, been used for nothing more than his own glory. He later said, "My first years in Parliament, I did nothing—nothing to any purpose. My own distinction was my darling object."[16] Now, considering the implications of Christian faith, Wilberforce found himself at a professional crossroads.

Meanwhile, the social evils of late eighteenth-century Europe were stunning. Children as young as five years old were employed for twelve- to fourteen-hour days in new factories. Public displays of animal cruelty passed for entertainment. Alcoholism was epidemic, as was sexual trafficking of women. In the late eighteenth century, a full 25 percent of single women in London were prostitutes, with an average age of sixteen.[17]

Motivated by newfound faith and Milner's influence, Wilberforce began to explore what it meant for the way he understood his world and how he chose to live his life. Abandoning drinking and sexual promiscuity were relatively easy choices for him; he had already discovered they did not satisfy. But he struggled with larger questions of meaning and purpose. Wilberforce considered abandoning his political career for the ministry.

As he considered his career plans, he had a conversation with another old friend: John Newton, former Atlantic slave trader, now one of Wesley's Methodists and rector of a local church. Twelve years earlier, Newton had written what was to become one of the most recognizable songs in the English-speaking world, "Amazing Grace." In a meeting, Newton urged Wilberforce to continue working where his skills were at their finest and to enact change as a parliamentarian, not a preacher.[18]

Thus, Wilberforce took up the calling God placed on his heart and life. He wrote in his journal, "O God, deliver me from myself! When I trust to myself I am darkness and weakness."[19] His spiritual conversion deepened, and in 1787, he decided to stake his life not on his own distinction but on two new, daring "Great Objects": the suppression of the slave trade and the moral renewal of British society.[20] He joined Sharp's Abolition Society and quickly became its public voice. Two years later, in 1789, Wilberforce introduced a bill in the British Parliament to outlaw the transatlantic slave trade. The anti-slavery bill was defeated. But Wilberforce was not. Building on slowly changing public opinion, he started another association to galvanize like-minded people, the Clapham Saints, whose purpose was "to apply their faith in Jesus Christ to personal, social, political, national and international matters."[21] The work was arduous.

A few weeks prior to Wilberforce's first abolitionist argument on the parliamentarian floor, Olaudah Equiano published his autobiography.[22] Equiano was both a prophet and an entrepreneur. He understood that the market was key to social change. In the same way that the trial of the *Zong* had brought to light a different story, told not from the view of the "up and in" but from the view of the "down and out," Equiano understood that life beyond slavery could be made possible "by the very market that brought him to the New World as property."[23] A free African and former slave living in London, Equiano was a fellow Methodist, having come to Christian faith in Georgia in 1765 after hearing George Whitefield preach.[24] Displaying brilliant economic adaptability, Equiano found subscribers for the development of his manuscript, wrote his own story, kept his copyright, and navigated it to publication.[25] To use contemporary parlance, Equiano changed the narrative.

Wesley read Equiano's autobiography, and then wrote Wilberforce.[26] It was to be his last letter, composed in February 1791, five days before his death. Wesley wrote,

> Unless God has raised you up for this very thing, you will be worn out by the opposition of men and devils. But if God be for you, who can be against you? Are all of them together stronger than God? O be not weary of well doing! Go on, in the name of God and in the power of His might, till even American slavery (the vilest that ever saw the sun) shall vanish away before it.[27]

Wesley acknowledged the forces of the status quo that opposed Wilberforce's work to enact positive social change.

Convicted of the need to enact change, and with the support and encouragement of Wesley's letter and the Clapham Sect, Wilberforce reintroduced the same bill every year over the next eighteen years.[28] During this generation, Wilberforce became a deeply unpopular man, and it took a severe toll on his health.[29] His reputation changed in the public eye from charismatic leader to embittered crusader. Yet empowered by his dedication to scripture, prayer, a community of fellow believers, and Wesley's letter, Wilberforce continued. Finally, in 1807, the Clapham Sect finally achieved their goal and passed a law abolishing the slave trade.

As theologian Willie James Jennings observes, Christianity offers a "breathtakingly powerful way to imagine and enact the social,"[30] yet has consistently failed to live up to its own transformative social potential for intimacy with God and one another. An honest assessment of late, eighteenth-century London does not show a high correlation between Christians and people who resisted slavery. Historically, faith has not proven sufficient motivation for those in power to change personal and institutional behavior, and the institutional church has too often spoken from positions of power, unable to see the perspective of people like Equiano and the slaves who begged for their lives aboard the *Zong*.

> Historically, Christian faith has not proven sufficient motivation for those in power to change personal and institutional behavior, and the institutional church has too often spoken from positions of power.

Perhaps the problem with the too-often failed witness of the historical Christian faith is the resistance of followers of Christ to apply a "down and out" ethos to their own identity.[31] The story of Christianity is found in positions of both resistance and change, as is visible in the protests of 2020, where we saw people claiming the name of Jesus on both sides of sometimes violent conflict. Too often, we Christians think we can follow Jesus while maintaining the comforts of "up and in." We try to follow Jesus' teachings without living Jesus' life.

It is one thing to have an idea to make something better, but the inertia of the gilded couch is powerful. Innovation is harder from a state of comfort. What creates such sustained conviction? Good coaches, for example, recognize the slippery safety of success. Much of the work of coaching is navigating the varying psychologies of positive and negative motivation. This motivation needs a personal dimension to be sustainable. But ultimately, a coach or another outside force can do only so much. Wilberforce would not have made it through eighteen years of introducing the same bill to his government body, at cost to his reputation and even his personal health, with only a coach in his ear. He needed a driving internal force. His personal experience with abolition was the internal force that motivated him—his source of "unpeace". Innovation also requires a critical mass, in which enough people become sufficiently dissatisfied with the status quo and motivated to create a better solution to move toward change, whether the motivation is material or spiritual. At least one eyewitness saw the *Zong* massacre live from his port window and did nothing. That person was assuredly invested in the status quo.

Innovation is portrayed by some as a corporate endeavor, detached, business like, an intellectual or material pursuit. But this is not accurate. Innovation does not originate with just any problems but with personal problems. It rises from awareness of human suffering, and solutions require our blood, sweat, and tears. Innovation requires skin in the game. It requires dissatisfaction with the status quo. Most innovators are not out to change the world. Their dreams are not that big. They just cannot abide the status quo any longer. The catalyst for change is not just recognition of need but moments when problems become personal, which happen through powerful stories. The slave ship *Zong* provided such a moment, its story of suffering a powerful narrative for those seeking change. It motivated the "up and in" of the Clapham Sect to choose to make themselves "down and out" for the sake of greater things. [32]

> Most innovators are not out to change the world. Their dreams are not that big. They just cannot abide the status quo any longer.

For the Christian innovator, conviction comes from a specific source: the Holy Spirit, which both comforts us in our suffering and challenges us to better ways of living. The Holy Spirit is the animating force that turns stories into lasting conviction; the follower of Christ who prays for change may discover that she gets more than she wished for. Faith in Christ offers us a security that is more powerful than the illusions of power and position. With faith, we become free from worry about protecting cultural contexts and customs. We come to empathize with those who live outside of its benefits. People who seek justice are either those who have never experienced it or those who have fully experienced it, know peace in their own lives, and want others to share in it. Jesus identified with the tax collector over the Pharisee (Luke 18:9-14) not because the Pharisee was concerned with customs but because he had lost sight of the main thing: people.

The goal is for all people to be "up and in." Jesus gave a glimpse of this final vision to three disciples up on the mount of transfiguration. C. S. Lewis describes the beauty of this image in his Narnia series, when the protagonists are invited to "come further up, come further in."[33] Jesus modeled a life with the "down and out" in order to bring all "up and in." A focus on the needs of people raises us beyond our customs and cultures. As the apostle Paul writes,

> In your relationships with one another, have the same mindset as Christ Jesus:
> Who, being in very nature God,
>> did not consider equality with God something to be used to his own advantage;
> rather, he made himself nothing
>> by taking the very nature of a servant,
>> being made in human likeness.
> And being found in appearance as a man,
>> he humbled himself
>> by becoming obedient to death—
>>> even death on a cross!
> Therefore God exalted him to the highest place
> and gave him the name that is above every name.
>
> (Phil 2:5-9)

If Jesus is the way, truth, and life (John 14:6), if Jesus abides with us, and if Jesus chose to hang out with sinners—the "down and out"—then this means we bring life with us when we go to "down and out" places. It is down-and-out where flourishing begins. Faith in Jesus as the source of positive change matures us from concern for personal security into concern for others who have yet to receive the benefits of life up-and-in. Over time, this transformation occurred in Wilberforce: faith in Jesus, hearing the stories of Jesus and others, personal experiences with Jesus and others, living in the power of the Holy Spirit, living in a Christian community, and presumably more.

For the Christian, dissatisfaction with the status quo is often understood as concern for the well-being of others, which we describe using the language of justice. In *Think Like a 5 Year Old*, I describe this jolt of pain as "unpeace." Sustainable motivation to create positive change does not live outside of us in extrinsic obligation to higher ideals but in the immediate, intrinsic desire to fix problems that cause harm to others.

The Thing Itself

How do we avoid the traps of comfort and stasis? To maintain concern for the problems of the world, it is not necessary to reject the world entirely, embrace asceticism, and become like monks. But it does suggest that the way to overcome the temptations and corruptions of the comfortably "up and in" is to constantly look "down and out" for stories of human suffering. While Christ offers us the security to fully love one another, and moral conviction leads us to dissatisfaction with the status quo, a desire for positive change needs a catalyst. Faith that moves others to action emerges when problems become personal for an entire group of people. The best vehicle for this are moments of narrative power. To innovate, begin with telling stories of need! Moral conviction is stirred by narrative power, which leads us to empathize with the needs of others over concern for our own safety.

The story of the slave ship *Zong* was such a catalyst. The power of story to open hearts to human suffering and create empathy for others is the key to inviting the "up and in" to overcome their natural desire for stasis and collaborate with the "down and out" to create change.

While the passage of the law abolishing the Atlantic slave trade in 1807 may have satisfied some, Wilberforce kept at the work of abolition, dissatisfied not just with the inhumane acquisition and selling of humans in trade, but with the institution of slavery itself. In an age in which equality is the *cause célèbre*, it is hard now to capture the magnitude of Wilberforce's will, which had been transformed by a new understanding of the world, defined by community over power. The view of the world according to the economics of power is the tragic story of the human condition, and slavery can be understood only in this context. As such, it has been deeply embedded in cultures since before recorded history.[34] In spite of the soaring rhetoric of the American Declaration of Independence, the equality of all humans was not a shared value in most cultures—even African ones. Indeed, the country of Liberia was founded by former American slaves who themselves became slaveholders. Yet Wilberforce soldiered on, and twenty-six years later, in 1833, on his last day of conscious life, Wilberforce received word that Parliament had passed a law, making slavery illegal.

To this day, the name Wilberforce is synonymous with abolition. But British Parliamentarian William Wilberforce didn't set out to make his surname a brand. He simply responded to a deep personal problem, and his influence changed the laws on slavery, at great personal cost. Most important, he did not do this work alone, but with the ingenuity of Olaudah Equiano, the support of the Abolition Society, his Clapham Sect fraternity of like-minded abolitionists, and an untold number of unnamed others. In these groups, Wilberforce found the community support he needed to face those who opposed him.

All stories of innovation would end here, except for one problem. With the perspective of history, we know that the 1833 British law outlawing slavery may have made the practice illegal, but it did nothing to resolve the thornier question of the human heart. It did not and could not end discrimination itself. Though it created positive change, it did not end suffering, because no solution designed by humans is perfect; in fact, the imperfections of our innovations seed the next iteration of the cycle. Thus, in our imperfection, we continue to seek positive change. This is why new visions must come to each generation. Next, we will look at the role of vision.

8

Unreasonable Vision

How Do We Know What to Do?

Christian innovation depends on alternate visions of reality. To his closest disciples, Jesus gave a mountaintop glimpse—a vision—of the reality of the New Creation. It was so powerful that the disciples wanted to stay, but Jesus pointed them down the mountain to a hurting world. Having been given a vision, the disciples were sent "down and out." God's Spirit works by giving us visions and then calling us to join in the work of seeing them to fruition. The challenge is to train our spirits to listen for God's Spirit, which we learn to do over time by retraining ourselves to seek the presence of God first in our lives. Once we are aware of God's vision, we can respond by making goals to pursue. The practice of goal-making takes imagination, curiosity, and hope.

The ultimate story of vision comes not from contemporary leadership literature but from the time Jesus led three of his disciples "up to a high mountain, where they were all alone" (Mark 9:2). This happened shortly after Peter first declared that Jesus was the Messiah. As the group ascended the mountain, something very strange occurred. Suddenly, Jesus' clothes turned a white that was beyond anything the disciples had ever seen. The Gospel writer Mark describes Jesus' clothes as whiter than any bleach could make them (v. 3).

Then, something even more strange occurred. Elijah and Moses appeared with Jesus, and they began chatting like it was happy hour. The vision was overpowering for the three disciples. Luke's Gospel describes their reaction: "Peter and those with him were almost overcome by sleep, but they managed to stay awake" (Luke 9:32 CEB). Their rabbi was somehow talking with two men who they knew to be two of the biggest giants of their tradition—and who were both dead. Can you imagine?

Not knowing how to respond, Peter suggests building something (Mark 9:5), which perhaps sounds a bit curious in the reading. But this gives us a clue about what we do in moments of divine revelation. True revelation is so overpowering and brilliant that it is terrifying. Perhaps the next best version of divine revelation is the experience of falling in love, which, when it happens, is beautiful, all encompassing, and completely terrifying; yet it is a mere glimpse of God's presence. Peter stammers and stutters because he has no idea what is happening. Following the rabbi Jesus around has led to more than he bargained for. His only response is to put his hands to use. Drawing from his Jewish religious tradition, Peter decides that God needs a tabernacle to dwell in.

Peter's response is typical of us as well. Instead of dwelling in the moment, whenever we receive undeserved grace, we experience terrified sensory overload, followed by an urgent need to do something. One pastor who attended Ginghamsburg at the height of the Spirit's movement exclaimed, "I want to bottle this up and take it home!" Our well-meaning desire is to capture the moment, but as the wind blows where it wishes, so it is with everyone born of the Spirit (John 3:8). Revelation is uncomfortable because it doesn't come from within. It is out of our control.

> Revelation is uncomfortable because it doesn't come from within. It is out of our control.

The story ends in a cloud, which is a recurring biblical image of God's presence, and a voice, described elsewhere in the biblical narrative like thunder: "This is my Son, whom I love. Listen to him!" (Mark 9:7). Then the moment is over, except for the disciples, who lay in fetal positions on the ground.

What does this story of the transfiguration tell us about vision? It is significant for several reasons. First, the story tells us where visions of Christian innovation come from: not from us but from God. As I described in part 1, humanism suggests we make our own better future, but Christ is clear: the New Creation already exists. Vision is when we receive an invitation to the party.

The revelation of God's glory on the mountaintop brings together the Old and New Testaments with a returning cameo of the same two people who had previously seen God on a mountaintop (see Exodus 33 for Moses; 1 Kings 19 for Elijah). Some have speculated this repeat is significant. If the moment were merely a hall-of-fame preview of saints, many people could have appeared and begun to speak with Jesus. Since it was the same two people, what if, in some strange twisting of time, the transfiguration was the exact same moment experienced in three moments?[1] In the New Creation, time may not be as we understand it today. We need God's vision, because our ability to see is as in an ancient mirror: dimly (1 Cor 13:12).

Second, Jesus brings three disciples, not one, to the mountaintop, so there can be no arguing later about who had the vision and deserves the credit. The vision for Christian innovation is shared; if it is not shared, then this may be a test for whether it is from God or not.

Third, the transfiguration makes you second guess the conventional wisdom that being a visionary is all sunshine and lemonade. Indeed, a vision from the Lord is always beautiful, but also may be terrifying. No wonder the disciples wanted to stay and build something. It was the ultimate "up and in" moment. Once it was over, they had only one place to go—down, which tells us we must always come down the mountain after moments of revelation.

As they descended, the disciples were full of questions. The journey down the mountain from the visionary moment is full of confusion and questions. Revelation isn't something we acquire, as in knowledge, where we take time to figure everything out ahead of time. A vision from God has no user manual. It is merely an image, given to us. It changes our perceptions completely and leaves us confused, trying to make sense of it all.

To his closest disciples, Jesus gave a glimpse of the alternate reality of the New Creation. It was so powerful that the disciples could not move. In the fullness of time of the New Creation, everyone will be where the disciples were—in the presence of Christ, on the mountain, which is the ultimate "up and in" location. But Jesus did not let them stay. Instead, he pointed them down the mountain to a hurting world. Having been given a vision, the disciples were next sent "down and out." The purpose of vision is to give our faith the fortitude to descend. With a vision comes a sending to go down to valleys full of people in need. Vision is not for our edification but for others. Until all people are on the mountain, we must carry the vision downward for the sake of others. We must look for the lost sheep.

> The purpose of vision is to give our faith
> the fortitude to descend.

Last, vision is not a privilege given to a select few; it may happen to every person who claims the Lord as Messiah. God's Spirit works by giving us visions and then calling us to join in the work of seeing them to fruition.

Receiving a Vision

So much has been written about vision that it can be difficult to see the topic with fresh eyes. Like innovation itself, vision is something that many people think they understand but few practice. Contrary to popular imagination, visions are not ideas with grand scope described by industrial titans or gifts unique to a few. If anyone with God's Spirit may see a vision of the New Creation, how does this happen?

Whether we know it or not, each of us has a vision for future creative work. Creativity is the manifestation of visionary activity. God created us to flourish through creative expression. When we innovate as Christians, we are fulfilling God's vision for our lives, or cocreating with God. This means our creative work is not random but best understood in the context of an invitation from God, otherwise known as a *calling*. Vision and calling are interconnected.

The word *called* has traditionally been a word of the church, but in the past few years it has been showing up more in secular writing, perhaps because it is seen as noble. It describes work done for a purpose. What does it mean to be called? Let us look at another biblical story when God audibly called someone.

In the beginning of the story, we meet a boy named Samuel. Samuel lived during a time when, as the text says, "there were not many visions" (1 Sam 3:1). This description is both scene-setting and foreshadowing. Not many people had visions, and people had stopped creating. Building a better world depends on the people of God receiving and acting on visions from God. This call story was set in a time that was barren of creativity.

As Samuel lay in his bed, God spoke to him. God literally called his name (v. 4). One way of knowing you are hearing God speak to you is that you see a clear vision for the future, for yourself and for others. Samuel heard something but did not understand, so he said, "I'm here," then went to see his mentor Eli, thinking Eli was calling him (v. 5). When the beginnings of a creative vision first stir in our hearts, we may not recognize it, or we may mistake it for something else. It may not look or sound like what we expect. That is because we do not know how to listen. But kudos to Samuel. He lay still, and even though he did not know what was going on yet, he heard something. He was not distracted.

When Samuel visited Eli, Eli told him to go back to sleep (v. 6). Crazy kid, the elderly man must have thought. Stop waking me up. This exchange happened a second time. Here, the biblical storyteller interrupts the narrative to inform the reader that the word of God was not yet revealed to Samuel. Aha! So, calling can come first. This is good news, along with the realization that we need help recognizing our own passions.

After the second directive from Eli, Samuel again returned to his bed. Then a third time, God called Samuel, and a third time, Samuel visited Eli (v. 8). But a different result occurred. Eli realized that it was the Lord who was calling the boy. Eli helped Samuel understand what was happening (v. 9). This is important. Samuel never recognized his own calling, even after three times. He needed someone wise to help him, someone who was experienced in recognizing when God moves and speaks. We need Elis in our lives. Samuel's mentor helped him figure out what was happening.

I first received a distinct calling—a creative vision—when I was twenty-one. I had a thought and wrote it down in a journal. I experienced no emotional connection at first, just a natural feeling that what I had written down made sense as an idea to help me direct my energies and passions. I did not share it with anyone, primarily because I did not realize it was going to change my life. It wasn't until two years later, when I met two men who would become mentors, that I began to recognize what I had written in my journal. We likely do not recognize the noise we hear in our hearts and minds. We need mentors in our lives, men and women who have heard God speak before, who will help us make sense of our seemingly indiscriminate passions and interests.

Samuel's calling happened at night, quietly, in bed. This is not the language of drill sergeants and bullhorns. For some, the idea of *calling* connotes directives from the top. When we talk about listening to a call from God, it is easy to imagine that we are on the receiving end of orders from the boss, ready to do the right thing if we can only understand the command. Instead, think of the Holy Spirit as a loving parent or mentor, who coaches and teaches us within the context of relationship. The Holy Spirit nudges and suggests and lets us discern the truth in time.

> Think of the Holy Spirit as a loving parent or mentor, who coaches and teaches us within the context of relationship.

Eli told Samuel to return to his bed and say, "Speak, LORD, for your servant is listening." Samuel did this (v. 10), and what Samuel heard next was horrifying: judgment was to come upon Eli and his family (v. 12). The first word from God was a surprise. As with the disciples on the mountaintop, vision is not all fun and games. The contemporary concept of knowing and pursuing personal passions may be misconstrued as doing what you want and hoping God will sanctify your desires. Sometimes when God speaks to us, it has nothing to do with us. As Samuel learned, the thing we are called to do is not just the thing that gives us pleasure. Instead, it may be the source of our unpeace. It's the thing that keeps us up at night. Joy is a part, certainly, but not the primary raison d'être. We are called to do something, not for purposes of consumption or our own comfort, but for purposes of creation and the building of community. It is for God's glory and the benefit of the New Creation. This is a test for the call you believe you hear. If the main benefit appears to be your comfort, it may not be from God.

After God finished speaking, Samuel was afraid to talk about it (v. 15). If we can learn how to listen, and we receive a word from God, we may not like it, or we may be shy to share it. God's vision was not pleasant for Eli. Perhaps what we hear is not helpful for those around us, so we are reluctant to share. In fact, if the vision leads to innovation, it is likely unsettling to the status quo for somebody. We may want to dismiss it or pretend it will go away.

God has spoken to me a few distinct times in my life. When I say "spoken," I don't mean an audible voice. Instead, I have experienced a rush of vision. On one occasion, I was driving on the highway, having returned from a visit to a ministry colleague, and I had so many ideas flying through my head and such *energy* that I pulled off into a rest area and wrote for an hour. Each time this has happened to me, it hasn't been for me but for the sake of the church. When I was younger and it happened, I would get excited and emotional. As I have gotten older, my need for a personal, emotional experience as a sign of God's presence has shifted to concern for the impact of God's vision on the people around me.

The epilogue to the story of Samuel is that, after that big night, time passed. A lot of time. Samuel grew. Our creative vision does not come to pass quickly. It may take a generation. In fact, if it is the kind of thing that can be built in a month, then it may be too small and not, in fact, a creative vision from God. We each have a set of good things that God has designed for us to do with our lives (see Eph 2:10). These tasks are creative, and they are re-creative. When we are called, the Holy Spirit gives us vision and then an invitation to join in the work of seeing it to fruition. This is the work of the New Creation.

Learning to Listen

While the story of Samuel is a helpful place to begin with vision, how do we learn to do the work of listening to God's Spirit in our lives? It is not often that we lay in bed at night and hear an audible word from the Lord. The challenge of receiving vision is to train our spirits to listen for God's Spirit. This is something we can learn to do.

The presence of the Holy Spirit is often described as wisdom. Scripture makes repeated reference to a "secret" knowledge or wisdom that comes only through the Holy Spirit, for example, "But we impart a secret and hidden wisdom of God, which God decreed before the ages for our glory" (1 Cor 2:7 ESV). The knowledge of God is not acquired through education or research; it is revealed.

The word *secret* is challenging because it is often associated with darkness and abuse. The word *mystery* may be better (the Greek is *mustérion*) because the way we acquire the secret is not visible to most. Yet the mystery of God's revelation to us is not just the fact that it is hidden. The word *secret* also hints at the knowledge aspect of what is happening. Wisdom is not just a state of mind but a knowledge of the spirit, a specific intelligence combined with the good judgment to know how to respond.

These secrets, according to the apostle Paul's writings in his letter to the church at Corinth, are foolishness to the world (see 1 Cor 1). For example, consider that Jesus says we must give to gain and lose to win. Jesus reveals these secrets to his disciples. He also speaks of them at the Sermon on the Mount, and the middle of John's Gospel is full of them. Are they something you can document? Sure, you can make a list. But the ability to apply the teachings of Jesus to life comes not through a list but through the leading of the Holy Spirit. David hints at this in the Psalms: "So teach us to number our days / that we may get a heart of wisdom" (Ps 90:12 ESV).

We do not just acquire wisdom or spiritual knowledge; rather, we receive it as a gift from God as we seek God. This happens over time, by renewing our minds, as we seek the presence of God in our lives (Rom 12:2). This seeking happens in humility. Our brokenness is critical for listening, because brokenness brings openness. From the perspective of an infinite God, we are pretty small. The best we can do is to name our vulnerability and ask God to shape us and give us not just human knowledge but glimpses of God's mysterious and powerful wisdom.

Twenty years after receiving my calling, I found myself at a difficult time in my life. I felt desperate for an answer, for God to tell me what to do. I prayed, as sincerely and as fervently as I had ever prayed. In return, two odd words popped into my head: "Seek first." It was not what I expected, and, at first, I was annoyed. I wanted to fix a problem, but instead God said, "Hello." The first thing to wait for is not marching orders but God's presence. If we are still and give our full attention, God will speak to us.

The language of "seek first" comes from the end of the Sermon on the Mount, when Jesus summarizes his entire body of teaching with a simple phrase, to "seek, however, first the kingdom of God and the righteousness of him, and these things all will be added to you" (Matt 6:33, my translation). If we define the kingdom of God not as a place but as God's presence, then this is best understood as an invitation to discover the New Creation, which is hidden in plain sight before us. If we do this consistently, then Jesus promises us we will find it (Matt 7:7) and all the wisdom of Jesus that is available to us.

> Obedience to God's vision, not our prowess and talent, is what bears fruit for innovation.

The problem is consistency. The reason we find it hard to hear God is not because God is hiding but because God is divine (completely holy), and we are human (in various stages of holiness).[2] It is easy to fall back into sinful habits of self-sufficiency. Obedience to God's vision, not our prowess and talent, is what bears fruit for innovation. In a separate story of Jesus and the disciples, Jesus instructs Simon the fisherman to cast his net in a different sort of way. Simon says yes, then sees nets full of fish. Simon is the professional, yet he lets the rabbi teach him how to do his job (Luke 5:1-11).

It is hard to be consistent and humble when you are used to believing only your five senses and unaccustomed to listening with your spirit. Here is a big difference: whereas innovation of the world is entrepreneurial and focused on speed to market, Christian innovation is marked by spiritual listening, patience, and a willingness to obey.

> Whereas innovation of the world is entrepreneurial and focused on speed to market, Christian innovation is marked by spiritual listening, patience, and a willingness to obey.

In my experience, the sinful habit of self-sufficiency manifests as a form of spiritual hurry. It is easy to get addicted to the rush of creative ideas: What new big thing will happen today? What email or phone call will I receive this week? An obsession with the thirty-thousand-foot view of vision can set you spinning, exhaust your colleagues, and alienate your family. However, if we continue to "seek first," we stay in relationship with the leading of the Holy Spirit and avoid running ahead on our own. A reaction of reverence and trust is a learned response.[3]

As we learn to wait for and listen to the vision of the Holy Spirit, we must then consider how to respond. For this, let us look at one more biblical story, from Numbers 13–14.

Learning to Respond

The people of Israel wandered the wilderness. One day, God said to Moses, their leader: Send some men to explore a land called Canaan. I am going to give it to you. So twelve men went. The men were heads of their respective tribes, hand-picked by Moses, and presumably capable and wise leaders. Moses told them to do the following:

Assess the land: What is it like? Are there forests? Fruit? Is it abundant or harsh?

Assess the people: Who's there? How many? Are they strong or weak?

Assess the cities: Are there camps or towns with fortified walls?

After a long period, the men returned with a report for Moses and the people. They said:

Land: Favorable. The land is abundant to overflowing, an amazing place. They brought back a branch with so many grapes on it that it took two men to carry it.

People: Unfavorable. The people are gigantic and fierce.

Cities: Unfavorable. Huge, well-fortified, and placed on strategic hills.

Ten of the men exclaimed, "We can't go there, or we will be killed!" But two, Joshua and Caleb, said, "Let's go up and take the land—*now*. We can do it."

After the meeting was over, the ten men began to spread rumors. The community began to riot, because, as preacher C. H. Spurgeon once said, "A lie will go 'round the world while truth is pulling its boots on."[4] They advanced on Caleb and Joshua to kill them. At the last minute, God showed up. God considered killing the ten men and their entire tribes but relented on one condition: no one above twenty years old, including the ten leaders and all their people, would receive the gift of entering the land. Then God told Moses to send Caleb and Joshua and their tribes on an alternate, round about path to the land. Moses told the two leaders, and they departed.

Imagine the other ten at this point, saying, "Well if we had known about the other path, we would have believed you!" When Moses told the ten about God's decision, they refused to accept the bad news. They decided to march on the land and take the gigantic people of Canaan head on. Moses tried to discourage them, but they went anyway. The result was tragic and violent: the ten leaders and their people were struck down.

> Vision is a clear, God-given image of the future, based on our source of unpeace, that inspires others to join in co-labor to realize God's redemptive gift.

What can we learn from this story of creative vision? Every one of the twelve men who scouted the opportunity saw the same abundance and the same challenges. One kind of leader—characteristic of the ten—dismissed the vision because of its challenges. Those leaders wanted a ready-made package. They didn't want to have to put anything together. They didn't want to work for it. The other type of leader—exemplified in Caleb and Joshua—saw the situation, not for what it was, but what it could be. They had vision, and this story gives us a good definition of vision. Vision is a clear, God-given image of the future, based on our source of unpeace, that inspires others to join in co-labor to realize God's redemptive gift. In the case of Caleb, the vision was for a better future for the Israelites.

Based on the story, here are some characteristics of creative vision:

It is from God.

It is specific.

It is related to our passions.

It is redemptive.

It is inspiring.

It is unrealized.

It is borne from struggle.

It is for the good of the community.

It is going to require significant work.

So how do we learn to respond to a vision from the Holy Spirit? Here are some suggestions.

1. Look for God's Revelation

Here is a noncomprehensive list of tests, according to the story of Caleb and Joshua, of whether a creative vision is from God:

It may initially seem to come out of nowhere.

It may seem audacious.

The majority of people do not think it is possible.

You are not fully qualified for it.

The path to start is clear.

The path to end is not.

It protects and serves those in your care.

It honors God and gives glory to God.

It is true to the character of God as contained in Scripture.

2. Use Your Imagination

Ten of the leaders made the mistake of looking for a solution lying around like a $20 bill on the ground that nobody else wants to pick up. That is not going to happen. The Holy Spirit typically doesn't deliver a five-star meal; rather, the Holy Spirit sends ingredients and asks us to be the sous chef. This means that the first step is to assess the circumstances and then imagine what might be done differently. Caleb and Joshua saw more than reality; they saw possibility. The promised land was not already built, empty and waiting for the Israelites to occupy it. People were already in it. God's people needed to participate, not by charging into the land, but by trusting and listening.

3. Get Curious

After getting inspired, the leaders were left to figure out the specifics. Deconstruct your inspiration. What would it take to seize on the opportunity? The keyword at this point is *curiosity*. A new creative vision begins by looking outward to the marketplace of ideas and activities.

For example, we know the name of Thomas Edison today because, as a young man inspired by the telegraph machine, he didn't just sit in a telegraph office and dreamily click a button to talk to somebody in Poughkeepsie.[5] He had to understand how the machine worked. He broke the telegraph down and ended up creating iterations that improved its performance. Later, he used this same pattern—love something, then tear it up to understand why—in service to a massive list of world-changing inventions.

Another approach is in asking good questions. The inventor of the Rubik's Cube says, "There are two ways to create change: Either find a new answer for an old question or find a new question that has never been asked."[6]

4. Have Hope

Finally, you need the spark to make it happen, which comes from hope. But be careful about the cynicism that may come with age and experience. Age can do terrible things to vision because we learn through experience the danger of challenging powerful coalitions of stasis. And so, we need to combine courage with hope when we are no longer blissfully unaware of the dangers. Then age and experience bring wisdom rather than cynicism.

Even as a young man, Martin Luther King Jr. wasn't blissfully unaware, riding a dreamy cloud. He was fully cognizant of the dangers he faced. Yet he plowed ahead because he had something even better than an imagination. To quote the book of Joel, he dreamed a dream. King didn't just "change the world" by impertinence, as it may appear, but by hope and the courage to name the problem. While ignorance may be bliss, at some point we all become aware of coalitions of stasis. The only way to overcome these forces is by remembering that the vision we seek is not of our own making but the work of the Holy Spirit. This remembrance comes through prayer.

Vision is helpful only when, like King, we have the courage to act. This means we are called to move according to the inspiration of God's Spirit. The next step in this process, after listening to God, is to take risks. It is to this that we will turn next.

9
Faith Leaps
How Do We Learn to Take Risks?

As a society, we have tried to remove risk-taking. The story of the sons of Jack Abernathy shows how our culture has shifted to an emphasis on failure prevention. Obsession with safety ironically creates atrophy and inhibits new and more robust ideas from flourishing. Conversely, flourishing is highly correlated with the ability to risk. The problem is that we tend to make choices out of fear. Failure prevention is an illusion, because it is self-defeating, while innovation involves learning to take spiritual, intellectual, and material risks. When we take risks, we become adaptable and better able to respond to crises. Most important, the willingness to jump depends on faith. The best way to develop faith is to keep our eyes on the destination, which is Jesus. The Holy Spirit gives us the courage to take risks. Faith leads to an attitude of abundance not scarcity.

United States Marshal Jack Abernathy was one of Theodore Roosevelt's famous Rough Riders. He would hunt down a wolf on his horse, jumping on it and capturing it with his gloved hands, as a cowboy would curb a steer.[1] Roosevelt later remarked that it beat anything he had ever seen, and he had seen a lot.[2]

Abernathy passed on his adventurous spirit to his two sons, Bud and Temple. In 1910, when Bud was ten and Temple was six years old, the two boys decided they wanted to ride their horses from the family ranch in Frederick, Oklahoma, to New York City to greet their father's friend Roosevelt on his return from an African hunting expedition.[3]

Jack said, "Sure," and gave them a few simple guidelines:

50 miles a day, maximum

No water crossings without an adult

$5 carry at a time

No Sunday travel[4]

Jack wrote them a note to show adults, stating they were not runaways. The boys left home in April with clothes, bedrolls, oats for the horses, bacon, and bread. As Oklahoma historian LeRoy Jones recounts, "Temple was so small he had to mount his half-Shetland pony from a porch and slide down its left foreleg to dismount."[5] They slept outside, sometimes on the free and open range. On the way, they stopped at their father's friends' houses, such as Quanah Parker, the last chief of the Comanche, and Wilbur Wright, the aviation inventor. As they rode on the free range, word rode ahead, and after a while they began to be greeted by families who invited them in for a meal.

In New York, at the end of their journey, they met the future president. The *New York Times* announced, "Abernathy Boys Put Ban on Kissing" with the sub headline, "Fearless Youngsters, Who

Have Ridden Here from Oklahoma, Mobbed By Women."[6] Roosevelt put the boys in the middle of his Rough Rider parade down Fifth Avenue. After the parade, the boys put their horses on a train back home. From Oklahoma, Jack bought them a car, and the boys, without their father, drove the 2,512 miles back to Oklahoma over the next twenty-three days.[7]

Ten years old and six years old.

It goes without saying: this would never happen today. No parent would allow it, and no municipal government would miss the opportunity to jail such a parent for endangerment. As a society, we have tried to remove risk-taking. It is as though the world is now run by insurance adjustors. Maybe it is.

Why are we so obsessed with failure prevention?

Failure Prevention

Former risk analyst and information theorist Nassim Nicholas Taleb argues that our desire for a risk-free society is harming us by making us more fragile and vulnerable to crisis and loss. He writes, "The more comfortable you are with looseness and uncertainty, the less fragile your environment is. . . . complex systems are weakened, even killed, when deprived of stressors."[8] Taleb's book *Antifragile* was published in 2012, and events since then seem to support his thesis. Current society, with its tall fences, tightly wound structures, and ideological certainties, has become quite fragile, and we are witnessing the breakage.

Journalist Malcolm Gladwell claimed the same thing twenty years prior in an article for *The New Yorker* called "Blowup." Gladwell's thesis asserted that it is a myth to believe we can manage the errors out of complex systems, whether in corporate settings or in personal relationships. His controlling story—the "blowup" reference of the title—was the O-ring failure that caused the space shuttle *Challenger* to explode, which was not caused by negligence or amoral behavior but by an ever-increasing organizational conformity that fostered an inability to consider problems and alternative scenarios.[9]

The premise of both authors is the same: obsession with safety creates atrophy and inhibits new and more robust ideas from flourishing. When your highest value is failure prevention, whether preventing the failure of systems or the loss of ideological viewpoints, one little problem can ruin everything. A high correlation exists between the obsession with safety and the stifling of ideas in the public square. For example, some journalists today are more concerned with advocating for their understanding of the truth over presenting alternative ideas and what one journalist described as the "pretense of objectivity."[10] Perhaps the concept of intellectual safety helps to explain "triggering" and the desire among some to cancel opposing viewpoints.

Conversely, flourishing is highly correlated with the ability to risk. Thus, the first necessary condition for innovation is the willingness to make leaps guided by faith. By "leap of faith," I do not mean blind action but action animated by a generosity of spirit and willingness to consider alternative ideas; to let go of existing technologies, programs, and systems; to risk; and to try new approaches. Innovation does not arrive on our doorstep in nicely designed packages. As we have discussed, it begins down the socioeconomic ladder and out on the margins, not up and in the corridors of institutional authority. It creates volatility to the status quo; from that volatility new life emerges. New life cannot, in fact, emerge without this volatility.

If we can recognize that volatility is essential to new life, why do we continually suppress it? To understand this, let us fast forward one hundred years from the risky journey of the Abernathy boys to another outdoor environment: high school football.

> If we recognize that volatility is essential to new life, why do we continually suppress it?

Coach Kevin Kelley never punts. He does not believe in it. Instead, he believes the advanced analytics that say going for it on fourth down gives football teams a better chance of winning games. Kelley became head coach of Pulaski Academy in Little Rock, Arkansas, in 2003. In 2005, his teams quit punting. They were already a championship team. In the nine years after he quit punting, his team compiled a record of 102–18–1 and two state titles. As his rationale, Kelley cited a study by a University of California, Berkeley scholar, which analyzed two thousand football games over a three-year period and concluded that a coach should never punt.[11]

A quick football lesson for non fans: in American football, a team has four plays, or downs, to advance the ball at least ten yards down the field. If they succeed, the team gets a new set of four plays, starting from the ball's location on the most recent successful play, which is called a first-down conversion. If the team fails on their fourth play, the other team takes over at the ball's spot.

There is a deeply held, conventional wisdom in football that a failed fourth-down play is a good way to lose the game—and get fired, if you are the coach. So, after three downs, if the team has not gained the requisite ten yards, most coaches will opt to use their fourth down to punt, or kick, the ball all the way to the other end of the field, which forces the opposing team to travel a much longer distance back across the field to score points. Kelley bucks this conventional wisdom. His approach is that opportunity is limited (in football and in life), so you should use every chance you are offered to its maximum potential.

If going for it on fourth down instead of punting makes so much sense, why do other football coaches not avoid punting? Kelley believes that it is because of peer pressure or conventional wisdom. Everyone else punts on the fourth down. Punting is deeply ingrained in the sport of football with coaches and fans alike. Kelley once defied his own logic and punted, and the crowd gave him a standing ovation.[12]

Most collegiate and professional football coaches do not take such risks. As with those who put up fences, the open field is intimidating. Yet statistical analysis reveals that coaches should go for it more often. With all other variables being equal, in fact, a team that never punts will defeat a team that punts most of the time.

Statistician Brian Burke offers three theories on why coaches choose not to go for it more often:

1. *It is outdated and uninformed thinking.* In the old days of football, much lower final scores decided games. Since teams did

not score often, punting nearly guaranteed the opponent could not march the field and score on their next possession. This is called "playing field position." Now, games are much higher scoring, and teams would be smart to maximize every chance they get to score.

2. *Decision makers are more worried about job security than winning.* A failed fourth-down conversion attempt is on the coach, while a punt indicts the players on the field. The main, hidden agenda of most coaches (and bosses), more than success, is job security.

3. *It is an example of Prospect Theory.* Economist Daniel Kahneman won a 2002 Nobel Prize for his work in developing Prospect Theory, which is a theory of economic behavior that suggests people tend to fear losses disproportionately more than they value equivalent gains. In other words, if you have to choose between activity designed to gain $1,000 in the stock market or activity designed to avoid losing $1,000 in the stock market, you will typically make decisions to avoid the loss, not achieve the gain.[13]

The bottom line: for many of us, our highest value is failure prevention. It is not success, or even safety, but fear of failure that drives our behavior. We side with protection and live like insurance adjustors. We keep an eye on worst-case scenarios and dismiss new thinking. We fear judgment. Fear is a powerful governor. It causes us to make decisions based not on positive visions of what might be but on negative visions of what might go wrong.

Fence Wars

Consider the vast American plains through which the Abernathy boys rode. Up through the 1870s it was almost completely free range. On the vast plains, cattle ranchers grazed their herd wherever it seemed best, and ownership was defined by herd of cattle, not geographical location. This changed (as all innovation and change occurs) because of the confluence of two things: a new technology—the invention of barbed-wire fencing—and a disruptive new historical development—the Texas drought of 1883. The drought created scarcity, which led some ranchers to use new barbed-wire technology to claim watering holes, corral their head of cattle, and prevent access by competitors. Soon, cattle owners were putting up fences indiscriminately, including across public roads and in places that blocked access to schools and churches. In response, others began snipping fences. The resulting "Fence Cutting Wars" caused over $1.5 billion dollars of damage in today's dollars.[14] Federal laws intervened in 1890, and, along with the rise of the railroad, we began slowly to section off the country. Like anything else, fencing has history. The Abernathy boys made their trip over a rapidly dwindling free range. One could travel over the open West and still navigate around fencing at that time. Now, a century later, a football field is the biggest grassy area some of us ever walk on. Suburbia is filled with zero lots with ten-foot-tall wooden fences so that no one can see or talk to their neighbor.

Tall fences are not the norm further east in the United States. Suburban Tennessee, for example, is typically open yard. When we lived in suburban Nashville, our children would roam all over the neighborhood. We got to know a lot of families that way. Compared to their life in Texas, our kids were "free range" in Tennessee.

While fencing helped cattle owners, they were not foolproof by any means, as the fence cutters proved. Fencing created an illusion of protection then, and still does so today. It gives us comfort and makes us think we are safe from the dangerous, outside world. A fence is firm, visual, and suggests that we will not experience loss or failure. But fencing also cuts us off from others—and ultimately from life.

The Scriptures have a lot to say about failure prevention. For example:

> Then he got into the boat and his disciples followed him. Suddenly a furious storm came up on the lake, so that the waves swept over the boat. But Jesus was sleeping. The disciples went and woke him, saying, "Lord, save us! We're going to drown!"
>
> He replied, "You of little faith, why are you so afraid?" Then he got up and rebuked the winds and the waves, and it was completely calm.
>
> The men were amazed and asked, "What kind of man is this? Even the winds and the waves obey him!" (Matthew 8:23-27)

The disciples were afraid of the danger. And who are we to judge them? They were literally drowning. We want safety. There are real dangers in life and in the world. That seems perfectly reasonable. Yet what happens in the story? No matter how dangerous circumstances became, Jesus was in the boat with them, calm to the point of sleeping, heart rate about sixty beats per minute or so; he was there to say, "Have faith."

Clearly, the willingness to take risks is not a call to foolishness. For example, we abate the power of the coronavirus when we wear masks in public. There is a place for discernment and protection, and this is not a political choice but a common-sense reality. However, studies have shown that excessive use of hand sanitizer may help to create stronger germs.[15]

> The attempt to make safety
> our highest value is self-defeating.

A large church pastor once told me he wanted only uplifting music for worship. I thought, what about the psalmist's laments? He insisted on only positive, safe messages. Three years later, he had an adulterous affair and left the ministry. Like the O-ring disaster, his worldview was built for failure prevention, and eventually, what happened? He blew up.

The attempt to make safety our highest value is self-defeating. There is value in the openness to uncertainty, even danger. We try to remove risk, but we cannot. Bad things will happen. When our primary value is safety, we also get increased fragility, atrophy, and ultimately the very failure we so desperately want to avoid.

Risk-Taking

Innovation, including Christian innovation, involves taking emotional, intellectual, and material risks. Taleb writes that new ideas and their resulting "technology is the result of antifragility, exploited by risk-takers in the form of tinkering and trial and error. . . . Engineers and tinkerers develop things. . . . We will have to refine historical interpretations of growth, innovation, and many such things."[16]

No, I would not let my children ride a horse from here to New York, then take a car back. But neither do I wish for my children to live a life free of danger. Today, our children sit in closed-off rooms staring at screens all day while pediatricians and psychologists decry how poorly they are doing. We have become scared of letting our kids roam.[17]

Just as we have taken the free range out of our children, we have taken free range out of our society and our church. We put up all kinds of fences. We want to create an environment in which we do not have to worry. But is that possible? Or are we just fencing off life? All of our rules and boundaries have endangered the very thing we want to protect. When we lock things down, whether our kids or our faith, we make them fragile.

Awareness of the damage that our obsession with safety causes is increasing. There is now a movement called "free-range parenting."[18] It is the anti-helicopter-parent model. It seeks to encourage parents to raise independent and, therefore, resilient children. Taking creative risks goes hand in hand with new life. If you want to be able to handle the future, I recommend adaptability. Growth comes from learning to navigate the free range, not from creating fences.

Perceived Pain

Pip Coburn wrote on the premise that people change only when the pain of their existing situation exceeds the *perceived pain* of changing to a new situation.[19] Risk-taking may be a bad idea when the benefits of the current situation outweigh the perceived benefits of a new situation, but it becomes an important strategic alternative when the existing situation's benefits become questionable. Potential risks posed by a new environment are often better than known risks in the existing environment because, while each presents hazard, the benefit of the old environment has already peaked, while the new environment at least holds the possibility for a better future.

Declining Protestant denominations are a study in scarcity. For example, after the turn of the century, the average age of the local pastor in my faith tradition, United Methodism, increased ten years in ten years. In healthy settings, the average would stay the same or even go slightly down. To age an employment population ten years in ten years is the equivalent to adding no new people in the entire time. The average pastor in my tradition is now around sixty years old, and—while younger Millennial-aged pastors are emerging—my generation (Gen X) is somewhat absent.[20] The result is that Boomer-aged leaders are hanging on. This is true in a variety of sectors.

This demographic challenge has created scarcity and led to a kind of thinking that favors grasping onto what exists, even as it declines. With an aging population, what happens when already burdened pension plans take on the additional weight of the bulk of the bell curve of those entering retirement? Who is going to provide the working base? The demographics of working populations in many sectors today suggests serious change ahead. While there is some recognition of this, it is late and inadequate.

No one likes to make unnecessary risks, so at what point does it become necessary? How do you find the moment to take the risk? Here is a hint: it is almost always earlier than you think. The strategic leader recognizes decline early instead of waiting until it is too late to turn it around. The question for every leader, whether the setting is corporate, church, or home, is where are the current trendlines pointing? If they are pointing down, is it an aberration or the new reality? And if it is the new reality, then what changes need to happen to fix the problem before it becomes too late? Responsible leadership involves making hard, risky choices to create a healthy future.

Adaptability

If we are not honest about loss, risk, and pain—danger—then we are not honest at all. We need to free range our kids, our companies, our society, and our churches. As Taleb says, "Antifragile systems are hurt when they are deprived of their natural variations (mostly thanks to naive intervention)."[21]

We do not want to be naive or foolish stewards of that with which we have been entrusted, so how do we balance sensible stewardship with risk-taking? The goal is a third way: not fragility or antifragility but a robust approach that can adapt to risk as it arises. To create an environment that can handle the future well, focus not on safety but on adaptability.

Our ability to adapt is our key to the future. The business sector has recognized that the rate of change is accelerating, and the lifespan of a large company is shrinking: Fast Company reports that, while in 1965, corporations in the S&P 500 Index lasted for an average of thirty-three years, this number has been shrinking for fifty years and is projected to hit fourteen years by 2026. The key to thriving in such an environment is adaptability.[22]

The reason for this acceleration is the reach of new technology, which is ever more global. Biographer Walter Isaacson notes, regarding the rise of computing, that it is a teleological fallacy to ascribe intention to inanimate creations: "A system of open networks connected to individually controlled computers tended, as the printing press did, to wrest control over the distribution of information from gatekeepers."[23] In other words, the rise of new technologies creates unforeseen consequences that usually do the most harm to those in "up and in" places.

Technology is not an animating force or something to be feared, but merely the way change occurs. As stated, technology is a force for both good and evil, a reflection of human nature. The more we create, the bigger the reach of our creations, the more people are affected by the rise of new technology, and the faster new disruptions disseminate. The coronavirus has not caused the changes we now experience. It has spread across the world faster than any previous virus, and the resulting impact has been more instantaneous. If it feels like changes keep coming faster and faster, it is because they are. The only way to thrive is to adapt by innovating, which requires a willingness to make leaps driven by faith.

The message that we need to explore new ideas is not new. But the problem, at least in the church, has been that we tend to confuse adaptability with adoptability. Consider my anecdotal history of the last sixty years of church life:

1960s—the emergence of contemporary music

1970s—the Moral Majority and a new emphasis on ethical standards

1980s—the church as a 24/7 mall of programs and activity

1990s—the rise of media and experience (the attractional church)

2000s—big data and analysis

2010s—a new social consciousness

What is common about this list of innovations in church life over the last sixty years? It mimics the business world and follows it by about ten to fifteen years, in every case. The corporate world is the best model for innovation in America today, and in response, the church tends to adopt corporate practice. Church consultants can make a living, and have done so, by merely repackaging corporate innovation for church consumption. Yet what has been the result? Not much; in fact, continued decline.[24]

The problem in church life has been that we try to adopt business ideas wholesale. When we do this, we end up achieving business goals. In other words, we create church customers and consumers. Christians can and should do better. It is not that business is bad, because we can learn a lot from what is happening in business. The problem is that we need to bring our unique theological perspective to new ideas, vetting them and adapting them to higher purposes. In his study of the history of computing, Walter Isaacson notes that the best innovators had the ability to both source a lot of good ideas and adapt them to their own needs.[25]

Adaptability is the skill of finding good ideas in lots of places, then changing them and using them to meet our needs.

This is what *adaptability* means. Not that we take ideas wholesale and apply them to our context; we change them to meet our needs and our goals. Adaptability is the skill of finding good ideas in lots of places, then changing them and using them to meet our needs. Christian innovation and lasting growth do not come from parroting another sector with different goals. They come from introducing new ways of living that fit our own unique setting.

Believe in Me

The way to respond to crises is not to put up fences and protect assets. The church of the last sixty years has been obsessed with failure prevention. In the process, it has lost faith. Instead, the key is to listen to Jesus in the boat, or as Jesus told Thomas in the locked room, "Stop doubting and believe" (John 20:27). With faith, we are free to learn to adapt to change as it comes. The more we adapt, the more robust we become in our ability to respond, or to be responsible innovators.

But how do we do this? The reality is that we struggle with faith daily, even with evidence of God's activity. To help us with the struggle to have faith, let us consider a third story of a group of people on an open range: the Israelites after leaving Egypt. Has there ever been a time when God's activity has been as clear as when the Red Sea split in half and the Israelites crossed unharmed? Yet, what happened three days later?

> Then Moses led Israel from the Red Sea and they went into the Desert of Shur. For three days they traveled in the desert without finding water. When they came to Marah, they could not drink its water because it was bitter. (That is why the place is called Marah.) So the people grumbled against Moses, saying, "What are we to drink?" (Exod 15:22-24)

The human capacity for going without appears to be quite small. As Norman Borlaug taught us, as soon as resources become scarce, people tend to replace faith with fear. In response, Moses cried out to the Lord, and the Lord provided. Then, the Lord gave the newly freed slaves a promise:

> If you listen carefully to the LORD your God and do what is right in his eyes, if you pay attention to his commands and keep all his decrees, I will not bring on you any of the diseases I brought on the Egyptians, for I am the LORD, who heals you. (Exod 15:26)

The Israelites received this promise. Yet they needed continual reminders. A few weeks later, the desert travel was becoming too much for them. They again cried out, this time going so far in their complaints as to suggest Egyptian slavery was preferable to the uncertainty of their desert travel. Studies show that "Egyptians enjoyed their food . . . with at least forty different kinds of bread and pastries, some raised, some flat, some round, some conical, some plaited. There were some varieties made with honey, others with milk, still others with eggs."[26] Slavery with access to fine dining seemed preferrable to freedom with bland food. Yet again, God provided: this time with food, freshly delivered each morning (see Exod 16:18). Yet, some hoarded: "They kept part of it until morning, but it was full of maggots and began to smell" (Exod 16:20).

Hoarding reflects a spirit of scarcity. It is the attitude of the "risk manager" who speaks in terms of "tolerance" or "appetite." We cannot quantify a vacuum or an unknown future. Any attempts to do so are fabricated. When we try to remove an uncertain future, our present turns to rot. The only way to overcome the fear that leads to atrophy, failure, and loss is to live by faith. In the end, the Israelites made it to the promised land, not because of their great faith, but because of the faith of Moses. Moses focused on the Lord, intervening on behalf of the Israelites, as the Lord led the people forward each day through their journey.

The Abernathy boys' trip was successful for a few reasons. First, they operated with their father's few simple rules. As Jack Abernathy provided for his sons, God provides us with a few simple guidelines for our journey. Our task is to mind these guidelines as we keep our eyes on the destination, which is the fullness and presence of Christ. Second, they navigated the free and open range. Third, they kept their eyes on the destination. In the same way, while easier said than done, I have found that the best way to avoid losing faith is to keep my eyes on Jesus. The key to new life is not to focus on protection against failure, but to get up every morning and saddle up, as the Abernathy boys did and as Moses did. Danger is part of the package. Life is dangerous. Jesus does not promise us a danger-free life. In fact, he takes us out into dangerous waters. Instead of looking for safety,

Jesus invites us to look at him. After a few near-death experiences while following Jesus around, perhaps we will become robust indeed.

The willingness to make faith leaps is the starting point for acting on God's visions of the New Creation. But once we are willing to move, what do we do next? It is to the practical work of creativity that we will now turn.

10

Fresh Connections

How Does the Creative Process Work?

Even though he was already known as an innovator, few people believed in Walt Disney's crazy theme-park idea. Like nursing before Florence Nightingale, amusement parks were considered seedy, sinful, and low class. But Disney made something new by combining two known things together in a fresh way. In this way, creativity is like chemistry, and the kernel of the creative process is the unique, explosive combination of previously known elements. The explosions can lead to what I call First Order and Second Order innovations. Each is a necessary part of health and growth. When we follow the Holy Spirit's fresh breath of inspiration, we both refresh tradition and discover new ideas. The challenge is to learn to evaluate new ideas well.

Opening day at Disneyland on October 17, 1955 was a disaster. Heat soared to 101 degrees Fahrenheit. Twice the expected audience showed because of counterfeit ticket sales. Some people's shoes literally began to stick in the soft asphalt. Others tripped over thick television cables. Water fountains were dry. Frustrated parents tossed their children over heads to get them onto rides.[1] Attendees on that first day may have been forgiven for not realizing they were witnessing the launch of one of the most significant entertainment innovations of twentieth-century America.

Disneyland started because Walt Disney had a personal problem. According to his daughter, Diane, when Walt's girls were small in the late 1930s, they would spend weekends at Griffith Park in Los Angeles: the girls on a merry-go-round, the dad sitting on a nearby park bench, eating a bag of peanuts and watching.[2] Disney dreamed of an outdoor park for children and their parents to play in together. As with many visionaries and entrepreneurs, Disney's dreams outpaced his capacity, however, and his park idea sat on the back burner for a time. He tinkered with prototypes of staged versions of his films in the course of his other work. For example, he had a dwarf's cottage built outside a theater for the premier of *Snow White* in 1939.[3] But innovation requires problems of sufficient need, and the consuming need for several years were simply the films themselves. Studio operations kept him busy, but they no longer satisfied his vision, which burned at a high rate. After *Snow White*'s premiere, with his studio vision achieved, Disney's mind began to wander. For the next several years, he watched over subsequent films and tinkered on outdoor spaces around his home, which included construction of a miniature railroad.

As the success of his studios grew, people began to send him letters. One day in 1948, he received a letter from someone, asking permission to come and visit his studio. The studio itself was uninspiring. What would guests do, watch artists draw? Disney remembered his park inspiration and began to consider a space adjacent to his studios in Burbank, California, where he could create staged and designed sets of his films for guests to play in with their children. Looking for inspiration, he visited Henry Ford's Museum and Greenfield Village in Dearborn, Michigan. Afterward, he sketched out a drawing that would become the basis for Disneyland.[4]

At the time, outdoor parks offered two options. The first, like today, were simple constructions like the city-owned merry-go-round his girls rode on. These contraptions offered little opportunity for children and parents to spend quality time together. The second were "amusement parks" such as the famous Coney Island in New York. The original American amusement-park model had peaked in popularity decades prior, and many had slid into a dilapidated, seedy state—not necessarily the kind of place a parent would feel comfortable visiting with young children, much less dropping them off for four or five hours.[5] On one such park outing with his children and a family friend, Walt said, "One day I'm going to build an amusement park—and it's going to be clean!"[6]

There was one exception to Disney's experience: the Tivoli Gardens in Copenhagen, Denmark, the second-oldest, continually operating amusement park in the world,[7] which opened in 1843. Disney, along with entertainer Art Linkletter, visited Tivoli and marveled at its clean, family-like atmosphere.[8] Inspired, Disney solidified his vision: a new type of amusement park, based on the stories of his films.

Over the next seven years, Disney marinated the idea of a park near his studios that would feature his film's characters. After many prototypes, iterations, setbacks, and leaps forward, Disney opened what he called his "theme park" in 1955. Despite its opening day trauma, Disneyland was a success. A new era of outdoor amusement parks emerged, and Disneyland has since been lauded (and criticized) as a high-water mark of American, twentieth-century entertainment and popular culture. One developer told a Harvard audience that it was the greatest piece of urban design in the nation.[9] As with all innovation, to use Isaacson's definition: it functioned, it worked for a long period of time, and it was the alpha dog on which subsequent innovation emerged.[10] Disneyland launched an entire era of the "theme park."

Let's review the story of Disneyland with the principles of innovation so far. Innovation emerges from **personal problems**. Walt Disney wanted a fun place to play with his girls, but for many years, knowledge of the problem itself was insufficient motivation. It had less relevance to his day-to-day existence than the existing demands of his animation and film studio. He'd had an **unreasonable vision**, but it took a significant moment—a letter from a fan wanting to visit the studio—to catalyze his dissatisfaction with the status quo. While he'd previously tinkered with miniature railroads on his property, the moment he committed significant capital to the idea, he made a **faith leap**. The end result was an explosive combination of storytelling, outdoor amusement parks, and interactivity: the theme park.

There is perhaps no better person to look at to understand the creative process than Walt Disney. While Walt experienced the first three components of innovation—personal problems, unreasonable visions, and faith leaps—Disneyland was successful because it represented an explosive new creative combination of ideas. Let us look more closely at the chemistry of creativity that leads to such innovative thinking.

The Chemistry of Creativity

For a while, my children and I played a mobile game called "Little Alchemy." In the game, you begin with four basic elements: earth, fire, water, and air. To play, you drag one element on top of another, and something new emerges. For example, water and air create mist, water and earth create mud, and so on. There are hundreds of combinations. Eventually, you can achieve modern technologies, and even go to space. The game is a nifty way to illustrate a basic premise of creativity and a theological truth: it is the new mixture of existing elements that creates unique and sometimes explosive new combinations.

Great periods of creativity and innovation, regardless of industry, begin with a crazy combination of unexpected things. Consider twentieth-century popular music: Elvis Presley combined postwar crooning with the blues-driven drums and bass of the African American gospel tradition. Lyricist and singer Bob Dylan set poetry to acoustic guitar, and then electric guitar. For decades, the music industry experienced one amazing chemical reaction after another as people combined styles in new and exciting ways.

Of course, not every combination of elements produces a notable reaction; rather, specific synchronicities spark new elements. Often, these elements are hidden in plain sight. At a creativity workshop I taught, I asked the attendees to write down five keywords that summarized their current problems, passions, and unsolved mysteries of life—professional or personal. One of the workshop attendees was a worship coordinator at a local church. She shared that two of her five keywords were "ministry" and "middle school." She had never considered her passion for middle schoolers in the context of her work in ministry, and the new combination left her stunned. A creative explosion had happened in her mind. The limitation of reducing a myriad of ideas and thoughts into five keywords forced a new kind of clarity. New combinations emerge, and the result is discovery.

The mobile game and the workshop attendee's experience illustrate a fundamental attribute of creativity: all new ideas come as combinations of existing things. A common misconception of creativity is that it happens *ex nihilo*, or that something appears out of nothing—whole cloth—in a blinding flash of inspiration, like Edison and the myth of his light bulb. In truth, we do not actually make things from nothing. It is false to believe that creativity comes from nowhere, although it sometimes seems that way. In Christian theology, the ability to create *ex nihilo* is restricted to the Creator God, YHWH. We mortals draw from multiple sources—*ex materia*—the transformation of existing matter into a new form with a purpose. Even inventor Thomas Alva Edison said, "My so-called inventions already existed in the environment. I've created nothing. Nobody does."[11]

In other words, good ideas that drive innovation are not magical but chemistry experiments of existing ideas that result in new expressions. What we make is a new combination of old thoughts and ideas, often gleaned from other objects, people, and writings.

> Good ideas that drive innovation are not magical but chemistry experiments of existing ideas that result in new expressions.

As the author of Ecclesiastes reminds us, there is nothing new under the sun (Eccl 1:9). The creative process is not mysterious. The way it works is simple: creativity is a three-part process of input, waiting, and connection. God provides the basic building blocks. Human creativity happens when we observe and absorb ideas and then mix and match them in our minds to create new combinations of old things. An understanding of the properties of each element certainly aids this experimental work, but it is not necessary. The man usually given credit for inventing the telegraph, Guglielmo Marconi, was known not for his pure scientific knowledge but for a relentless spirit of experimentation.[12] Disney created something new by reimagining one old thing (amusement parks), moving something from one setting to another (storytelling), and adding participation.

> Creativity is the process of mixing disparate things together into fresh connections. It is the ability to connect dots well. It is not about eurekas but about connections.

Creativity is the process of mixing disparate things together into fresh connections. It is the ability to connect dots well. It is not about eurekas but about connections. If you ask a group of people if they are creative, many will say no, but this response comes from fear or ignorance. Everyone has the ability to pay attention and make new connections.

First Order and Second Order Innovation

When you hear the word *innovation*, perhaps you think of a few grandiose examples such as the wheel, electricity, and indoor plumbing. According to George Day of the Wharton Business

School, there's a spectrum for innovation that includes both "Little i"—incremental improvements—and "Big I"—sector-wide disruptors.[13] Both "Little i" and "Big I" are necessary. For example, while the airplane and the internet are "Big I" innovations that changed the world, the respective industries that emerged from each of these inventions have required many iterative improvements, refinements, and perfections.

Each is distinct. Most people are focused on "Little i" innovation and incremental growth, such as a better process for retaining guests, a more efficient way to track paper costs, or a social media strategy that results in incrementally better engagement. According to Day, "Little i" accounts for 86 percent of all organizational resources.[14] These are necessary for healthy, functioning organizations, including churches. Industries can spend decades working on fine-tuning improvements that refine and squeeze out better returns on our work. Most of us strive to create "Little i" innovations every day.

Yet, while "Little i" innovation is necessary and takes up most of our time, it is "Big I" innovation that results in entirely new movements. It disrupts industries, creates jobs, and impacts thousands of people. "Big I" innovation gets the entrepreneur going in the morning. While only 14 percent of all organizational resources go to "Big I" innovation, it results in 61 percent of all growth. Day writes, "It's the risky, 'Big I' projects—new to the company or new to the world—that push the firm into adjacent markets or novel technologies."[15] While "Little i" practitioners rarely create "Big I" opportunities, "Big I" thinkers need "Little i" iterations and improvements.

Because the terms *big* and *little* seem like value judgments, another way to consider this is to distinguish those who excel at First Order innovation, or first drafts from blank sheets, and those who excel at Second Order innovation, subsequent drafts that solve problems, improve features, and polish style. One way to distinguish this work is to consider First Order innovators "Starters" and Second Order innovators "Maximizers." Such First Order and Second Order innovations exist in every field. One might say, for example, that Haydn was a Starter and Mozart a Maximizer.

Stories of innovation tend to highlight Starters such as Walter Rauschenbusch, Norman Borlaug, and Florence Nightingale for good reason. Starters introduce new combinations that kick off years of growth, either by creating an entirely new category or by redefining a category. For example, the Wright Brothers are rightly celebrated for their discovery of human-powered flight.[16] Less well known is Frank Whittle, who redefined flight when he filed a patent for a turbojet engine. A Maximizer, his idea sat in a lab for a decade but eventually inaugurated the golden age of modern airline travel, which lasted thirty years and ended only when the government deregulated the industry, invited competition, and led to the inevitable downshift to focus on price.[17]

Healthy endeavors, organizations, and industries need both Starters and Maximizers. Each type of innovation brings its own share of risk, and often innovators do not reap the fruits of their own work. Yet their visions change millions of lives. Because of the desire for failure prevention, however, organizations gravitate toward the perceived safety of smaller and smaller innovations, refining and processing until there's little improvement left. It is a select few big ideas that create the sea-change upgrades on which organizations, societies, and civilizations become new.

Consider the local church. When a congregation is new, everything is an innovation. Some ideas are bigger, and some are smaller. If a church is good at navigating the innovations happening in the world of church and the world of culture at large and knows how to apply them to their own environment and context, that church will grow. But eventually time and structure take over, and new ideas start to flatline. Ideas begin to lose resonance with new generations of the "down and out." According to one study, the vast majority of new congregations start to plateau after their fifteenth year, as noted by the number of adult baptisms that occur at the church.[18] So if your church is more than fifteen years old and you want it to grow, what do you do?

First Order innovation is something different entirely: the promise of and calling to greater things.

Usually, church leaders focus on the "Little i" of achievable improvements to existing, dysfunctional, status quo environments.

Building effective systems to create order from chaos is necessary and good. Second Order innovations for churches, based on my research of fast-growing churches, may include better parking lot visibility, a focus on creating new groups, both big and small, and planting new churches, among other things. These are needed suggestions. But the real growth of First Order innovation does not emerge from little refinements and improvements. First Order innovation is something different entirely: the promise of and calling to greater things, and it is this type of innovation that is less common.

Explosive Eras

The twentieth century was a period of First Order American innovation. In the last one hundred fifty years, a wide variety of sectors and industries have made significant leaps forward in technical capability. Consider this quick list of advancements:

1870s–1890s: oil and electricity

1880s–1910s; 1940s–1960s: automobiles

1910s–1930s; 1960s–1980s: film

1920s–1940s: chemistry

1950s–1960s: electronics

1950s–1980s: popular music

1990s–2000s: computers

2000s–2010s: mobile technology

Some of the dates here are arguable. But consider the characteristics of these cycles.

(1) An era of explosive innovation begins with a new, First Order combination of existing ideas, such as the combination of blues music with electric instruments. Disney's new theme park reinvigorated the dilapidated amusement park industry by combining it with his unique form of storytelling. His technical and service innovations included a clean and safe park atmosphere; custom-designed and built stages and sets for storytelling; enough activity for an all-day, family visit; the concept of a visitor as a guest; and a "50-25-25 formula for

revenues: half from novel attractions with a storytelling theme, and a quarter each from food service and retail sales."[19] Though Disneyland offered a myriad of improvements in the small details of the amusement park industry, Disneyland's key innovation was not its Second Order fixes but something much more fundamental: the combination of visual storytelling and interactive experience. Walt Disney reinvigorated the old amusement park industry with his brand of visual storytelling and created multisensory storytelling experiences: films that come to life in space. This innovation spawned an entire industry.[20] If you are leading a church, are you focused on Second Order improvements at the expense of true First Order innovation?

(2) First Order innovation leads to an explosion of Second Order ideas and improvements, as innovators experiment with the newly introduced category. For example, the Dr Pepper museum in Waco, Texas, highlights the hundreds of oddball cola beverages on the market in the first decade of the twentieth century. One of the signs of innovation is the rise of many small companies. But remember the two rules about innovation: they are confined by time and space, and they help some while hurting others. No innovation lasts forever. The activity of a new category consolidates into empires, the chemical spark fades, and creativity becomes commodity.

(3) One sign of the end of an era of innovation is the presence of empires. When you are in the middle of an empire era, it may feel like the powers that be are all-powerful. Currently, the digital behemoths Google, Facebook, and Apple seem all-powerful. But as we learned earlier, the life span of an S&P500 company is getting shorter and shorter. These digital corporations reflect a period of innovation in communications, but like the companies that preceded them on the S&P500, odds are only a few will last past this generation. In previous eras of innovation, companies rose to amazing heights, yet their "up and in" status prevented them from seeing emerging needs.

The Best Story Told in the Worst Way

Let us return to Walt Disney and consider one effect of his First Order theme park innovation. Disney's theme park led to regional and local parks in metropolitan areas throughout the United States. For example, several theme parks emerged in the Dallas-Fort Worth metropolitan area in the decades following the opening of Disneyland. Here is a brief listing:[21]

Storybook Land (1956–1964)

Six Flags Over Texas (1961– present)

Penny Whistle Park (1967–1995)

Sandy Lake Amusement Park (1971–2018)

Lion Country Safari/International Wildlife Park (1972–1991)

Seven Seas (1972–1976)

Sesame Place (1982–1985)

White Water (1982–1986)

Six Flags Over Texas was the biggest and is the only one from the original era of innovation that has lasted to the present; though to survive, it has had to consolidate and has gone through several corporate and in-venue lives. The power of Disney's immersive, storytelling approach bled into other sectors, as well, such as retail, restaurant, sports, and even roadside gas stations.[22]

The cultural impact of Disneyland reached its peak in the 1980s when I was a teenager. Localized Disney-esque experiences in the Dallas-Fort Worth area had a big influence on me. I attended some of these parks and thrilled at the opportunity to engage with stories in interactive ways. To cite a common Gen X trope, I was a "Choose Your Own Adventure" child.[23] I loved immersive, narrative, interactive experience.

Though I could not fully articulate it at the time, as I attended these parks, I was engaging in my creative process of input, waiting, and connection. In chapter 1, I talked about dissatisfaction with the status quo that arises from personal problems. My personal problem came in the form of deep dissatisfaction with the way the church conducted one of its most basic functions: how it witnessed or told the story of Jesus. It seemed to me that the church had the best story but told it in the worst way. This emerging awareness of the problem occurred over several years and peaked in 1991, when I heard God speak to me as I read Scripture. I wrote down a statement, which became a mission: to use oral, written, and visual means to tell the story of Jesus Christ.

At first, I was not sure how to proceed. But I had new eyes for the world around me and a newly emerging purpose: how to combine the emerging set of tools of a storytelling culture with biblical storytelling. Though few understood my problems and passions, I obstinately stuck with it, and after several years of experimentation, I found an opportunity to work on my problem. After seminary, a door opened for me to take a full-time job filling a large screen in a sanctuary with weekly visual images for worship—something unheard of in 1995. This was a Holy Spirit directive. At Ginghamsburg, I finally got an opportunity to develop my passions and participate in one of the biggest innovations in church in the last two generations.

To many people, our work in worship seemed to be a radically different approach for the church, but I saw it as *ex materia*—a new combination of existing ideas. In this way, we both introduced new ideas to worship and reinvigorated tradition. When we follow the Holy Spirit's fresh breath of inspiration, we both refresh tradition and discover new ideas. Ginghamsburg's innovations were First Order, at least in our faith tradition of United Methodism. Since then, many have made Second Order improvements to our early efforts at immersive, multisensory storytelling.

How to Evaluate a New Idea

How do you discover which elements to combine to do greater things? First, understand that, in my experience, it took years and was largely the result of unexpected opportunities that seemed to fall into my lap. In other words, the Holy Spirit does the leading. The question, then, is about paying attention well. We need awareness and the ability to listen, and then obey. Here are some suggestions on paying attention.

Writer Paul Graham makes several good points about the feasibility of a creative idea and how to avoid wasting your valuable creative energy. He writes for the market, but the lessons apply to mission. In Graham's experience, bad ideas happen because:

> You created the first thing you thought of (in other words, you were impatient).

> You were ambivalent about being "in business" (which means creating ideas to meet people's needs, not just because you felt like it).

> You deliberately chose an impoverished market to avoid competition.[24]

I have done all three. My hunch is that most people pursuing a creative idea have done these in some form or another. As I stated, our work cannot be just for our benefit, but for a world in need. Here is a short list of feasibility considerations.

1. Does Your Idea Respond to Specific Problems and Needs?

Forget about the difference between good ideas and bad ideas. We often dream of ideas because they sound cool. "Cool" is a bad barometer of the value of an idea. Graham shares an old British idiom given by his father: "Where there's muck, there's brass." This means that unpleasant work pays. It is a simple law of supply and demand. Work people like does not pay well, because there is so much supply. This sounds bleak, but Graham offers some hope:

> This is not to say that you have to do the most disgusting sort of work, like spamming, or starting a company whose only purpose is patent litigation. What I mean is, if you're starting a company that will do something cool, the aim had better be to make money and maybe be cool, not to be cool and maybe make money.[25]

You can create all day long for your own personal benefit, which can be great for your psyche. But if you want your creative ideas to have an impact on the world—to change hearts and lives—then you need to make something people need. This is why it is so important to stay attuned to the world around you.

Part of creativity is learning to spot a good idea. A prime candidate for a good idea is that it solves someone's problem. This applies not just to entrepreneurialism but to any endeavor. You can be in a salaried position, working for a corporation, nonprofit, or church, and spend significant time on a bad idea that meets no direct need in the lives of your people. Instead of starting with your idea, start by thinking of problems. Graham suggests the front page of the *Wall Street Journal* as a good source for finding problems to solve. Regardless of your sources of input, the point is to be curious.

I discover problems when talking to people and in my daily morning web surf. As common themes emerge, I start to save them in a folder. Then I test my concepts with an informal focus group called Colleague Nagging, where I bounce questions and ideas off people I work with and see how they respond. If they stare blankly, I shelve it. I have hundreds of unpublished blog posts. If they get excited and started responding, perhaps I am on to something.

2. Are You Paying Attention to Your Own Nagging Questions?

I don't mean to suggest that you should create only as a response to the market. As I stated early, problems must be personal in order for you to sustain the energy to solve them. It is only in our personal experience that we find the passion necessary for any great work. So how do you solve this paradox between personal art and public need? The way I handle the tension is to pay attention to my own nagging problems in addition to keeping eyes open to other people's problems. If I have a personal question that won't go away, I start to pay attention to it. I begin with a few months of taking notes and saving links. The best solutions show up in the Venn diagram overlap of public problems and personal dissatisfaction.

3. Are You Avoiding a Crowded Arena?

I have fooled myself into thinking I could create a need through sufficient passion. (In my book on worship and technology, I tried to name my solution "Digital Age Worship." Bad idea.) It is not likely that you will discover a dark corner of the world where creative sunshine has never shone. If no one has ever addressed the need, it may not be an actual need. The question instead is, Has anyone ever done it like you want to do it? Remember, *ex materia*, not *ex nihilo*. Don't look for an empty arena; instead, look for a fresh angle or approach in a busy arena. This book is one of many on innovation; hopefully, it is asking questions in a new way.

To summarize using the characteristics of innovation: we begin by seeking the presence of Jesus. We pay attention to the needs of the world around us and listen to the source of unpeace in our own heart. We are patient and wait for the inspiration of the Holy Spirit. After a period of discernment that our ideas are from God, we set goals and make a leap of faith. We seek connections, analyze the viability of ideas within cultural context, and state what impact we hope to create.

Then what? The example of Disney and the work of fresh connections may suggest that the work of greater things is private, an individual endeavor. Certainly, there are myths about the lone creative genius who has a blinding eureka of inspiration on which the future turns. But the reality is that we are not capable of doing greater things on our own. The work of Christian innovation requires the shared abilities of teams of people, working together for the benefit of God's vision. It is to this topic we turn next.

11

Shared Abilities

What if We Aren't Creative Geniuses?

When we listen to the Holy Spirit, God leads us to community, and it is in community where we find validation for the full range of our gifts and talents. Our ideas are not about us but about the larger community, which is both affirming and humbling. Our task is to learn to get out of the way of the Holy Spirit and the vision at hand, to put our egos aside, and to allow the community at large to share ideas and innovate together. Unleashing creative potential in ourselves and others requires us to shed old values of efficiency, shift from a myth of superhero production to one of patience, and invite one another to use our full gifts and skills for the purpose of God's glory.

Forrest Pool had been trying to get hold of his friend and pastor, Arthur Jones. He wasn't sure how to say it, but after talking it through with his wife he was considering what it might look like to leave the corporate world and work for a local church. The idea seemed crazy. After all, he was at the precipice of a successful career in a premier tax consultant firm in the Dallas area. His family's future seemed secure. Yet he couldn't shake the feeling he'd had one day that what he was doing was leaving him unfulfilled.

For the last few years, Forrest and his wife had been casually attending St. Andrew United Methodist Church. Recently, they had joined a small group with some other couples their age. One of the couples was the associate pastor of the church, Arthur Jones, and his wife, Becky.

The church had been looking for a new chief operating officer for over nine months, and Arthur had brought it up as a struggle he was navigating at work. Several weeks went by, then Forrest's wife, Dana, suggested he talk to Arthur about what it might look like for him to take on that role. He decided to reach out to Arthur about it but couldn't seem to connect.

That night, at their small group gathering, Arthur looked at Forrest at one point and said, "Can we step outside and talk?" The question came out awkward, like an invitation to an after-school fistfight. Forrest laughed and said, "Sure." They stepped outside, and Arthur said, "I want to talk to you about becoming the church's chief operating officer." Forrest smiled and said, "That's why I was trying to call you this afternoon."

Arthur and Forrest experienced a movement of the Holy Spirit that evening. It was a moment in which they each saw how Forrest's unique skill set could be used as part of the New Creation. In Arthur's invitation, Forrest saw potential for a new kind of work that could offer validation for the full range of his gifts and talents. The same validation had happened years prior for Arthur, and now he had the pleasure of sharing the experience with a friend. In that evening, outside on the back patio, each friend saw himself not as he did each morning in the mirror but as God saw him: uniquely made yet designed to be with and serve a larger community.

Stories such as these may seem explainable as coincidence when seen in isolation or outside faith. Yet to those with faith, these moments are sure signs of the Holy Spirit's leadership. Jesus says the sure sign of the Spirit's leading is "fruit that will last" (John 15:16). I am convinced that similar stories of serendipity occurred in the lives of Nightingale, Borlaug, Equiano, and in every story of Christian innovation. Greater things happen when a group of people are set in motion by the presence of the Holy Spirit. When we listen, the Holy Spirit leads us to places of wholeness, where we find validation for the full range of our gifts and talents. Yet the opportunities we are given are not about us but about the larger community. While the world looks for superhero giftedness, Christian innovation requires becoming a valued part of a community of people with shared abilities. Next, let us analyze how to encourage an environment where such stories happen to flourish.

The Superhero Myth

When my children were younger, one of their favorite cartoons was Disney's *Phineas and Ferb*, which featured the lovable mad scientist, Dr. Doofenshmirtz. Doofenshmirtz is an archetypal personality of evil innovation, a person with intellectual superpowers who harnesses magical technology to achieve the impossible, usually with tragic consequences.

Roots of this archetype began in 1818 with Mary Shelley's *Frankenstein*, which was written at the height of an age of incredible industrial innovation. Shelley's Doctor Frankenstein says, "So much has been done—more, far more, will I achieve: treading in the steps already marked, I will pioneer a new way, explore unknown powers, and unfold to the world the deepest mysteries of creation."[1] The mad scientist archetype is someone who is drunk on the belief that he or she harnesses the creative power of a god.

In the 1890s, science fiction author H. G. Wells created a similar character in *The Island of Doctor Moreau*. This was after a generation of rapid technological change, which had introduced electricity, the automobile, indoor plumbing, the airplane, radio, and much more. The inventor had come to be seen as a sort of magician in the public consciousness, harnessing the mysterious powers of the universe to improve the life of the everyday person. Wells based his character of Moreau on Thomas Alva Edison.[2] Edison's renown was worldwide; people named their kids after him. I should know. My middle name, Alva, comes from my mother's father, who was named after Edison.

The mad scientist archetype is a superhero of innovation. It reflects a myth about the origins of new life and an expectation that a single person, a "great man" (and they were nearly all painted as male), can emerge who will lead the community out of its current struggles and into a peaceful and prosperous future. While the narrative tradition of the superhero traces to the rise of the Superman comic books of the 1930s, the concept of a superman is much older. The idea is rooted in the "great man" philosophies of the 1800s, out of which emerged a secular alternative to Christian theology.[3] The idea of a powerful, salvific figure is ancient. As the Israelites wandered in the wilderness, they came to demand a king from God. God didn't want the people to be led by a human king; God's design was for God to lead the people. But, lacking faith, they demanded a strong, tall leader they could see (1 Sam 8). Reluctantly, God gave them Saul, who stood a head taller than other men and whose charisma attracted all who saw him (1 Sam 9:2).

As we have learned, creativity is not about making something from nothing but about making fresh connections. This happens one of two ways: either we are a self-sufficient source of all good ideas, or we need other people. Of course, the former is as limited as each person's individual giftedness, talent, and pool of personal resources. When we watch stories of superheroes and look for single leaders to fix our problems, we have the same expectation today. But this was a destructive falsehood to the Israelites, and it remains so today. The stories in this book sometimes hide teams of supporting cast members, as no one person has the necessary skills to solve the problems

of society. Innovation does not come from mad scientists with superhero powers. Solving the problems of a society happens through
shared abilities, not lone genius leaders.

The Hebrew word for create, *bara*, contains the same root that
translates as covenant. The movement of creation is itself a movement into relationship, and to create is to be in community with
others. Creativity is not something we do with our hands, apart from
ourselves. It is part of us. Everyone who has ever created understands
this fundamental truth. The closest metaphor we have for the artist's
creation is giving birth, which literally takes life from the mother to
the point of death. Like childbirth, creativity is an act of self-emptying. Just as a newborn baby is removed from its mother, we remove
a part of ourselves when we make something new. As God designed
it, then, work is perhaps best understood as a form of creativity in
which we empty ourselves fully into another, to the point of dying,
so that others may live. When Philippians says Jesus lowered himself
to the point of death, this is in part its meaning—that Jesus went
"down and out" for others, by giving of himself to create a better
world. Jesus, by God's creative force, sacrificed himself unto death to
create the salvific New Creation.

> The movement of creation is itself a movement
> into relationship, and to create is to be in
> community with others.

The beauty of sacrifice in God's design is that it is mutually reinforced. When one person only gives, that person dies. When others only receive, the community withers. But when all give to one
another, everyone lives and the community flourishes. This is the
design of the New Creation.

The corruption of sin marred this design, as people's focus shifted
from others to themselves. When the people demanded a king,
they rejected God's preferred way of leading the people, which was
through relationship and love. The people wanted someone to lead
in power. God granted this wish and anointed Saul. God later regret-
ted it—the only time in the Scriptures, other than the flood, when
God expressed regret for divine actions (see 1 Sam 15:11). Why did

God regret it? Saul never sought a relationship with God. He only took advantage of his position. Saul was oriented toward power—a fundamental orientation toward the self, rather than love—a fundamental orientation toward others. Saul used God's Spirit to exert more power in the world. This also suggests that God's Spirit comes alongside a human spirit instead of taking it over, and that we retain individual autonomy and the ability to make our own choices.

As one of the three persons of the Trinity, God's Spirit is about *kenosis*, self-emptying in a mutual relationship of love. The three persons of the Trinity model all relationships by fulfilling one another in the perfect sacrifice of love. The core metaphor of the New Creation isn't a place or a building but a set of self-giving relationships. Theologian Leonard Sweet writes,

> The Scriptures introduce us to a God known by his relationships, a God revealed and experienced in three relational ways (God causing us, God for us, God near us), and where everything stands in relation to everything else. God even exists in relationship, and everything that God makes exists in relationship. By yourself, you are nothing; in relationship, you are everything. True selfhood requires community.[4]

In the use of our gifts, we are faced with two unavoidable choices, both related to our stance with the community. We are either fundamentally giving to the community or we are taking for ourselves. To return to the three mistakes the church makes, when our orientation is toward retreat, rule, or self-reliance, we miss the beauty and the opportunity of true community (see chapter 3). The design of the New Creation is that our orientation is toward the community, and our attitude is love.

Of course, life in community is not easy to sustain. Rightly understood, the glue that connects community together is religion. Though many see religion as a set of rules, it is better understood as the way we reorient our stance toward the community from taking to giving. The Latin word *ligare* (to "bind") is where we get our words *religion*, *obligate*, and *ligament*. Think of Paul's image of the body of Christ as a set of parts of one body. As Paul writes, "From him the whole body, joined and held together by every supporting ligament, grows and builds itself up in love, as each one does its part" (Eph 4:16). Without the connectivity of ligaments, a body would fall to pieces. Ligaments hold us together just as our shared core convictions hold us together in covenant.

At the same time, ligaments are meant to be stretched. Without stretching our shared connection, we atrophy, as many religious muscles have done. The stretching is how we get stronger and healthier. It is how we grow. Growing, whether the inner work of personal maturity or the outer work of society, is done in community, with others, perfected in love.

From Arthur's perspective, Forrest was a perfect match for the needs of the church. The congregation was at a crossroads and had the opportunity to grow into new ways of operating that could create great things. But it needed a head administrative leader who could also manage a large and growing team of talented staff. Forrest was ideal for this role. This does not mean that Forrest was somehow going to single-handedly save the church or solve every problem. It would have been easy for either Forrest or Arthur to adopt a superhero myth about their work at the church, and indeed some do this, which feeds the ego at the expense of the community. Instead, they opted for community.

Even the supposedly nonfiction image of Edison as a mad scientist with superpowers is myth. Edison's public persona was carefully cultivated, a product of public manipulation of messages we might today call marketing.[5] We picture Edison doing the work by himself, but in reality, he had a lab called the Invention Factory that started with a few people and grew to a staff of two hundred at its peak. As biographer Neil Baldwin writes, the history of Edison's work on the electric light is hardly Archimedes' "Eureka" moment.[6] Legend has it that he tried six thousand different light bulb experiments, but even if true, this was conducted in a lab with two hundred people.

Eureka moments don't happen to the madcap lone genius in a studio but within the context of a daily work schedule, shared with many people. This is not necessarily a revelation, though we sometimes still tend to look for a lone superhero who will save our situations and organizations. Many people have recognized that the myth of a lone superhero or genius is unhelpful. Creativity researcher Linda Hill writes,

> If a problem calls for a truly original response, no one can know in advance what that response should be. By definition, then, leading innovation cannot be about creating and selling a vision to people who are somehow inspired to execute that vision. . . . Instead of trying to come up with a vision and make innovation happen themselves, a leader of innovation creates a place—a context, and environment—where people are willing and able to do the hard work that innovative problem-solving requires. One of the leaders we studied neatly summed this up by repeating a line he had heard from the CEO he admired. My job, he said, is to "set the stage, not to perform on it."[7]

By definition, innovation is social. The idea of communities of people working together began to take off in corporate settings in the 1980s, often expressed through the metaphor of teamwork. But while a lot of ink has been used in service of creating collaborative, teams-based work environments, many people, organizations, and churches struggle with truly achieving their goals using team-based work environments. Why?

The question is the challenge of learning to get along with other people.

The Problem with Teams

It's no secret that the reality of teamwork is often much worse than the rhetoric. Just ask any industrious student saddled with a "group project." Professional settings presumably contain successful students, yet the same problem reappears. For adults, perhaps the inability of teams to function well is a factor of corporate cultural environment. This is assuredly tied to Frederick Winslow Taylor, one of the least recognized, most influential figures in American history.

Taylor was the premier business consultant of the early twentieth century. He was known as the "Optimizer."[8] Prior to Taylor, most craftspeople were artisans. They maintained their own tools, their own methods, and they interacted directly with people who had needs, hand crafting "custom" solutions, tailored to the needs of each "customer." Inspired by the efficiency of industrial manufacturing, Taylor sought to overhaul labor by applying empirical thinking to standardize solutions, increase efficiency, and ease production. He believed there was one best way to do things. As a consultant, he advised businesses to break down production into a series of tasks and assign workers ideal times to complete each task. Taylor despised the workers associations and their attempt to establish horizontal bonds between other workers and their customers, because they reduced efficiency and created too many potential divergences from the overall plan. In Taylor's world, workers should have no awareness of or incentive toward organizational goals: the lower you fell in the organizational chart, the smaller the scope of your knowledge and role should be.

There were certainly benefits to Taylor's work. With a focus on efficiency, Taylor's methods were instrumental in the exponential growth of manufacturing in America. His emphasis on efficiency was crucial to the ability of the United States to quickly equip and deploy armies to defeat the Axis powers in World War II.

Yet Taylor's thinking was dehumanizing and has proven to be detrimental. A continued reliance on command-and-control leadership and operational efficiency still dominates most organizational thinking today. Rather than transparency and collaboration, organizations tend toward "siloed" operations and "need to know" communication culture. The lack of a truly transparent, collaborative environment limits workers' ability to bring their entire set of gifts and talents to a problem.

Despite the buzz about teams, workplace culture has so far not been able to sufficiently overcome Taylor's philosophy. Our conversations about teams today are influenced by an unstated value system that emphasizes high productivity through maximum efficiency and is guided by a command-and-control, centralized leadership style characteristic of military and sports settings. This is true in church and ministry organizations as well. While many communities extol teams of people who work together, they are confined by a larger, restrictive "command of teams."[9] Like characters in the Marvel Universe, the ideal team for many organizations is a superhero collection of five-star talents with special powers. We merely extend the superhero myth to a group.

> Like characters in the Marvel Universe, the ideal team for many organizations is a superhero collection of five-star talents with special powers. We merely extend the superhero myth to a group.

According to retired general Stanley McChrystal, even the military has come to realize the limitations of a command-and-control leadership style, as it creates rigidity and an inability to quickly adapt to changing circumstances.

True collaboration shares abilities. Instead of reducing people to workers who execute tasks, shared mission elevates people to leaders who grow a vision. Management theory has come to recognize this. Taylor was an "X theory" manager who believed people were basically lazy; to increase efficiency, you needed to reduce their role and influence on the organization. In healthy work environments, everyone across the community, from the lowest to the highest, all grasp the overarching purpose. In management thinking, this approach is called "Y theory." It believes that workers, when empowered to do what they are gifted to do, are intrinsically motivated.

True team-based leadership cultivates creative leaders, not simply people who are skilled at executing commands. The fundamental shift is from the control of the information or management based on the "need to know" to transparency as an organizational value. In a team of teams, everyone must see the entirety of the system for the plan to work.

In this environment, a leader is less chess master and more gardener, whose primary purpose is not to move every piece but to create the ecosystem in which other leaders can grow. Instead of (vainly) searching for a group of superheroes, like an all-star team made up of hall-of-fame players, a gardener-leader cultivates the talents of each person.

> Everyone has a genius to bring to the shared mission; an effective leader recognizes and cultivates each person's potential contribution.

In one of his parables, Jesus describes people who are given talents to use: some have one talent, some two, and some five. Those with the talents are challenged to use them to bear fruit. The one with five and the one with two multiply them; the one with a single talent acts out of fear, buries the talent, and is chastised by the homeowner for his poor decision (Matt 25:14-30). Everyone has a genius to bring to the shared mission; an effective leader recognizes and cultivates each person's potential contribution. In the community of Christ, there are one-, two-, and five-talent people, but each person has something to contribute. Not only is there no lone genius, but everyone has a part. Or as creativity expert and author Elizabeth Gilbert says, everyone has a genius.[10] It's not that everyone *is* a genius, but everyone *has* a genius-level skill that can be offered to a community and used for good. This is true for churches, organizations, and even informal startups of groups of people who are trying to create something new.

Let the Spirit Lead

If the New Creation emerges through Holy Spirit–led communities in which every person understands the mission and brings their whole set of gifts and talents, then how best can we equip one another to do greater things? This is a question of leadership: What is our understanding of the leadership of the Holy Spirit in the household of God? How are we to listen to God together? We learn to do this in two ways: one, by getting out of the way, and two, by shifting from production to patience. Here are ways to make this shift:

1. Commit to Working in Community

I am still learning what it means to live in a community. Maybe it is growing up in an army officer/preacher's family and moving a lot. Maybe it is a fear of being known. It could also be that, sometimes, I have believed the superhero myth, which teaches that the only truly great work comes out of grinding loneliness and isolation. This image is destructive to Christian innovation. The truth is that all great creative work lives in a community bound by time and space. It is formed by the lives and relationships and opinions of a group of people with unique challenges and unique joys. Great innovators all had a community. Mozart had lovers and friends and enemies, bosses, a hometown, and a doctor. Even the mythology of the lonely twentieth-century artist, like Hemingway, is false. As a young man, he hung with a group of fellow creatives. As an old man he had friends in all sorts of low places. Besides, Hemingway died poorly in the end, so let us agree his is not a good model to follow.

While the superhero myth suggests community is not necessary to the work of the New Creation, the opposite is true. You can understand a great work only when you understand its time and space. In fact, it is the very flawed nature of community that allows great art to flourish. The combination of safety and limitation, of understanding and misunderstanding, creates the tension that is the basis for great creative work. Creativity is best lived in the rhythms of the flawed people with whom you live your life, in the place where your own flaws can be known. Get to know the flawed people around you, and let people know your flaws. Allow your opinions and thoughts and feelings to fuel someone else's creativity. Do not choose the illusion of success over the beauty of relationships. Community isn't just good for you, like castor oil; it is the kitchen in which the ingredients of all great work, and the great works of others, come together.

> Do not choose the illusion of success
> over the beauty of relationships.

2. Change Your Source of Validation

Creative environments that lead to innovation are environments in which people feel worthy. This is an ongoing leadership task, perhaps the most important one. If exercising creativity is to become a "star" talent, then to unleash Christian innovation is to be a creative leader and oriented toward maximizing one another's talents. As a leader, set the stage for others to work. Creative cultures emerge when everyone practices a habit of shared abilities.

In my experience and in working with other people, validation precedes a true self-assessment. Validation is important for everyone. People need to know that their contribution is both good and needed. This goes beyond assuaging ego, which is the language of the world and the language of power. It also goes beyond a sincere sense of gratitude or thank-you to one another for doing a good job. Consistent verbal feedback to one another about a good job is important, but to help one another maximize gifts, we must truly know one another. In fact, people in positions of leadership who don't make the effort to truly know their staff and colleagues should perhaps no longer be in a position of leadership because of the damage they can do. I have seen leaders, including pastors of churches, attempt to continue their work without the hard, messy work of really knowing one another in community, and it leads only to harm.

> In my experience and in working with other people, validation precedes a true self-assessment.

Instead, love one another, which includes helping one another to find worth. This means truly understanding one another's gifts and putting one another in positions to maximize gifts and contributions. This is what it means when the Scriptures say, "outdo one another in showing honor" (Rom 12:10 NRSV). This is not a command to minimize yourself but to highlight others' gifts.

3. Lead as a Steward, Not as an Overseer

The apostle Paul writes about building one another up (Eph 4:12). Mutual edification and building one another up are critical for teams to live out their creative potential.

The building image can be troublesome though. We tend to think of construction metaphors when we consider what it means to build. But the Greek word Paul uses here, *oikonomos*, is different. Rather than construction, where everyone is faced outward, doing their own task, the word has a more intimate connotation. It more accurately means to *steward*, as in managing a household. To be a steward changes the context of the work to social. Christ is the head of the household, and we are managers. As husband to one and father to four, I am not the king of my castle. Christ is the king. I am the steward, the manager. My job is to raise up, to *oikodomē*, my four kids, into fully mature followers of Christ.

This is the shift that we need to make in the church. We have allowed construction to become a dominant metaphor for how we understand our work. But we're not overseers. We are not people working on a cathedral. We are *oikonomos*—stewards. Further, the dwelling we are building, *oikos*, is the metaphor for God's kingdom. It is the house where we live as God's children, with Christ as the head. It is a relational word.

4. Move from Efficiency to Communication

One of the problems with Frederick Winslow Taylor's view of work is that it is, by nature, anti-creative. An emphasis on "best practices" means the starting point is last year's work, what has been done before. A focus on efficiency is anti-innovative. Some opt for efficiency, though, because it's more convenient for the leader. By opting for the most efficient answer, a leader may justifiably circumvent communication and a need to bring others along. He or she can just force a vision through. But this is not the way of Jesus. And in my experience, it does not work for a sustained period anyway.

Starting with "best practices" is by nature
anti-innovative.

The way around this kind of static thinking is to create consensus by communicating with others. The downside is that communication takes time; creating a healthy culture of shared abilities requires the kind of time that you cannot give if you are spending the bulk of your time maintaining old programs that are on the long tail of decline.

Admittedly, this is a catch-22. You absolutely need to kill some things to start new things, but people are more likely to align with a new thing once it is off the ground and has demonstrated success. This means you may have to double up by building the new thing while maintaining the old one, a practice commonly known as "building the new plane while flying it," or perhaps more accurately "building the new plane while flying it and flying the old one too."

Another technique for introducing change in social settings is to use outside narratives to justify ending old things. The arrival of the pandemic, even with all its tragic consequences, offered a boon to those who understood the opportunity. It was a chance to let something old go in order to free up necessary resources to start the new thing.

Shared abilities outpace superhero mythologies. But this doesn't mean the final results will be perfect. They never are. Next, we will look at the life cycle of creative work and how to deal with the fact that the final result is never quite perfect.

Almost Perfect 12

When Are We Finished?

Innovation is an iterative process of achieving good and improving outcomes rather than perfect results. This process is a journey, from the explosion of a new idea to the finished product, which is never quite perfect, but which creates positive change and influences others. Because the context in which we create constantly changes, this is not a one-time journey either. Rather, we are called to a lifetime of commitment to the work of the New Creation. An ongoing life cycle of innovation is best understood as incarnation. When we follow the lead of the Holy Spirit, we will find ourselves called down into new problems and projects throughout our lifetimes. This journey gives us joy, purpose, and meaning.

More than seventy-five-years old, Smokey the Bear is still one of the most recognizable faces in America. Smokey was the brainchild of the War Advertising Council, a taskforce of media executives gathered by President Franklin D. Roosevelt during World War II. The council was responding to public fear of wildfires after Japanese submarines bombed the Ellwood Oil Fields, a small refinery off the Santa Barbara coast.[1]

While the bombing is now merely an interesting historical anecdote as the first attack on the US mainland during World War II, at the time the incident led to widespread public fear about fire-based Japanese attacks along western coastal American forests. Aware of the influence of mass communication in the war effort, Roosevelt commissioned a council to partner with the US Forest Service. Their primary task was to create an advertising campaign to reduce the frequency of human-caused forest fires.

It took five years for the council to discover the right combination of images and copy. The Advertising Council's first campaign looked a lot like other wartime advertising. Released in 1943, the council crafted slogans such as "Another Enemy to Conquer: Forest Fires" and "Our Carelessness: Their Secret Weapon." The latter showed larger-than-life caricature images of Hitler and Japanese General Hideki Tojo staring down at a forest fire. After several months, they recognized the campaign wasn't working. They needed another approach.

For a second campaign, the Advertising Council opted for a celebrity endorsement. The council recruited Bambi, Disney's diminutive deer, who had been introduced into the public consciousness the previous year. Bambi worked, but endorsements are rarely a long-term solution. Endorsements are like renting; they needed to own. They needed their own platform.

For a third campaign, the Advertising Council introduced their own cartoon: a bear in a ranger's hat and dungarees. Smokey the

Bear launched in August 1944 in an ad that showed him pouring water on a campfire and declaring, "Care will prevent 9 out of 10 fires." Inspired by the design style of Disney and other illustrations of the day, the bear resonated with the public. They had found their spokesperson.

For a fourth campaign, the Council redesigned Smokey the Bear and added some new advertising copy. The next year, the war ended. Roosevelt encouraged the council to continue its efforts, which covered a variety of campaigns and messages. Two years later, they returned to Smokey. The threat of Japanese fire bombing was over, but they continued the message about the danger of forest fires with a new forest fire campaign. They kept the bear but gave him a new tagline: "Only you can prevent forest fires."

This fifth campaign was a huge success. Brand recognition soared. People wrote songs about him. By the mid-1960s, Smokey was getting so many letters from children that the US Postal Service gave him his own zip code. The present-day Advertising Council estimates that 96 percent of American adults recognize Smokey the Bear—which is on par with Mickey Mouse and the president.[2]

The story of Smokey the Bear offers some clues about the nature of introducing new change. Business management consultant Peter Drucker once observed that there are only two tasks in business: innovation and marketing, which may be understood as making something and sharing it with people.[3] Each involves a creative process.

> There are only two tasks in business: innovation and marketing, which may be understood as making something and sharing it with people. Each involves a creative process.

This process is a craft, not a transaction. In a transaction, you pay someone for a product or service. People enter a transactional relationship with the expectation of a return on investment. But as stated in the previous chapter, people who make something new, whether through marketing or innovation, cannot know what is going to happen. Often, the work does not resonate. (Perhaps this is why the median tenure of a typical chief marketing officer is only thirty months.[4])

One way to overcome the uncertainty of the future is to test a lot. Successful innovators engage in a constant process of creating and testing. The War Advertising Council consisted of some of the nation's premier media executives. Yet this high-powered brain trust needed several tries before discovering the right combination that led to Smokey the Bear's success. Their approach was to test by launching campaigns and then evaluating what happened. This process of iteration is an important principle of innovation.

A publishing industry executive once shared with me an anecdote about the product plan that enabled Rick Warren's *The Purpose Driven Life* to become the highest-selling book of the first decade of the twenty-first century. The executive tried the exact same template for several other products, and none worked. A successful plan may do nothing for the next product because the cultural environment in which the plan is executed changes rapidly, including the context, channels, and codes.

Any attempt at creating something new, whether in innovation or marketing, is a craft in which the variables are complex and changing. It will likely take several attempts to create just the right combination of messaging that resonates with an audience. This iterative work requires deep knowledge of the cultural environment, the company or organization doing the marketing, the audience, the specific product or service, and constantly changing signs and codes of written and visual language. This is what church culture writers Leonard Sweet and Michael Beck describe as "contextual intelligence," or CQ.[5] How do you develop intelligence for a constantly changing cultural context?

The Characteristics of Innovation

Let us look at the first five key characteristics of Christian innovation using the story of Normal Borlaug, the Christian and agricultural engineer who invented better food production techniques that saved millions, if not billions, of people as the world population soared in the decades after World War II:

(1) Personal Problems. As a young college freshman, Borlaug witnessed grown men resort to rioting out of basic hunger. Later, he observed firsthand the destructive power of famine in postwar Mexico, and then in the exploding populations of the Asian subcontinent. Throughout his life, Borlaug saw suffering firsthand. People's pain sustained his passion, kept it personal, and compelled him to fix a problem that some said could not be solved.

The problem of food production was severe. As the *Dallas Observer* notes, "Many prominent thinkers recommended abandoning famine-threatened India and Pakistan as hopeless causes." Instead, they "advocated a 'lifeboat' theory of survival, a sort of global triage whereby desperate basket cases would be allowed to perish so that precious resources could be funneled to those nations deemed salvageable."[6] The problems Borlaug faced were overwhelming.

(2) Unreasonable Visions. Initially, Borlaug studied forestry at the University of Minnesota, but one night he attended a lecture by Elvin Charles Stakman, the head of plant pathology. The evening changed his life. He ended up getting a doctorate in plant pathology and becoming premier in his field at eradicating agricultural disease.[7] His attempts to practice this expertise were initially thwarted by World War II. Yet during the war Borlaug learned how to innovate, as he led a team that led a team that invented a special saltwater-resistant glue to solve a problem in which ocean food drop packages in the Pacific theater were coming apart because the salt water was destabilizing the glue holding them together.

(3) Faith Leaps. His passions led him to turn down a promising corporate position at DuPont after the war. Instead, he decided to lead a risky new program to help Mexican farmers, sponsored by the Rockefeller Foundation. At first, he thought he had made a significant career mistake.[8] He wrote to his wife that, "The soils were depleted, the crops were ravaged by disease, yields were low and the farmers could not feed themselves, much less improve their lot by selling surplus."[9]

(4) Fresh Connections. The first two years in Mexico were difficult. He started by using the same methodology he had learned with the saltwater-resistant glue, which is the same methodology the

War Council had used to discover Smokey the Bear. Borlaug planted crops, waited, tested, and planted again. But the process of evaluation was taking too long. To speed up the process, he worked in two different agricultural zones within the country.

The breakthrough happened when he made a fresh connection. Borlaug and his team combined two varieties of wheat into a new plant. As *Dallas Observer* journalist Mark Stuertz writes:

> Dramatic progress came when Borlaug hit upon the idea of incorporating Japanese dwarf wheat varieties into his breeding program. Nature favored tall wheat grasses as they can better compete for sunlight. But tall wheat is inefficient from a grain standpoint and has a tendency to fall over, resulting in spoilage, especially when the plant sustains vigorous growth spurts from nitrogen fertilizer. So Borlaug bred his wheat for shorter, stronger stalks that could better support fatter seed heads, allowing growers to charge the plant with water and fertilizer. Yields tripled.[10]

(5) Shared Abilities. The Rockefeller-funded program recruited a team of four, including a corn breeder, an agronomist, and another plant pathologist. Reflecting on Borlaug's Nobel Peace Prize in 1970, *Science* magazine described the team as "one of those fortunate coincidences of a few talented people brought together and, as a result, influencing in a major way the course of history."[11] Those with eyes to see recognize more than a coincidence at work. Borlaug and his team pooled their knowledge and resources and began to work. In the end, Borlaug spent sixteen years in Mexico. When he arrived, Mexico imported 60 percent of its food. Eight years later, they were self-sufficient; by the end of his work, they were feeding other countries.[12]

All five steps of these characteristics were critical to Borlaug's innovation.

The Life Cycle of Innovation

Now, finally, let us look closely at the sixth step, the life cycle of innovation. This process captures my own lived experience and was the origin of this book. It is perhaps the most "how to" part as well.

While some who study innovation talk about it as a factory, with successful ideas as widgets that move down a conveyor belt to completion, I prefer to think of innovation as a story. The stages of innovation are milestones in the structure of storytelling. The experience of moving from initial realization of a problem to completed resolution is not linear like gears on a factory floor but organic and messy like raising a child. It has highs and lows, moments of confusion and moments of clarity. As we have discussed, the story begins on a mountaintop and ends on a hill we may call finished, which is never quite perfect yet creates positive change and influences others.

Like any good story, you can plot it. I have tried to, below. The X-axis is Time, starting at the beginning of an idea and extending outward to all eternity. The Y-axis is Awesome, starting from 0 percent awesome and extending upward to infinitely awesome, like so:

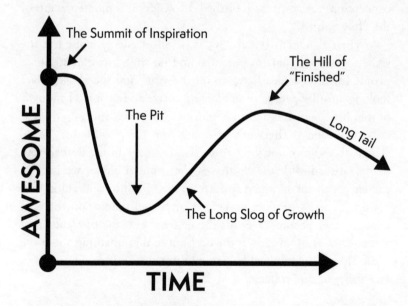

The Mountain Range

First, survey the landscape: What is the situation, the problem that necessitates a change? The problems of any context are myriad, which forces you to be specific about your aims.

Borlaug's problems were immense yet specific. The primary problem was hunger, due to the Great Depression. This was further compounded by the emergence of rust fungus, which was destroying plants, and the rise of the Dust Bowl in the American Midwest, which, at the time, was considered a consequence of new technology; in retrospect it is known to have been caused by poor agricultural methods. This is the context within which you operate. Here is where you name needs and make problems personal.

The Summit of Inspiration

Here is where creativity begins. Within the range of possibility, something specific happens. Every new thing starts with a brilliant spark, a metabolic reaction, a flash of light in your mind—like the kind scientists have discovered happens at the moment of human conception.[13] A new idea is birthed. I consider this moment a gift of the Holy Spirit.

When an idea is brand-new, it is full of energy, poised at the starting line, with lots of potential and no time investment. Some people leave their idea here, up on the vista, and spend their lives looking at other people's completed projects and saying, "I thought of that first!" which is a form of glory-seeking avoidance.

Innovation is the work of doing something with this "Little Bang," this glimpse of the Creator God's image in us. Rather than being satisfied with the beauty of the thought alone, we harness the energy of the moment to activate the idea into something real, a work of art, a product or service, an actual innovation that can change other people's lives for the better. Thus, the first and most difficult act of innovation is the decision to do something about the idea. This takes an incredible amount of courage and willingness to face suffering and ridicule.

The first and most difficult act of innovation is the decision to do something about the idea.

If you find yourself on the summit of inspiration, don't wait long! There is an activation energy at this point, but if you let it dissipate into the atmosphere, it will likely not return. You never know what the inspiration may lead to once you get started. Google Docs, the first fully online word processing software, began with activation energy, but it was not until the prototype was built that its creator discovered its unique benefit of real-time, multi user document interaction and collaboration.[14] In Borlaug's story, while he knew of a range of issues related to plant pathology, Stakman's lecture gave him a flash of inspiration.

The Pit

Innovation scholars disagree on what should happen after the arrival of the new vision. In business, some suggest that most attempts to innovate fail because the visionary does not meet the practical demands of business. In the business world, an idea must pass a validity test. This entails extensive investigation and planning, including technical and market research and an exact definition or scope of the project. Others suggest that the problem with planning, as the saying goes, is that everyone has one until you get punched in the mouth. While it is true that to fail to plan means to plan to fail, it is also clear that too much planning can become a substitute for action. Jesus calls us down the hill. No amount of planning can avoid the pit of the valley. My experience is that it is better to start immediately and then build the thing as you go.

Regardless, in every story of innovation, almost immediately after leaving the summit of pretty vistas, you almost always fall hard. Ideas are like baby birds. They always crash into the ground cover on their first try. Your initial work will send you tumbling into a pit of discomfiture,[15] an in-between, that seems to go on forever. "Down and out" in the valley is where the true, unglamorous life of creating happens. Your idea is young and ugly. You spend a lot of time working it, but sometimes it just seems to get worse or perhaps it levels off at low-level bad.

Often, and tragically, we quit somewhere in this pit. Veteran Proctor and Gamble innovation expert Robert Cooper reports that, of every seven new product or service projects, about four enter development, one and a half are launched, and only one succeeds.[16]

Perhaps the idea really stinks. Or perhaps there's a kernel of greatness in it, but we give up too soon. We decide the idea wasn't that good to begin with, or we cannot figure out the questions of implementation, or perhaps we are just not that good at spotting ideas.

Every work of value I have ever helped to birth has, at some point, felt like a total disaster. Before I knew about the pit, I just figured I stunk at creating things. Then I began to realize other people experience it too. If you are making a prototype widget or writing a song or crafting a business plan to quit your day job, you will at some point think it is not worth the pain and want to quit. Luckily, if you persevere and if what you are making is legitimate, meets real needs, and is produced with a sense of craft, something interesting may begin to happen.

The Long Slog of Growth (The 8 "I" Steps)

Like a flower in a sidewalk crack, the good idea finally begins to grow. Perhaps it is something serendipitous and unforeseen, such as the real-time, collaborative writing feature that eventually became Google Docs. Perhaps it is simply gut-level stubbornness, where you refuse to let your original flash go. Whatever it is, if you stick with it long enough, eventually the idea trends upward, and what you end up with is, if not as good as the original flash of infinity that got you started, a finished project worth sharing with another.

The long slog is where most innovation books focus. In my experience, the way this happens is through a repetitive process:

- *Ideate.* This means you dream up a bunch of ways of solving the problem. This is the whiteboarding work of generating creative ideas, or ideas that are both original and have value. When I led a team of creatives to design a new type of outdoor church Christmas event because of COVID-19 restrictions, we began by talking about all the cool things we always dreamed of doing at Christmas.

- *Invent.* Of course, you have a deadline, so eventually you will need to narrow the ideas into a prototype plan, also known as a proof of concept. (If you don't have a deadline, make one.) In the case of the outdoor Christmas event, we named a series of zones around the church campus, each of which offered a different type of experience of the Christmas story.

– *Influence.* Someone needs to be sold. You will likely need to do this more than once, but the need to gather influence must happen no later than this point, once you have a basic invention in mind.

– *Implement.* The next step is to create the first working version. In the case of the Christmas live event, this meant dates on the upcoming December calendar. As live events require so many resources to get off the ground, we had no choice but to present our 1.0 to the public.

– *Inspect.* Listen to people and get their feedback. If necessary, give it to them for free, or at a reduced rate, in exchange for their participation in an incomplete product and a review.

– *Iterate.* Based on feedback, create a second draft. (Return to a previous step.)

– *Install.* Put the final version into practice. This is as much lament as lightning bolt. It is the point at which you reach the "hill of finished." What you have made is not the same thing as what you saw back on the mountain, but it is done. More on this in a moment.

– *Integrate.* Last, reorder your existing systems around the new innovation, and, if successful, watch as the idea gets adopted on a wide scale. Note that wide adoption usually requires additional iteration and perhaps abandonment of some of your early, favorite features.

If this sounds time-consuming and difficult, that's because it is. It usually takes years. Borlaug sped up the process by doubling the growing seasons—one in southern Mexico, one in northern Mexico. You may find ways to speed the process up, but if you shortcut it, you will undoubtedly fail to achieve your goal. Inevitably, it is a long slog in the same direction.

Last, not every group or organization is good at every step in this process. Each step requires distinct gifts. For example, economist Joseph Schumpeter argues that there's a significant distinction between "invention" and "adoption." The former is the actual work of making something new. The latter is the ability to get it to market and gain acceptance for the invention. For example, Xerox was once the home of an amazing amount of invention. Most of the amazing stuff that came from there, though, never made it into their product line. They had a culture of invention but not implementation and integration.[17]

The Hill of Finished

Notice that the word *perfect* is nowhere to be found in the above process. Perfect, as the axiom goes, is the enemy of good. Recognizing our own imperfection allows us to relax in the grace of the only One who is perfect. Instead, I prefer to talk about something being "almost perfect." The pursuit of perfection can stifle innovation; instead, look for quality and speed to market.

I know an academic who missed a manuscript deadline every year for thirteen years. He could never decide his work was good enough to share with others. When you make things, there is a fallacy of finished. Your idea never finishes, per se; you just decide to quit working on it. This decision to end can be extrinsic; often it is only a deadline or a commitment to share it with other people that keeps you from slaving on an idea forever.

It's unlikely that the final product is as pure and brilliant as your initial idea, but it's possible. Maybe it is even better. The point is, it is finished, and it has been released into "the wild."

The Slide

After an idea becomes a true innovation, which according to Isaacson's definition means it works for a long period of time and is the basis for subsequent development,[18] it eventually starts to fade into a long tail where it generates an afterglow of benefit to you and others. This afterglow can last for years, even decades or centuries. Culture may be understood as a sort of collection of innovation afterglows. For example, opera is a continued afterglow of what was once a dominant musical innovation.

Why does the slide happen? One problem is that we struggle with the growth and introduce problems that inhibit continued success. *Harvard Business Review* named three reasons we struggle with growth:

(1) Attribution error. We puff ourselves up. We think our success was due to our talents and our current model or strategy, and we give short shrift to the part that environmental factors and random events may have played. (I'd phrase that last part to factors beyond our control, which is most of them.)

(2) Over confidence bias. We become self-assured and believe we don't need to change anything. We get stuck in our ways. History is littered with stories of successes who didn't see disruptive change coming.

(3) Failure-to-ask-why syndrome. When we experience success, we quit deconstructing our work. We stop asking the tough questions. In short, success ruins us. After we've seen it, we know what it looks like. We want it again, but without the work.[19]

Another reason that the success of our work slides over time is that *the culture changes.* No innovation is perfect. In the business world, there are still people who use competitor products and services. In the world of Christian innovation, it is because there are still people lost and in need in the valley below. Meanwhile, our efforts start the long slide away from the time and space in which they first appeared. Recognizing the change and adapting to it before it is too late is the most difficult part of the process.

The solution to avoid this long slide is to make another leap of faith, but the trick is to do it not from the bottom of the slide, when it is too late, but from the hill of finished. This is counter intuitive, because it means you are called to begin the next idea while the previous idea is peaking. This is called the Sigmoid Curve, and I write about it in *Think Like a 5 Year Old*. To offer a brief recap using the chart above, the goal is to begin every new project before you completely reach the hill of finished on the previous project. Because of the necessity of jumping into the pit, starting while the previous project is peaking keeps you from periods of decline and stasis.

Of course, this is counter intuitive. You intentionally put yourself through the pain of creating something new just as you are reaping the rewards of your previous work. This entails more pain since growth always involves pain to some degree. It doesn't appear to make sense to change just as you are doing so well. There is even, perhaps, a sense of loss. Why throw away something that is mature and bringing reward for something untested and new? While, in a sense, this decision is about loss, because we are leaving behind our work without fully enjoying its fruits, it is a necessary step to continue to invest. For those of us in ministry or with a sense of ultimate purpose about work, this is part of our calling to realize a better future. Most organizations and groups do not do this, though, which is why they suffer periods of decline. As baseball executive Branch Rickey supposedly said, "It is better to trade a player a year too early rather than a year too late."[20]

Successful innovators regularly reinvent themselves, rising to new challenges and pushing through painful new phases of growth. The junction between the first and second is not easy or clean. There is always a period of confusion, where the first curve is being abandoned and the second one embraced. This is a time of overlap, ambiguity, and confusion.

The theological way of understanding this constant adaptation is through incarnation.

Incarnating

When I was in Cambridge studying for my doctorate, I worshipped in a very old church, built in the twelfth century. At the church, they burned incense. While incense is now a regular part of the Catholic worship tradition, I learned there that it wasn't introduced in worship for sacramental or liturgical purposes. Its roots are much more earthy. In an age before bathing was common, when people gathered on hot days in tight indoor spaces, body odor became a problem. The stench interfered with people's ability to worship. Priests would begin worship by throwing incense around the room to make it smell beautiful, which created a much better atmosphere for worship. Now it's just part of the tradition for most worshippers.

Most of what we do in church is full of such customs that began with real human experience and ended up as rituals and rites of religious activity. The purpose of a symbol is to remind a person, in a visceral, experiential way, about why they do what they do. It's to create meaning or aid in the experience. When rituals lose their meaning, they become purely self-referential. They make someone think of only the symbol itself and not of the reality to which it points. The Protestant reformers were called *iconoclasts* (literally, "image breakers") not necessarily because they hated images, though some went to this extreme, but because they hated symbols and images that became idols, ritualistically pointing to themselves and not to Christ.

Some of us find comfort in such rituals. Others of us, and I am one of the latter, want to understand the symbols, break those that have lost their meaning, and create new ones, rooted in today's time and space, that can point people to Christ.

Innovation is like the work of making new symbols that connect to today's culture. Because the context in which we create constantly changes, we are called to a lifetime of commitment to the work of the New Creation. This process is best understood through the theological lens of incarnation. *Incarnation* is "God taking a nosedive into raw human experience" to speak to us in a language we can understand—the language of a person, Jesus of Nazareth.[21] With incarnation, God modeled how to become present in finite time and space so that people might discover an infinite God. In this way, to innovate is to love. Our job is not to be keepers of a kingdom but to be the reconnaissance team that goes out into the surrounding countryside, looking for people to invite to the banquet feast. We do this by giving them the gift of grace, meeting them where they are, learning their language, and addressing their needs, and then inviting them to come.

> With incarnation, God modeled how to become present in finite time and space so that people might discover an infinite God. In this way, to innovate is to love.

Sometimes, this means stepping off the mountain of known success and down toward the unknown valley. I have lived this. In 2011, after some years of marketplace "success," I recused myself from my own platform. I had begun to feel disconnected from my own creative work. I turned inward for a while and just focused on writing. Eventually, sometime after I made this decision, a surprising thing happened. I began to see good new ideas. I was no longer trying to develop ideas for the sake of turning a profit or to sustain previous success, like I had been doing, but for the pure joy of the work. I'd overcome my own success, and the result was new growth.

What I'd experienced was exactly what author Henri Nouwen describes in his book *Bread for the Journey* as "fruit." Nouwen discusses signs for knowing that what you are making is fruitful and not simply successful. Counter to the three traps of growth above are three ways of discovering new wells of creative energy:

(1) It comes from weakness and vulnerability. You might phrase this as the struggle. Good work is candid, not packaged. It is born in and shaped by the mess. Success must have struggle.

(2) It is unique. Your unique contributions are related to your vulnerability. Your work comes not just out of your gifts but through your struggles. When it comes to making new things, the mess you own is just as important as the gifts you have been given.

(3) It brings you joy. While the creative process has lows, and isn't necessarily about happiness, it is about a deep contentment in knowing you're doing what you're supposed to be doing.[22] This knowledge is as good as it gets. The joyous irony is that, when we stop worrying about success and just focus on the work, we are more likely to find success.

When we follow the lead of the Holy Spirit, we will find our-selves called down into new valleys throughout our lifetimes. This journey gives us joy, purpose, and meaning, even if we don't "change the world." Last, I look at this phrase and a way to measure our work.

13

Changed Lives

What if We Fail to Change the World?

Christian innovation is not necessarily tied to personal achievement but may occur through the work of faithful followers over the course of generations. When we do not see the fruit of our labor, we may think we have not been successful in changing the world. But change is the outcome of a life of faithful *ora et labora*, prayer and work. Instead of focusing on achieving results, we gain joy and fulfillment by faithfully living life in God's Spirit.

The Sleepy Hollow Cemetery in Concord, Massachusetts, houses some of America's great sons and daughters. Gravestones with names such as Hawthorne, Alcott, Emerson, and Irving line the walks. One of the headstone names is the little-known Ephraim Bull. His tombstone reads, "He Sowed, Others Reaped." By his own understanding, Bull was not successful in changing the world.

Bull had been dissatisfied with the state of the grape in early America. Native North American grapes were so abundant, Viking explorers named their discovery Vineland.[1] But they were tiny, not lush, and untrusted by European settlers, who opted to import cut vines from the old world.

Growing a good grape was a critical agricultural concern. As had been the case since antiquity, water sources were often contaminated,[2] and with little understanding of bacteria and the concept of purification, alcoholic beverages were safer. As tea was the drink of the English overlords, and coffee was for morning, beer and wine had become the daily beverages of choice. Alcohol was served with meals, and colonialists drank a variety of spirits as part of a healthy diet.[3] The later temperance movement, which culminated in Prohibition, was a direct response to the heavy consumption of alcoholic beverages in colonial America. At the time, though, drinking itself was not considered evil, only its excess. Distilled liquors were popular, as was hard cider and to a lesser degree beer. Wine, however, was not popular. In the period just before the revolution, Americans consumed only a tenth of a gallon per capita of wine per year.[4]

The reason for the unpopularity of wine, despite the high rate of alcohol consumption, was the poor quality of the American grape, combined with the problems of growing European grapes on native soil. Wet rot, dry rot, beetles, mealy bugs: after two centuries of failed attempts, one horticulturalist claimed that the European vine could not be grown in the New World.[5]

Yet people tried. Bull's father was a silversmith who planted roots in Boston after the revolution, raised a large family, and grew American grapevines in his backyard. His oldest son, Ephraim, born in 1806, learned the metalworking trade but preferred hanging out in his father's garden. At age thirty, doctors advised that he leave the city for health reasons, so he moved out to Concord, where the revolution had begun. There he set up a farm and gradually let go of his metalworking trade in exchange for farming. His passion was growing a good grape, particularly grapes that could better withstand the "early frosts and severe winters" of rural Massachusetts, "though hundreds before him had tried and failed at this task."[6]

The problem with growing a better grape was the turnaround time. Every new seedling had to wait until the vine bore fruit, which takes two growing seasons. Select seeds and cross-pollination created a new iteration, which went back into the ground for another try. The process was excruciatingly slow. In 1849, after seven years of tinkering and six years of intentional growth of a northern fox grapevine, Bull discovered one seedling that yielded good fruit—over an inch in diameter, and sweet. He shared it with a neighbor and called it the Concord grape. They celebrated together, but afterward Bull continued to tinker for four more years. In 1853, he decided to show it off to the Massachusetts Horticultural Society as a seedling from a native grape. It created a sensation.[7] The grapes soon went on sale, and local grocer C. M. Hovey cut him a check for $3,200, the equivalent of more than $100,000 today.

Unfortunately, Bull took sick the day of the expo and decided not to attend his grape's big debut. Shortly after the grapes went on sale, as historian Paul Collins writes,

> Something strange happened. Sales went down—just a little at first. Then a little more. And then, inexorably, the sales dwindled to nearly nothing. The realization slowly sank into Bull: it wasn't just amateurs who had been sending in orders to Hovey. His competitors had been buying the vines.[8]

Others had stolen his grapes. Soon, horticulturalists around southern New Hampshire were growing their own version of Bull's plush American grape. Unlike some creative ideas, it was impossible for Bull to keep his methods a secret. All people had to do to make their own was stick their purchase in the ground. By 1855, "Concord grapes" were everywhere. Bull turned to politics. The next year, he was elected to the Massachusetts House of Representatives, where he stayed for almost forty years. Perhaps this was motivated by his new discovery of human nature.

What does Bull's innovation, and the history of the Concord grape, tell us? Something significant about the way positive change actually works. For one, the Concord grape was not a failure but a massive success. It just so happened that Bull was not the financial beneficiary.

Very Few of Us Actually Change the World

Today, much talk is given to the idea of pursuing your dreams and changing the world. Popular media teaches us to find something we love to do and pursue it. Secular literati search for humanist language for what is essentially a spiritual pursuit, and the most common word is usually *passion*. Though we've diminished the term to erotic sensation or personal ambition, *passion* is a word from the Christian tradition, which means "suffering." In its best understanding today, passion means discontent, a problem that stays alight as a fire in our gut and compels us to work. When people talk about finding passions or pursuing dreams, this is what they're talking about.

Having a passion means suffering for your visions. It could be vocation or avocation, but our passion compels us to seek positive change. We do not do it just because it is a job; we are compelled because it is personal. Success is ancillary, and far from guaranteed. When it happens, success is merely the outcome of the need to engage in the creative process. Bull was discontented with existing grapes, so he made a new grape. We innovate for lots of reasons, but lasting change comes from personal connection, because only a personal, lasting commitment gets us through the pit and up the long slog.

But since we are imperfect, our solutions are imperfect. The hard truth is that, despite the rhetoric, very few of us change the world and live to tell the story. Bull's dissatisfaction with the status quo of American grapes never went away. He continued to grow grapes the rest of his life and planted almost twenty thousand seedlings. Of these, he considered twenty-one to be valuable. The first was the Concord; the rest he kept to himself, unable to trust local nurseries from cheating him of the profits of his labor.[9] In 1893, at the age of eighty-seven, he invested his last remaining savings in one last attempt to release a new variety of grape commercially, but it, too, failed. Bull died poor, and—according to his tombstone, which he commissioned—bitter. He was unable to enjoy the fruits of his labor.

We are not guaranteed to see the fruits of our work. In the biblical story, the grapes of the promised land were so big it took two men to carry a vine back to the Israelites. Yet Moses didn't get to enter, which begs the question: why try?

New Life

By the mid-nineteenth century, alcoholism was becoming a concern. Thomas Bramwell Welch was tired of seeing his clergy friends getting wasted on leftover Communion wine. The Lord's Supper was a central act of worship, but its drink too often led to a drunkenness offensive to the temperance of his Methodist faith.

Early Methodists were largely teetotalers, and the church's first *Discipline*, or rule book, in 1843, called for unfermented wine—grape juice—for Communion. This injunctive was difficult to fulfill for most local congregations. Grape juice naturally turns alcoholic as it sits and ferments, and it was too difficult to make fresh, unfermented wine every time. Besides, most congregants had grown up drinking wine at the Lord's Supper, like their Christian brothers and sisters had for the previous 1800 years, and they saw nothing wrong with it.

What really bothered Thomas, though, was how his clergy friends were prone to imbibing the leftovers. Their reasons were theological—they couldn't throw away consecrated Communion elements—

but their drunkenness was practical. One night after a clergy friend stopped by his house in a stupor, Thomas was sufficiently upset to do something about the problem.[10]

Some years prior, Thomas had been a practicing Methodist minister. Now he was a dentist with medical and divinity degrees and interested in the intersection of church and science. He began to explore how to bottle a juice that would not ferment. Fortunately, in the previous generation, two disparate creative innovations had developed, without which his problem might not have had a solution.

The first trend was Bull's development of the Concord grape. His debut in Hovey's market in 1853 quickly spread across the Northeast, and Bramwell Welch got wind. The second technological development occurred in France nine years later in 1862. Louis Pasteur had received a good amount of press for his new drink preparation method, in which he heated juice just enough to kill most of the bacteria that caused spoilage. After the boiling process, bacteria wouldn't reappear. Pasteur's work was being used for milk, for keeping wine from going bad, and for keeping juice from becoming alcoholic.

Welch read about Louis Pasteur's new process and wondered about its potential for removing fermentation from the winemaking process.[11] Through experimentation, Welch figured out how to combine Bull's concord grapes and Pasteur's process in a painstaking set of tasks:

- squeeze (a lot of) raw grape juice
- pour it into a bottle
- seal it with cork and wax
- place the bottle in boiling water

His method killed the yeast responsible for fermentation, leaving a fine juice suitable for Communion. The iterative process of discovering this simple set of tasks almost killed his family. His son Charles later wrote to his father, "For three years, you squeezed grapes; you squeezed the family nearly out of the house; you squeezed yourself nearly out of money; you squeezed your friends."[12]

But Thomas had found a product and slapped a label on his idea: "Dr. Welch's Unfermented Sacramental Wine." He asked for $12 a bottle. It was 1869. The new grape juice bombed. Three possible reasons: It was too expensive. Its market didn't yet exist. Worst of all, church people thought unfermented wine wasn't appropriate for the Eucharist. Some even called it heresy. Broke and broken, Welch stored his bottles away and returned to his medical business.

An entire generation had passed when Thomas Bramwell Welch's son Charles had an idea. Partly due to Methodist influence in America, temperance had become a trending topic by the 1890s, and, in the trend, Welch's son saw an opportunity to reintroduce his father's idea. The fatigued father gave a warning, but Charles ignored his father's caution and plowed ahead. He found his big break at the 1893 World's Fair, where he introduced a new batch of "Welch's Unfermented Wine"—minus the "Dr." on the bottle—not just as a sacramental drink but as a juice for common consumption.

The Welch family overturned centuries of church traditions based on the need for temperance in a highly indulgent society.

This time, Welch's Grape Juice was a sensation. Soon, for the first time in nearly nineteen hundred years of church history, Christians began to drink a non alcoholic version of wine on Sunday worship, and Charles Welch became a millionaire. There are few stories of such significant innovation in Christian history. The Welch family overturned centuries of church traditions based on the need for temperance in a highly indulgent society. What may we learn about Christian innovation from the Welch story?

(1) Welch leveraged his gifts and talents to solve a personal problem. You don't have to operate from a position of authority or hold credentials or a title to introduce something new. Although he had attended seminary and worked professionally as a minister for a short period, Welch was a long-time layman by the time he made his unfermented juice, and his son had no professional history in the church. They just saw a need. Thomas Bramwell Welch was intensely bothered by the hypocrisy of a church moral code that preached ab-

stinence yet served alcohol in its most sacred worship ritual. It was his source of unpeace. He was compelled to do something.

(2) Limitations may seem bad but can be actually good and even necessary for creativity to occur. We all have handicaps. We think they hinder our ability to create, but they might be helping it. Welch's juice didn't flow from an industry of abundance like the vineyards of Europe but from the land with the worst grapes—America. This limitation led to problem-solving and a new vision based on emerging technologies. The temperance movement, of which Methodism was a part, gradually grew in influence throughout the nineteenth century until, by the 1890s, it was the concern of not just a denomination of Christians but the whole society. It was not until the temperance movement had become a national trend that Welch's juice took off.

(3) While the stasis of "up and in" may seem sacred, it does not mean change is impossible. Christians had consumed alcohol at Communion for nineteen hundred years. Was this necessary or mere cultural custom? Many Christians believed that to drink anything for the Lord's Supper other than what Jesus served his disciples in the Scriptures was heresy. The church had practiced the use of wine for almost two millennia, and it was the model Jesus had established in Scripture. Yet nothing in the words of Jesus or the Scriptures mandated wine. Welch overturned centuries of tradition and now, one hundred years later, many conservative denominations make the practice of drinking non alcoholic wine just as holy and immutable.

(4) Keepers of tradition sometimes respond best to ideas introduced by the general market. When it was introduced to church people as an alternative to a time-honored ritual, it bombed. When it became a beverage common to everyday life, clergy and laypeople naturally saw its benefits for church use. Welch's source of unpeace had no initial impact on church life. Yet forty years later, his creative idea changed the Communion experience for millions of believers.

(5) Innovation doesn't occur in a vacuum but works with and builds upon the work of others. Welch's spectacular innovation was merely the combination of two previously new ideas. He built on

Bull's grapes and Pasteur's process. Creativity is current, it lives in time and space, and it depends on shared abilities.

By their own perspective, Bull did not change the world, nor did Thomas Bramwell Welch. But their work set the stage for something that did.

Change Is the Outcome, Not the Goal

An online meme poked fun at Christian innovation by pretending that an ancient Middle Eastern church, seventeen hundred years old, had rebranded its name to match an American, non denominational megachurch.[13] While funny, the unspoken criticism of the image is directed toward church leaders who advocate change on a trendline with the accompanying loss of the church's traditions. I agree with the parody-makers that such change is a bad idea. We should not reject tradition for the sake of relevance, which reflects a poor theology of *new*. The problem is that a lot of what passes for innovation in the contemporary church is a backward, outside-in approach to creative thinking, and invariably it fails.

The problem with the meme's mockery of the contemporary Christian church, however, is that the image implies there is one perfect incarnation of a Christian congregation, aloft, above time and space, when, in fact, there is not. There is a universal body of Christ, but the form that the body of Christ takes is through local congregations, and each congregation is incarnational in its own way. It lives in a time and space and trades in ideas limited by that time and space. These ideas get old as time and space changes.

What the church needs is people being who they are made to be, creating. While this is our calling, results are not guaranteed.

The phrase "change the world" has been a popular slogan for activity that improves the human condition. While something can certainly change the world for the worse, the phrase generally connotes positive change. Not every innovation changes the world. In fact, few do. Conversely, not everything that changes the world comes from innovation. Sometimes it comes from resistance, such as Telemachus, the Christian monk who ended gladiatorial contests in the year 404 by walking onto the arena floor, though he certainly could have predicted it would have resulted in his death.[14] We do not innovate because we seek to "change the world." We are called to innovate because it is who we are as creative beings. We do not work eschatologically because we are trying to inaugurate some future end. We do it teleologically because the end has already been fulfilled in us through Christ's resurrection.

> We are called to innovate because it is who we are as creative beings. We do not work because we are trying to make some future end. We do it because the end has already been fulfilled in us through Christ's resurrection.

Change that works isn't a trend to adopt or a technique to add or a committee or staff person to acquire. Innovation comes from within, from our inherent creativity. Creativity is what we are called to do and how we are called to live. Part of the beauty of redemption in Christ is that, in Christ, we have the freedom to rediscover the creative wonder we were given in the beginning and from the beginning.

Creativity is raw material, the process of having new ideas with value. Most of us lose sight of our creativity and become content with following, maintenance, comfort, and even consumption. We lose track of our capability to generate new ideas. Innovation is the process of acting on new ideas. When we create in God's Spirit and we make new things, we may call the result "Christian innovation." It may be a new product or program, a new service that leads to new attendees, a new communication system, a medical service, a new law or policy, and so on.

I don't know many people who set out to upset those who prefer the status quo. I just know people who want to create. To be creative, to innovate, is to be a change agent, not because it is trendy but because it is what we are made to do. Change isn't the goal; it is the outcome.

> We are not called to change the world, but merely to bring our creativity to bear on the problems we see.

There are no guarantees that what we are doing will change the world. In fact, that is not our charge. We are charged only with bringing our creativity to bear on the problems we see. In this way, innovation doesn't break tradition, it builds on it.[15] Often, we do not see the fruit of our labor, and we think we have not been successful in changing the world. But change is the outcome of a life of faithful *ora et labora*, prayer and work. Instead of focusing on achieving results, let us make our goal faithful living in God's Spirit.

Epilogue
Six Ways to Engage in Christian Innovation

If Christian innovation is the work of the New Creation, what sorts of work should Christians engage in? If you are looking for where to start, here is a simple list of six powerful ways to create change.

1. Products and Services

The first response to the concept of innovation and to the needs of the world is to create a new product or service. Many of the examples in this book have been people whose work led to new products or services that benefited people and made their lives better.

A recent example that comes to mind from the world of communications and media is the YouVersion app, led by LifeChurch in Edmond, Oklahoma, which was a fresh connection of mobile technology and Bible reading. By any definition, with over 100 million downloads, the YouVersion app has done greater things for the New Creation.

2. Policy

Policy is the action of positional authority. Positional authority is what we have when we have a title or a place of authority among our peers. Pastors, by virtue of their position, find themselves placed in authoritative situations all of the time.

While it can be argued that culture has been steadily stripping away this authority for generations, and this is probably true at a public level, in closed communities and individual conversations, pastors still yield an immense amount of authority.

It is not simply the position that matters. Position alone does not lead to innovation; in fact, it is often the way that groups resist innovation. Policy is the structural action that we create from a place of positional authority to affect positive change. Policy dictates law, but more important even than law, it sets social norms and the exchange of money. This can happen at a societal level or even in the work of a local church. The primary example from this book is the work of the abolitionists who ended slavery in England.

3. Personality

At a basic level, this is a reference to *charisms*, which is our divinely given power or giftedness. Culturally speaking, personality is often seen as charm, or at a darker level as seduction or manipulation. But each person's gifts are uniquely part of the work of the New Creation. Change is not about just the position or the product; it is about your unique contributions. Your ability to affect change is as much a product of your ability to connect and influence others as it is your ability to structurally implement policy. This comes down to your passions.

4. People

While good ideas that can affect positive change can come from anywhere, some people have a special talent for putting the right people in the room together. I am thinking of a few such friends in my circles as I write this. These friends seem to have a special knack for bringing together people who ought to know one another directly.

One of my favorite ways to solve any problem is by considering the best *who* for the job, the right person to call. Realizing this is realizing the power of relationships, which is at the heart of the gospel.

5. Pictures

Image is the indigenous language of the mind. All ideas are conceived in the form of a vision of the future, which is an image not a sentence. This image solves a problem. The ability to describe this picture to others is at the heart of effecting change. This means, if you want to change, paint a picture. It can be an actual visual image or a picture composed of words. The power of pictures cannot be overstated.

6. Presence

Perhaps most important, we can affect change through Christian innovation with the power of presence. Human communication is the sharing of ideas. This is not a one-way street in which we are sending messages and others receive them. It's a dynamic, beautiful relationship in which we listen and learn from others. The listening and learning is, in fact, more important than the sharing and sending.

Works Cited

"Abernathy Boys Put Ban on Kissing." *New York Times.* June 12, 1910. https://
    www.nytimes.com/1910/06/12/archives/abernathy-boys-put-ban-on-kiss-
    ing-fearless-youngsters-who-have.html.

Andrew-Gee, Eric. "Your Smartphone Is Making You Stupid, Antisocial and
    Unhealthy. So Why Can't You Put It Down?" *The Globe and Mail.* January
    6, 2018. https://www.theglobeandmail.com/technology/your-smartphone-
    is-making-you-stupid/article37511900/.

Baldwin, Neil. *Edison: Inventing the Century.* New York: Hyperion, 1995.

Ball, Tom. "Top 5 Technological Advances of the 21st Century." *Computer Business
    Review.* February 8, 2018, accessed April 21, 2018. https://www.cbronline.
    com/list/top-5-technological-advances-21st-century.

Beinart, Peter. "The Left and the Right Have Abandoned American Exception-
    alism." *The Atlantic.* July 4, 2018. https://www.theatlantic.com/ideas/
    archive/2018/07/the-left-and-the-right-have-abandoned-american-exceptio-
    nalism/564425/.

Berkun, Scott. *The Myths of Innovation.* Boston: O'Reilly, 2010.

Bernard, Ian. "The Zong Massacre (1781)." *Black Past.* October 11, 2011. https://
    www.blackpast.org/global-african-history/zong-massacre-1781/.

Bertram, Geoffery, Robert Feilden, and Sir William Rede Hawthorne. "Sir
    Frank Whittle, O. M., K.B.E., 1 June 1907–9 August 1996." *Biographi-
    cal Memoirs of Fellows of the Royal Society* 44:435–52. https://doi:10.1098/
    rsbm.1998.0028.

Beuchner, Frederick. *Wishful Thinking: A Theological ABC.* New York: Harper and
    Row, 1973.

Birkinshaw, Julian, John Bessant, and Rick Delbridge. "Finding, Forming, and
    Performing: Creating Networks for Discontinuous Innovation." *Cali-
    fornia Management Review* 49, no. 3 (April 2007): 67–84. https://doi.
    org/10.2307/41166395.

Boorstin, Julia, "How Coronavirus Could Permanently Change the Movie Indus-
    try." *CNBC.* March 21, 2020. https://www.cnbc.com/2020/03/20/how-
    coronavirus-could-permanently-change-the-movie-industry.html.

"Borlaug and the University of Minnesota," University of Minnesota. March 10, 2005. https://web.archive.org/web/20050310043736/http://www.coafes. umn.edu/Borlaug_and_the_University_of_Minnesota.html.

Borlaug, Norman. "The Green Revolution, Peace, and Humanity." The Nobel Prize. December 11, 1970. https://www.nobelprize.org/prizes/peace/1970/ borlaug/lecture/.

Bourgon, Lyndsie. "A Brief History of Smokey Bear, the Forest Service's Legendary Mascot." *Smithsonian* (July–August 2019). https://www.smithsonianmag. com/history/brief-history-smokey-bear-180972549/.

Bowler, Peter J. *A History of the Future: Prophets of Progress from H.G. Wells to Isaac Asimov.* Cambridge: Cambridge University Press, 2017.

Boyle, John Hunter, *Modern Japan: The American Nexus.* Fort Worth: Harcourt Brace Jovanovich, 1993.

Brendlinger, Irv. "John Wesley and Slavery: Myth and Reality" (2006). *Faculty Publications-College of Christian Studies*, George Fox University. Paper 116. http://digitalcommons.georgefox.edu/ccs/116.

Brown, Lester R. "Nobel Peace Prize: Developer of High-Yield Wheat Receives Award." *Science* 170, no. 3957 (Oct 30, 1970): 518–19. http://doi. org/10.1126/science.170.3957.518.

Burke, Brian. "A New Study on Fourth Downs: Go For It." *New York Times.* September 17, 2009. http://fifthdown.blogs.nytimes.com/2009/09/17/a-new-study-on-fourth-downs-go-for-it/.

Burton-Jones, Simon. "What Can We Learn from William Wilberforce?" The Clewer Institute. September 26, 2018. https://www.theclewerinitiative.org/ news/2018/9/26/guest-post-what-can-we-learn-from-william-wilberforce.

Cannon, Walter Bradford. *Bodily Changes in Pain, Hunger, Fear, and Rage.* New York: Appleton-Century-Crofts, 1915. http://www.archive.org/details/ cu31924022542470.

Carter, Stephen L. "Destroying a Quote's History in Order to Save It." *Bloomberg Opinion.* February 9, 2018. https://www.bloomberg.com/opinion/ar-ticles/2018-02-09/destroying-a-quote-s-history-in-order-to-save-it.

Cawley, Brian D., and Peter J. Snyder. "People as Workers in the Image of God: Opportunities to Promote Flourishing." *The Journal of Markets & Morality* 18, no. 1 (2015).

Cep, Casey. "The Real Nature of Thomas Edison's Genius." *New Yorker.* October 21, 2019. https://www.newyorker.com/magazine/2019/10/28/the-real-nature-of-thomas-edisons-genius.

Chazanof, William. *Welch's Grape Juice: From Corporation to Co-operative.* Syracuse, NY: Syracuse University Press, 1977.

Christensen, Clayton. *The Innovator's Dilemma.* New York: Harper Business, 2011.

Christensen, Maria. "The Meiji Era and the Modernization of Japan." The Samurai Archives. n.d., https://www.samurai-archives.com/tme.html.

ChurchPOP. "POPNews: St. Peter's Basilica Renamed 'Tiber Creek Community Church'." September 17, 2014. http://www.churchpop.com/2014/09/17/st-peters-basilica-renamed-tiber-creek-community-church/.

Coburn, Pip. *The Change Function: Why Some Technologies Take Off and Others Crash and Burn*. New York: Penguin, 2006.

Coffey, John. "Evangelicals, Slavery & the Slave Trade: From Whitefield to Wilberforce," *Anvil* 24, no. 2 (2007): 101.

Cohen, Bernard. "Florence Nightingale." *Scientific American* 250, no. 3 (March 1984).

Coleman-Lochner, Lauren, and Eliza Ronalds-Hannon. "Mall Landlords, Authentic Brands in Talks to Buy J.C. Penney," *Bloomberg*. June 15, 2020. https://www.bloomberg.com/news/articles/2020-06-15/mall-landlords-authentic-said-to-be-in-talks-to-buy-j-c-penney.

Collins, Kenneth J., and Jason E. Vickers, eds. *The Sermons of John Wesley: A Collection for the Christian Journey*. Nashville: Abingdon Press, 2013.

Collins, Paul. *Banvard's Folly: Thirteen Tales of People Who Didn't Change the World*. New York: Picador, 2001.

Cooper, Robert. *Successful Production Innovation*. Product Development Institute, 2012.

Cormode, Scott. "Innovation that Honors Tradition: The Meaning of Christian Innovation." *Journal of Religious Leadership* 14, no. 2 (Fall 2015).

"Coronavirus Will Change the World Permanently. Here's How." *Politico*. March 19, 2020. https://www.politico.com/news/magazine/2020/03/19/coronavirus-effect-economy-life-society-analysis-covid-135579.

Crichton, Michael. *State of Fear*. New York: Harper, 2009.

Crouch, Andy. *Culture Making: Recovering Our Creative Calling*. Downers Grove, IL: IVP Books, 2013.

Crowe, Jack. "AOC: 'Is It Still Okay to Have Children' in the Age of Climate Change." *National Review*. February 25, 2019. https://www.nationalreview.com/news/aoc-is-it-still-ok-to-have-children-in-the-age-of-climate-change/.

Dalberg-Acton, John Emerich Edward. *Historical Essays and Studies*. London: Macmillan, 1907.

Davis, David Brion. "Slavery and the Idea of Progress." *The Journal of Southern Religion* 14 (2012): 9. http://jsr.fsu.edu/issues/vol14/davis.pdf.

Day, George. "Is It Real? Can We Win? Is It Worth Doing?: Managing Risk and Reward in an Innovation Portfolio." *Harvard Business Review*. December 2007. https://hbr.org/2007/12/is-it-real-can-we-win-is-it-worth-doing-managing-risk-and-reward-in-an-innovation-portfolio.

de Berker, Archy O., Robb B. Rutledge, Christoph Mathys, Louise Marshall, Gemma F. Cross, Raymond J. Dolan, and Sven Bestmann. "Computations of uncertainty mediate acute stress responses in humans." *Nature Communications* 7, no. 10996 (2016). https://doi.org/10.1038/ncomms10996.

Deeringer, Martha. "The Astonishing Ride of the Abernathy Boys." *Texas Coop Power*. January 2018. https://www.texascooppower.com/texas-stories/history/the-astonishing-ride-of-the-abernathy-boys.

Descartes, René. *Discourse on the Method of Rightly Conducting the Reason, and Seeking Truth in the Sciences*, 1637. http://www.gutenberg.org/files/59/59-h/59-h.htm, Part IV.

Dias, Victor. "St. Augustine on the Structure and Meaning of History." Master's thesis, Concordia University, 1996.

Douthat, Ross. *The Decadent Society: How We Became the Victims of Our Own Success*. New York: Avid Reader Press, 2020.

"Dreaming of Disneyland: How Walt arrived at his idea of a theme park." The Walt Disney Family Museum, archived from the original on May 18, 2006. http://disney.go.com/disneyatoz/familymuseum/exhibits/articles/dreaming-disneyland/index.html.

Duncan, Francesca E., et al., "The Zinc Spark Is an Inorganic Signature of Human Egg Activation." *Scientific Reports* 6, no. 1 (April 26, 2016): 24737. https://doi.org/10.1038/srep24737.

Easterbrook, Gregg. "Forgotten Benefactor of Humanity." *The Atlantic*. January 1997. https://www.theatlantic.com/magazine/archive/1997/01/forgotten-benefactor-of-humanity/306101/.

Ehrlich, Paul. *The Population Bomb*. New York: Ballantine, 1968.

Equiano, Olaudah. *The Interesting Narrative of the Life of Olaudah Equiano, Or Gustavus Vassa, the African, Written by Himself.* http://www.gutenberg.org/ebooks/15399.

Evans, Christopher H. *The Kingdom Is Always But Coming: A Life of Walter Rauschenbusch*. Waco, TX: Baylor University Press, 2010.

Fallows, James. "Is This the Worst Year in Modern American History?" *The Atlantic*. May 31, 2020. https://www.theatlantic.com/ideas/archive/2020/05/1968-and-2020-lessons-from-americas-worst-year-so-far/612415/.

Faubert, Michelle. "Granville Sharp's Manuscript Letter to the Admiralty on the Zong Massacre: A New Discovery in the British Library." *Slavery & Abolition* 38, no. 1 (January 2, 2017): 178–95. https://doi.org/10.1080/0144039X.2016.1206285.

Fiske, John. *Outlines of Cosmic Philosophy*. Cambridge: Riverside Press, 1902.

Foo Fighters. "Learn to Fly." *There Is Nothing Left to Lose*. Roswell RCA Records. 1999.

Fratto, Natalie. "Screw Emotional Intelligence—Here's the Key to the Future of Work." *Fast Company*. January 29, 2018. https://www.fastcompany.com/40522394/screw-emotional-intelligence-heres-the-real-key-to-the-future-of-work.

Gabler, Neal. *Walt Disney: The Triumph of the American Imagination*. New York: Vintage, 2007.

Gard, Wayne. "Fence Cutting." *Handbook of Texas Online*. http://www.tshaonline.org/handbook/online/articles/auf01.

Garfinkel, David. *Advertising Headlines That Make You Rich*. Garden City, NY: Morgan James, 2006.

Gathro, Richard. "William Wilberforce and His Circle of Friends." Knowing and Doing, C. S. Lewis Institute. 2001. https://www.cslewisinstitute.org/webfm_send/471.

Gerson, Michael. "The Last Temptation." *The Atlantic*. April 2018. https://www.theatlantic.com/magazine/archive/2018/04/the-last-temptation/.

Gilbert, Elizabeth. "Your Elusive Creative Genius." *TED*. February 2009. https://www.ted.com/talks/elizabeth_gilbert_your_elusive_creative_genius.

Gillis, Justin. "Norman Borlaug, Plant Scientist Who Fought Famine, Dies at 95." *New York Times*. September 13, 2009. https://www.nytimes.com/2009/09/14/business/energy-environment/14borlaug.html.

Gilson, Etienne. *The Spirit of Medieval Philosophy*. New York: Charles Scribner and Sons, 1936.

Gino, Francesca, and Gary P. Pisano, "Why Leaders Don't Learn from Success." *Harvard Business Review*. April 2011. https://hbr.org/2011/04/why-leaders-dont-learn-from-success.

Gladwell, Malcolm. "Blowup." *New Yorker*. January 15, 1996. https://www.newyorker.com/magazine/1996/01/22/blowup-2.

———. *The Tipping Point: How Little Things Can Make a Big Difference*. New York: Little, Brown, and Company, 2000.

"Governor Abbott Waives STAAR Testing Requirements," gov.texas.gov. March 16, 2020. https://gov.texas.gov/news/post/governor-abbott-waives-staar-testing-requirements.

Graham, Paul. "Why Smart People Have Bad Ideas." paulgraham.com. April 2005. http://paulgraham.com/bronze.html.

Gray, John. *Straw Dogs: Thoughts on Humans and Other Animals*. New York, Farrar, Straus, and Giroux, 2007.

Gregory, Brad S. *The Unintended Reformation: How a Religious Revolution Secularized Society*. Cambridge, MA: Harvard University Press, 2012.

Griswold, Daniel R. (@danielrgriswold). "What Christianity is about . . ." Twitter. September 30, 2019, 8:46 a.m. https://twitter.com/dannonhill/status/1178667425635733509.

Gurri, Martin. *The Revolt of the Public and the Crisis of Authority in the New Millennium.* San Francisco: Stripe Press, 2018.

Hammer, Joshua. "Thou Shalt Not Underestimate Florence Nightingale." *Smithsonian.* March, 2020.

Handy, Robert T. "Water Rauschenbusch," in *Ten Makers of Modern Protestant Thought,* ed. George L. Hunt. New York: Association Press, 1958.

Harris, Kara. "Fact Check: Did Bill Gates Predict the Coronavirus in 2015?" USAToday.com. March 22, 2020. https://www.usatoday.com/story/news/factcheck/2020/03/22/coronavirus-fact-check-did-bill-gates-predict-outbreak-2015/2890900001/.

Hartnell, Jack. *Medieval Bodies: Life, Death and Art in the Middle Ages.* London: Profile Books Ltd, 2018.

Hays, Richard B. *The Moral Vision of the New Testament: A Contemporary Introduction to New Testament Ethics.* New York: HarperOne, 1996.

Heath, Chip, and Dan Heath. *The Power of Moments: Why Certain Experiences Have Extraordinary Impact.* London: Bantam Press, 2017.

Hill, Linda A. *Collective Genius: The Art and Practice of Leading Innovation.* Boston: Harvard Business Review Press, 2014.

Himmelsbach, Adam. "Punting Less Can Be Rewarding, but Coaches Aren't Risking Jobs on It." *New York Times.* August 18, 2012. https://www.nytimes.com/2012/08/19/sports/football/calculating-footballs-risk-of-not-punting-on-fourth-down.html.

Hoonhout, Tobias. "Brooks Brothers Repurposes Factories to Produce 150,000 Masks Daily." *National Review.* March 30, 2020. https://www.nationalreview.com/news/brooks-brothers-repurposes-factories-to-produce-150000-masks-daily/.

Hopp, Christian, David Antons, Jermain Kaminski, and Torsten Oliver Salge. "What 40 Years of Research Reveals About the Difference Between Disruptive and Radical Innovation." *Harvard Business Review.* April 9, 2018. https://hbr.org/2018/04/what-40-years-of-research-reveals-about-the-difference-between-disruptive-and-radical-innovation.

Hunter, James Davison. *To Change the World: The Irony, Tragedy, and Possibility of Christianity in the Late Modern World.* New York: Oxford University Press, 2010.

Huska, Liuan. "Christians Invented Health Insurance. Can They Make Something Better?" *Christianity Today.* October 20, 2020. https://www.christianitytoday.com/ct/2020/november/health-care-insurance-reform-medical-system.html.

Imarisha, Walidah. *Angels with Dirty Faces: Three Stories of Crime, Prison, and Redemption.* Oakland, CA: AK Press, 2016.

Isaacson, Walter. *The Innovators: How a Group of Hackers, Geniuses, and Geeks Created the Digital Revolution.* New York: Simon and Schuster, 2014.

Ives, Nat. "Average Tenure of CMOs Falls Again." *Wall Street Journal*. May 27, 2020. https://www.wsj.com/articles/average-tenure-of-cmos-falls-again-11590573600.

Jaramillo-Echeverri, Juliana, Adolfo Meisel-Roca, and María Ramírez-Giraldo. "More than 100 Years of Improvements in Living Standards: The Case of Colombia." *Cliometrica* 13, no. 3 (2019).

Jennings, Peter, and Todd Brewster. *The Century*. New York: Doubleday, 1998.

Jennings, Willie James. *The Christian Imagination: Theology and the Origins of Race*. New Haven, CT: Yale University Press, 2010.

Jones, Arthur. *Solid Souls*. Plano, TX: Invite Press, 2021.

Jones, L. Gregory. *Christian Social Innovation: Renewing Wesleyan Witness*. Nashville: Abingdon Press, 2016.

Jones, LeRoy. "Abernathy Boys." *Heritage of the Great Plains/Heritage of Kansas (1957-Present)* 43, no. 2 (Emporia State University, December 6, 2012). https://dspacep01.emporia.edu/bitstream/handle/123456789/2214/Jones%20Vol%2043%20Num%202.pdf?sequence=1.

Jones, Timothy K. *Workday Prayers: On-the-Job Meditations for Tending Your Soul*. Chicago: Loyola Press, 2000.

Kawasaki, Guy. "The Art of Innovation." Lecture, Catalyst 2015, Atlanta October 9, 2015.

Keomoungkhoun, Nataly, "What happened to D-FW's theme parks? Curious Texas straps in to investigate." *Dallas Morning News*. August 19, 2020. https://www.dallasnews.com/news/curious-texas/2020/08/19/whats-the-history-of-d-fws-theme-parks-curious-texas-goes-for-a-ride/.

Kolbert, Elizabeth. "Climate Change and the New Age of Extinction." *New Yorker*. May 13, 2019. https://www.newyorker.com/magazine/2019/05/20/climate-change-and-the-new-age-of-extinction.

Kreider, Alan. *The Patient Ferment of the Early Church: The Improbable Rise of Christianity in the Roman Empire*. Grand Rapids, MI: Baker Academic, 2016.

Krikler, Jeremy. "The Zong and the Lord Chief Justice." *History Workshop Journal* 64, no. 1 (2007): 29–47. https://doi.org/10.1093/hwj/dbm035.

Krippendorff, Kaihan. "A Brief History of Innovation . . . And Its Next Evolution." May 9, 2017. https://kaihan.net/brief-history-innovation-next-evolution/.

Krupp, Steven. "Busting Leadership Myths in an Uncertain World." Heidrick & Struggles October 3, 2016. https://www.heidrick.com/Knowledge-Center/Publication/Busting-leadership-myths-in-an-uncertain-world.

Kuhn, Thomas S. *The Structure of Scientific Revolutions: 50th Anniversary Edition*. Chicago: University of Chicago Press, 2012.

Labarre, Suzanne. "MoMA curator: '[Humanity] will become extinct. We need to design an elegant ending'." *Fast Company*. January 8, 2019. https://www.

fastcompany.com/90280777/moma-curator-we-will-become-extinct-we-need-to-design-an-elegant-ending.

Larson, Edward J. *Summer of the Gods: The Scopes Trial and America's Continuing Debate Over Science and Religion*. New York: Basic Books, 1997.

Larson, Erik. *Thunderstruck*. New York: Broadway Books, 2006.

Lasch, Christopher. "Religious Contributions to Social Movements: Walter Rauschenbusch, the Social Gospel, and Its Critics." *Journal of Religious Ethics* 18, no. 1 (Spring 1990): 7–25. http://onlinelibrary.wiley.com/journal/10.1111/(ISSN)1467-9795.

Lewis, C. S. *The Last Battle*. New York: Collier Books, 1956.

MacCulloch, Diarmaid. *Christianity: The First Three Thousand Years, 1st American ed*. New York: Viking, 2010.

Makrides, Vasilios N. "Orthodox Christianity, change, innovation: contradictions in terms?" *Innovation in the Orthodox Christian Tradition? The Question of Change in Greek Orthodox Thought and Practice*. Surrey, UK: Ashgate, 2012.

Maney, Kevin. *The Maverick and His Machine*. Hoboken, NJ: John Wiley and Sons, 2003.

May, Todd. "Would Human Extinction Be a Tragedy?" *New York Times*. December 17, 2018. https://www.nytimes.com/2018/12/17/opinion/human-extinction-climate-change.html.

McCartney, Paul, and John Lennon. "Getting Better," *Sgt. Pepper's Lonely Hearts Club Band*. Recorded March 9, 1967. Parlophone EMI, 33 ⅓ rpm.

McChrystal, Stanley. *Team of Teams: New Rules of Engagement for a Complex World*. New York: Penguin, 2015.

McCullough, David. *The Wright Brothers*. New York: Simon and Schuster, 2015.

McFarland, Sam. "Abolition! Granville Sharp's Campaign to End Slavery." *International Journal of Leadership and Change* 7, no. 1 (2019). https://digitalcommons.wku.edu/ijlc/vol7/iss1/5.

McGavran, Donald. *The Bridges of God*. Eugene, OR: Wipf and Stock, 1955.

McGilchrist, Iain. *The Master and His Emissary: The Divided Brain and the Making of the Western World*. New Haven: Yale University Press, 2009.

McGinnis, Lindsey. "Why A Small City Made Bus Routes Free to Low-Income Residents." *Christian Science Monitor*. March 30, 2020. https://www.csmonitor.com/USA/2020/0330/Why-a-small-city-made-bus-routes-free-to-low-income-residents.

McRaney, Will. "Church Planting as a Growth Strategy in the Face of Church Decline." *Journal for Baptist Theology and Ministry* 1, no. 2 (Fall 2003): 69–93.

Metaxas, Eric. *7 Men and the Secret of Their Greatness*. Nashville: Thomas Nelson, 2013.

Miles, Michael. "The Lesson of the Sigmoid Curve." Dumb Little Man (blog). October 7, 2008. https://www.dumblittleman.com/lesson-of-sigmoid-curve/.

Miller, Tom. "The 1889 2nd German Baptist Church—407 West 43rd Street." *Daytonian in Manhattan* (blog). February 2, 2012. http://daytoninmanhattan.blogspot.com/2012/02/1889-2nd-german-baptist-church-407-west.html.

Morgan, Lewis Henry. *Ancient Society; Or, Researches in the Lines of Human Progress from Savagery, through Barbarism to Civilization.* New York: H. Holt, 1877.

Nagy, Evie. "How to Know If Your Dumb Idea Will Change the World." *Fast Company.* August 29, 2014. http://www.fastcompany.com/3035032/agendas/how-to-know-if-your-dumb-idea-will-change-the-world.

Nestor, James. *Breath: The New Science of a Lost Art.* New York: Riverhead Books, 2020.

Nielsen's Mobile Insights Survey. "Mobile Kids: The Parent, The Child, and The Smartphone." *NielsenIQ.* February 28, 2017, accessed April 21, 2018. http://www.nielsen.com/us/en/insights/news/2017/mobile-kids--the-parent-the-child-and-the-smartphone.html.

Norberg, Johan. *Progress: Ten Reasons to Look Forward to the Future.* London: Oneworld, 2017.

Nouwen, Henri. *Bread for the Journey.* New York: HarperCollins, 1997.

O'Kane, Sean. "How GM And Ford Switched Out Pickup Trucks For Breathing Machines." *The Verge.* April 15, 2020. https://www.theverge.com/2020/4/15/21222219/general-motors-ventec-ventilators-ford-tesla-coronavirus-covid-19.

Parker, Theodore. *Ten Sermons of Religion.* Boston: Crosby, Nichols and Company, 1853.

Peters, Adele. "Meet the women deciding not to have kids because of climate change." *Fast Company.* March 7, 2019. https://www.fastcompany.com/90315700/meet-the-women-deciding-not-to-have-kids-because-of-climate-change.

Pidot, Sacha J., et al., "Increasing Tolerance of Hospital *Enterococcus Faecium* to Handwash Alcohols." *Science Translational Medicine* 10, no. 452 (August 1, 2018): eaar6115. http://doi.org/10.1126/scitranslmed.aar6115.

Pinker, Steven. *Enlightenment Now: The Case for Reason, Science, Humanism, and Progress.* New York: Viking, 2018.

Polanyi, Michael. *Personal Knowledge: Towards a Post-Critical Philosophy.* Chicago: University of Chicago Press, 1958.

Poole, Steven. "How Leeches Made Their Comeback." *New York Magazine.* November 11, 2016. https://nymag.com/vindicated/2016/11/how-leeches-made-their-comeback.html.

Price, Harrison. "Walt's Revolution! By the Numbers." Stanford Graduate School of Business. May 2004. https://web.archive.org/web/20120117120900/http://www.gsb.stanford.edu/news/bmag/sbsm0405/feature_alumnibks_price.shtml.

Public Papers of the Presidents of the United States: Lyndon B. Johnson, 1963-64. Volume I, entry 357. Washington, D.C.: Government Printing Office, 1965.

Pugh, Jena. "5 Oldest Walt Disney Rides That Are Still Around Today." *Best of Orlando.* May 16, 2016. https://www.bestoforlando.com/articles/5-oldest-walt-disney-world-rides-still-around-today/.

Rabey, Steve. "Borlaug: Not by Bread Alone." *GetReligion.* September 15, 2009. https://www.getreligion.org/getreligion/2009/09/norman-borlaug-not-by-bread-alone.

Rauschenbusch, Walter. *Christianity and the Social Crisis.* New York: MacMillan, 1913.

———. *A Theology for the Social Gospel.* Nashville: Abingdon Press, 1917.

Ravina, Mark. *The Last Samurai: The Life and Battles of Saigō Takamori.* Hoboken, NJ: John Wiley and Sons, 2004.

Resnick, Brian. "Social Distancing Can't Last Forever. Here's What Should Come Next." *Vox.* March 30, 2020. https://www.vox.com/science-and-health/2020/3/26/21192211/coronavirus-covid-19-social-distancing-end.

Rhodes, D. (@dbryanrhodes). Twitter. May 17, 2020, 4:40 a.m. https://twitter.com/DBryanRhodes/status/1261954769561804800.

"Right Direction or Wrong Track." *Rasmussen Reports.* April 1, 2019. http://www.rasmussenreports.com/public_content/politics/top_stories/right_direction_wrong_track_apr01.

Riley, Naomi Schaefer. "America's Real Digital Divide." *New York Times.* February 11, 2018. https://www.nytimes.com/2018/02/11/opinion/america-digital-divide.html.

Robinson, Ken. *Out of Our Minds: Learning to Be Creative.* London: Capstone, 2011.

Romer, David. "Do Firms Maximize? Evidence from Professional Football." University of California, Berkeley. July 2005. https://eml.berkeley.edu/~dromer/papers/PAPER_NFL_JULY05_FORWEB_CORRECTED.pdf.

Roozen, David A., and C. Kirk Hadaway, eds. *Church and Denominational Growth: What Does (and Does Not) Cause Growth or Decline.* Nashville: Abingdon Press, 1993.

Rosen, Michael, and Helen Oxenbury. *We're Going on a Bear Hunt.* Avon, MA: Margaret K. McElderry Books, 2003.

Roser, Max, Hannah Ritchie, and Esteban Ortiz-Ospina. "World Population Growth." *Our World in Data.* May 2019. https://ourworldindata.org/world-population-growth.

Rothman, Joshua. "The Case for Not Being Born." *New Yorker.* November 27, 2017. https://www.newyorker.com/culture/persons-of-interest/the-case-for-not-being-born.

Rubik, Ernó. *Cubed: The Puzzle of Us All.* New York: Flatiron Books, 2020.

Rudy. Directed by David Anspaugh. TriStar Pictures. 1993. https://www.amazon.com/Rudy-Sean-Astin/dp/B00171R00O/.

Russell, William Howard. "The Crimea." *The Times.* October 12, 1854. https://www.thetimes.co.uk/archive/article/1854-10-12/7/3.html.

Salinger, Sharon. *Taverns and Drinking in Early America.* Baltimore: Johns Hopkins University Press, 2002.

Sawhney, Mohanbir, Robert C. Wolcott, and Inigo Arroniz. "The 12 Different Ways for Companies to Innovate." *MIT Sloan Management Review* 47, no 3 (Spring 2006): 75–81. https://sloanreview.mit.edu/article/the-different-ways-for-companies-to-innovate/.

Schlangenstein, Mary, Esha Dey, and Brian Eckhouse, "U.S. Airlines Face End of Business Travel as They Knew It." *Bloomberg.* July 20, 2020. https://www.bloomberg.com/news/articles/2020-07-20/u-s-airlines-face-the-end-of-business-travel-as-they-knew-it.

Schmidt, Eric, and Jonathan Rosenberg. *How Google Works.* New York: Grand Central Publishing, 2014.

Schumpeter, Joseph A. *Capitalism, Socialism, and Democracy.* New York: Harper and Brothers, 1950.

Scott, James C. *Seeing Like a State: How Certain Schemes to Improve the Human Condition Have Failed.* New Haven, CT: Yale University Press, 1999.

Servick, Kelly. "Cellphone Tracking Could Help Stem the Spread of Coronavirus. Is Privacy the Price?" *Science.* March 22, 2020. https://www.sciencemag.org/news/2020/03/cellphone-tracking-could-help-stem-spread-coronavirus-privacy-price.

Shelley, Mary Wollstonecraft. *Frankenstein, or the Modern Prometheus (Revised Edition, 1831).* https://en.wikisource.org/wiki/Frankenstein,_or_the_Modern_Prometheus_(Revised_Edition,_1831)/Chapter_3.

"Shields and Brooks on Obama's NewsHour interview, presidential legacy." *PBS NewsHour.* June 1, 2016. https://www.pbs.org/newshour/show/shields-and-brooks-on-obamas-newshour-interview-presidential-legacy.

Skenazy, Lenore. *Free-Range Kids: Giving Our Children the Freedom We Had Without Going Nuts with Worry.* San Francisco: Jossey-Bass, 2009.

Slaboch, Matthew W. *A Road to Nowhere: The Idea of Progress and Its Critics.* Philadelphia: University of Pennsylvania Press, 2018.

Slaughter, Michael. *Out on the Edge: A Wake-Up Call for Church Leaders on the Edge of the Media Reformation.* Nashville: Abingdon Press, 1998.

Smith, Ben. "Inside the Revolts Erupting in America's Big Newsrooms." *New York Times.* June 7, 2020. https://www.nytimes.com/2020/06/07/business/media/new-york-times-washington-post-protests.html.

Snow, Richard. "The History of Disneyland: How Walt Disney Created the 'Happiest Place on Earth'," *History Extra.* March 24, 2020. https://www.historyextra.com/period/20th-century/history-disneyland-when-open-how-built-walt-disney/.

———. *Disney's Land: Walt Disney and the Invention of the Amusement Park That Changed the World.* New York: Scribner, 2019.

Snyder, Howard A. *The Community of the King.* Downers Grove, IL: InterVarsity Press, 2010.

Spector, Bert Alan. "Carlyle, Freud, and the Great Man Theory More Fully Considered." *Leadership* 12, no. 2 (April 2016): 250–60. https://doi.org/10.1177/1742715015571392.

Spector, Dina. "The US Capitol Just Honored Norman Borlaug, The Man Who Saved A Billion Lives." *Business Insider.* March 25, 2014. https://www.businessinsider.com/who-is-norman-borlaug-2014-3.

Spurgeon, C. H. *Spurgeon's Gems: Being Brilliant Passages From The Discourses Of Charles Haddon Spurgeon.* New York: Sheldon, Blakeman & Company, 1859.

Stearns, Richard. *Unfinished: Believing Is Only the Beginning.* Nashville: Thomas Nelson, 2013.

"Steve Jobs." wikiquote.com. https://en.wikiquote.org/wiki/Steve_Jobs.

Stuertz, Mark. "Green Giant." *Dallas Observer.* December 5, 2002. https://www.dallasobserver.com/news/green-giant-6389547.

———. "Theme Puke." *Dallas Observer.* January 13, 2000. https://www.dallasobserver.com/restaurants/theme-puke-6396484.

Swayne, Josephine Latham, ed. *The Story of Concord Told by Concord Writers.* Boston: E. F. Worcester Press, 1906.

Sweet, Leonard. "Absolute Relative," *Napkin Scribbles: A Podcast by Leonard Sweet.* March 7, 2019. https://anchor.fm/napkinscribbles/episodes/Absolute-Relative-e2sggs.

———. *Me and We: God's New Social Gospel.* Nashville: Abingdon Press, 2014.

———. *So Beautiful: Divine Design for Life and the Church.* Colorado Springs, CO: David C. Cook, 2009.

Sweet, Leonard, and Michael Adam Beck. *Contextual Intelligence: Unlock the Ancient Secret to Mission on the Front Lines.* HigherLife Development Services, 2021.

Sweet, Leonard, and Frank Viola. *Jesus Speaks: Learning to Recognize and Respond to the Lord's Voice.* Nashville: W Publishing, 2016.

Taleb, Nassim Nicholas. *Black Swan: The Impact of the Highly Improbable*. New York: Random House, 2007.

———— *Antifragile: Things That Gain from Disorder*. New York: Random House, 2012.

Tannahill, Reay. *Food in History*. New York: Three Rivers Press, 1995.

Telford, John. *The Letters of the Rev. John Wesley, Volume 8*. London: Epworth Press, 1931.

Tetlock, Philip E., and Dan Gardner. *Superforecasting: The Art and Science of Prediction*. New York: Crown Publishers, 2015.

Thomas, Frank A. *American Dream 2.0: A Christian Way Out of the Great Recession*. Nashville: Abingdon Press, 2012.

Tirella, Joseph. *Tomorrow-Land: The 1964-65 World's Fair and the Transformation of America*. Guilford, CT: Lyons Press, 2014.

Trotsky, Leon. "Towards Capitalism or Towards Socialism?" *The Labour Monthly* 7, no. 11 (November 1925): 659–66. https://www.marxists.org/archive/trotsky/1925/11/towards.htm.

Trout, Jack. "Peter Drucker on Marketing." *Forbes*. July 3, 2006. https://www.forbes.com/2006/06/30/jack-trout-on-marketing-cx_jt_0703drucker.html.

Tuckle, Sherry. "Technology and Human Vulnerability." *Harvard Business Review*. September 2003. https://hbr.org/2003/09/technology-and-human-vulnerability.

US Congress. Congressional Record. 2007. 110th Cong., 1st sess. vol. 153, pt. 8, 10835–10839.

US Congress, Senate, Congressional Tribute to Dr. Norman E. Borlaug Act Of 2006. 109th Congress, 2006. Public Law 109-395. https://www.govinfo.gov/content/pkg/PLAW-109publ395/html/PLAW-109publ395.htm.

Valinsky, Jordan. "Brooks Brothers Files for Bankruptcy." *CNN*. July 8, 2020. https://www.cnn.com/2020/07/08/business/brooks-brothers-bankruptcy/index.html.

Van Doren, Charles Lincoln. *A History of Knowledge: Past, Present, and Future*. New York: Ballantine Books, 1993.

Vannoy, Karen, and John Flowers. *10 Temptations of Church: Why Churches Decline and What to Do About It*. Nashville: Abingdon Press, 2012.

" 'Virus-Fighting' Scientist Gets Magnets Stuck in Nose." *BBC*. March 30, 2020. https://www.bbc.com/news/world-australia-52094804.

Volf, Miroslav. "Work, Spirit, and New Creation," *Evangelical Review of Theology* 41, no. 1 9 (January 2017).

Vos, Geerhardus. *The Teaching of Jesus Concerning the Kingdom of God and the Church*. New York: American Tract Society, 1903.

Wallace, Daniel B. 1998. "Granville Sharp: A Model of Evangelical Scholarship and Social Activism." *Journal of the Evangelical Theological Society* 41 (4): 591–613.

Walters, Kerry, and Robin Jarrell. *Blessed Peacemakers: 365 Extraordinary People Who Changed the World*. Portland, OR: Wipf and Stock, 2013.

Walvin, James. *The Zong: A Massacre, The Law and the End of Slavery*. New Haven: Yale University Press, 2011.

"Watch the Colorado Symphony's Virtual Performance of Ode to Joy." YouTube. March 20, 2020. https://www.youtube.com/watch?v=kJ6-vRVgZLM.

"What REVEAL Reveals." *Christianity Today*. February 27, 2008. https://www. christianitytoday.com/ct/2008/march/11.27.html.

Wiener, Philip P., ed. "Ancients and Moderns in the Eighteenth Century." *Dictionary of the History of Ideas, Volume 5*. New York: Charles Scribner's Sons, 1968.

Wilberforce, Robert Isaac, and Samuel Wilberforce, *The Life of William Wilberforce*. London: John Murray, 1843.

Willis, Martin T. "Edison as Time Traveler: H.G. Wells's Inspiration for His First Scientific Character." *Science Fiction Studies* 26, no. 2 (July 1999): 284–94. https://www.jstor.org/stable/4240787.

Wilson, Len. "Rising to Heaven: The Ideology of Progress and the Semiotics of Church Growth" (2020). Doctor of Ministry. 396. https://digitalcommons. georgefox.edu/dmin/396.

———. "Top 25 Fastest Growing Large United Methodist Churches, 2019 Edition," lenwilson.us (blog). May 28, 2019. http://lenwilson.us/top-25-fastest-growing-large-umc-2019/.

———. *The Wired Church: Making Media Ministry*. Nashville: Abingdon Press, 1999.

———. *Think Like a 5 Year Old: Reclaim Your Wonder and Create Great Things*. Nashville: Abingdon Press, 2015.

Woolf, Virginia. "Mr. Bennett and Mrs. Brown," *Collected Essays, I*. London: Hogarth Press, 1966.

World Health Organization, "The World Health Report 2007: A Safer Future: Global Public Health Security in the 21st Century." Geneva: World Health. 2007. https://www.who.int/whr/2007/whr07_en.pdf.

Wright, Robert. "Why Pure Reason Won't End American Tribalism." *Wired*. April 9, 2018. https://www.wired.com/story/why-pure-reason-wont-end-american-tribalism/.

Wright, Ronald. *A Short History of Progress*. New York: Carroll & Graf, 2004.

Zhuo, Julie. "The Pit of Discomfiture: Or, Where Creatives Fall into Despair." *The Year of the Looking Glass, Medium*. February 18, 2014. https://medium. com/the-year-of-the-looking-glass/the-pit-of-discomfiture-d90ba0eb1974.

Notes

INTRODUCTION

[1] Brian Resnick, "Social distancing can't last forever. Here's what should come next," *Vox*, March 30, 2020, https://www.vox.com/science-and-health/2020/3/26/21192211/coronavirus-covid-19-social-distancing-end.

[2] Lauren Coleman-Lochner and Eliza Ronalds-Hannon, "Mall Landlords, Authentic Brands in Talks to Buy J.C. Penney," Bloomberg, June 15, 2020, https://www.bloomberg.com/news/articles/2020-06-15/mall-landlords-authentic-said-to-be-in-talks-to-buy-j-c-penney. For one example of a new business, see EFS Clean, which trades at https://efsclean.com/service/electrostatic-disinfection-services/.

[3] Here is one example. Mary Schlangenstein, Esha Dey, and Brian Eckhouse, "U.S. Airlines Face End of Business Travel as They Knew It," Bloomberg, July 20, 2020, https://www.bloomberg.com/news/articles/2020-07-20/u-s-airlines-face-the-end-of-business-travel-as-they-knew-it.

[4] "Coronavirus Will Change the World Permanently. Here's How." Politico, March 19, 2020, https://www.politico.com/news/magazine/2020/03/19/coronavirus-effect-economy-life-society-analysis-covid-135579.

[5] "Governor Abbott Waives STAAR Testing Requirements," gov.texas.gov, March 16, 2020, https://gov.texas.gov/news/post/governor-abbott-waives-staar-testing-requirements.

[6] Sean O'Kane, "How GM and Ford Switched Out Pickup Trucks for Breathing Machines," The Verge, April 15, 2020, https://www.theverge.com/2020/4/15/21222219/general-motors-ventec-ventilators-ford-tesla-coronavirus-covid-19.

[7] Tobias Hoonhout, "Brooks Brothers Repurposes Factories to Produce 150,000 Masks Daily," National Review, March 30, 2020, https://www.nationalreview.com/news/brooks-brothers-repurposes-factories-to-produce-150000-masks-daily/.

[8] Jordan Valinsky, "Brooks Brothers Files for Bankruptcy," CNN, July 8, 2020, https://www.cnn.com/2020/07/08/business/brooks-brothers-bankruptcy/index.html.

⁹ Kelly Servick, "Cellphone Tracking Could Help Stem the Spread of Coronavirus. Is Privacy the Price?," *Science*, March 22, 2020, https://www.sciencemag.org/news/2020/03/cellphone-tracking-could-help-stem-spread-coronavirus-privacy-price.

¹⁰ Julia Boorstin, "How Coronavirus Could Permanently Change the Movie Industry," CNBC, March 21, 2020, https://www.cnbc.com/2020/03/20/how-coronavirus-could-permanently-change-the-movie-industry.html.

¹¹ Lindsey McGinnis, "Why a Small City Made Bus Routes Free to Low-Income Residents," *Christian Science Monitor*, March 30, 2020, https://www.csmonitor.com/USA/2020/0330/Why-a-small-city-made-bus-routes-free-to-low-income-residents.

¹² "Watch the Colorado Symphony's Virtual Performance of Ode to Joy," Youtube.com, March 20, 2020, https://www.youtube.com/watch?v=kJ6-vRVgZLM.

¹³ " 'Virus-Fighting' Scientist Gets Magnets Stuck in Nose," BBC.com, March 30, 2020, https://www.bbc.com/news/world-australia-52094804.

¹⁴ See Nassim Nicholas Taleb, *Black Swan: The Impact of the Highly Improbable* (New York: Random House, 2007).

¹⁵ "Right Direction or Wrong Track," Rasmussen Reports, April 1, 2019, http://www.rasmussenreports.com/public_content/politics/top_stories/right_direction_wrong_track_apr01.

¹⁶ "Shields and Brooks on Obama's NewsHour interview, presidential legacy," PBS NewsHour, June 1, 2016, https://www.pbs.org/newshour/show/shields-and-brooks-on-obamas-newshour-interview-presidential-legacy.

¹⁷ Matthew W. Slaboch, *A Road to Nowhere: The Idea of Progress and Its Critics* (Philadelphia University of Pennsylvania Press, 2018), 2.

¹⁸ Elizabeth Kolbert, "Climate Change and the New Age of Extinction," *New Yorker*, May 13, 2019, https://www.newyorker.com/magazine/2019/05/20/climate-change-and-the-new-age-of-extinction.

¹⁹ Todd May, "Would Human Extinction Be a Tragedy?," *New York Times*, December 17, 2018, https://www.nytimes.com/2018/12/17/opinion/human-extinction-climate-change.html.

²⁰ Suzanne Labarre, "MoMA curator: '[Humanity] will become extinct. We need to design an elegant ending'," Fast Company, January 8, 2019, https://www.fastcompany.com/90280777/moma-curator-we-will-become-extinct-we-need-to-design-an-elegant-ending.

²¹ Adele Peters, "Meet the women deciding not to have kids because of climate change," Fast Company, March 7, 2019, https://www.fastcompany.com/90315700/meet-the-women-deciding-not-to-have-kids-because-of-climate-change.

²² Joshua Rothman, "The Case for Not Being Born," *New Yorker*, November 27, 2017, https://www.newyorker.com/culture/persons-of-interest/the-case-for-not-being-born.

23 Jack Crowe, "AOC: 'Is It Still Okay to Have Children' in the Age of Climate Change," *National Review*, February 25, 2019, https://www.nationalreview.com/news/aoc-is-it-still-ok-to-have-children-in-the-age-of-climate-change/.

24 Virginia Woolf, "Mr. Bennett and Mrs. Brown," Collected Essays, I (London: Hogarth Press, 1966), 320.

25 See Malcolm Gladwell, *The Tipping Point: How Little Things Can Make a Big Difference* (New York: Little, Brown, and Company, 2000).

26 Foo Fighters, "Learn to Fly," There Is Nothing Left to Lose (Roswell RCA Records, 1999).

27 Thomas S. Kuhn, *The Structure of Scientific Revolutions: 50th Anniversary Edition* (Chicago: University of Chicago Press, 2012), 92.

28 In one study, the authors make a distinction between disruptive and radical innovation, claiming the latter is completely new. I reject this distinction because nothing comes from nothing. We just can't see the predecessor ideas for some of them. See Christian Hopp, David Antons, Jermain Kaminski, and Torsten Oliver Salge, "What 40 Years of Research Reveals About the Difference Between Disruptive and Radical Innovation," Harvard Business Review, April 9, 2018, https://hbr.org/2018/04/what-40-years-of-research-reveals-about-the-difference-between-disruptive-and-radical-innovation.

29 Schlangenstein, Dey, and Eckhouse, "U.S. Airlines Face End of Business Travel."

30 Michael Rosen and Helen Oxenbury, *We're Going on a Bear Hunt* (Avon, MA: Margaret K. McElderry Books, 2003).

31 In the book, the group eventually reaches a cave, sees the bear, runs back home, gets under their covers, and decides not to go on any more bear hunts. They had reached the limits of their abilities. As carriers of God's Spirit, we have no such limitation.

32 Skunkworks is a business term, originating in the aerospace industry, that refers to small, experimental laboratories that operate independently from the main corporation.

33 I have a friend in the graphic-design business who left full-time church work and struggled to find a corporate graphic-design position. Nobody wanted to hire a guy with only "church" on his résumé. He finally got an entry-level position at the Travel Channel and, within a few months, had been promoted to Art Director. If you can make it happen in church, you can make it happen anywhere.

CHAPTER 1

1 Walter Isaacson, *The Innovators: How a Group of Hackers, Geniuses, and Geeks Created the Digital Revolution* (New York: Simon and Schuster, 2014), 81.

2 Though this is a popular meme, IBM denies Watson ever said this. See Kevin Maney, *The Maverick and His Machine* (Hoboken, NJ: John Wiley and Sons, 2003), 463.

[3] Isaacson, *The Innovators*, 82.

[4] This is Scott Berkun's definition of innovation. Scott Berkun, *The Myths of Innovation* (Boston: O'Reilly, 2010), xvii.

[5] Clayton Christensen, *The Innovator's Dilemma* (New York: Harper Business, 2011), xvi.

[6] Scott Cormode, "Innovation That Honors Tradition: The Meaning of Christian Innovation," Journal of Religious Leadership 14, no. 2 (September 2015): 81–102, https://arl-jrl.org/wp-content/uploads/2019/01/Cormode-Innovation-that-Honors-Tradition.pdf, 82.

[7] Sir Ken Robinson, *Out of Our Minds: Learning to Be Creative* (London: Capstone, 2011) 151.

[8] Cormode, "Innovation That Honors Tradition," 102.

[9] "Steve Jobs," wikiquote.com, https://en.wikiquote.org/wiki/Steve_Jobs.

[10] Isaacson, *The Innovators*, 81.

[11] Ross Douthat, *The Decadent Society: How We Became the Victims of Our Own Success* (New York: Avid Reader Press, 2020), 104.

[12] David Garfinkel, *Advertising Headlines That Make You Rich* (Garden City, NY: Morgan James, 2006), 57.

[13] Joseph A. Schumpeter, *Capitalism, Socialism, and Democracy* (New York: Harper and Brothers, 1950), 83.

[14] Mohanbir Sawhney, Robert C. Wolcott, and Inigo Arroniz, "The 12 Different Ways for Companies to Innovate," *MIT Sloan Management Review* 47, no 3 (Spring 2006): 75–81, https://sloanreview.mit.edu/article/the-different-ways-for-companies-to-innovate/.

[15] Julian Birkinshaw, John Bessant, and Rick Delbridge. "Finding, Forming, and Performing: Creating Networks for Discontinuous Innovation," California Management Review 49, no. 3 (April 2007): 67–84. https://doi.org/10.2307/41166395.

[16] Eric Schmidt and Jonathan Rosenberg, *How Google Works* (New York: Grand Central Publishing, 2014), 206.

[17] Philip E. Tetlock and Dan Gardner, *Superforecasting: The Art and Science of Prediction* (New York Crown Publishers, 2015), 26.

[18] Jack Hartnell, *Medieval Bodies: Life, Death and Art in the Middle Ages* (London: Profile Books Ltd, 2018), 16.

[19] Hartnell, Medieval Bodies, 15.

[20] Etymologically, modern means "measure," suggesting experimentation.

[21] Iain McGilchrist, *The Master and His Emissary: The Divided Brain and the Making of the Western World* (New Haven: Yale University Press, 2009), 336.

[22] For more on the shift in authority from the past to the future, see Len Wilson, "Rising to Heaven: The Ideology of Progress and the Semiotics of Church Growth" (DMin thesis, 2020), 396, https://digitalcommons.georgefox.edu/dmin/396.

[23] As gross as it sounds, leeches have been making a comeback in medicine. For one example with unnecessary photos, see Steven Poole, "How Leeches Made Their Comeback," *New York Magazine*, November 11, 2016, https://nymag.com/vindicated/2016/11/how-leeches-made-their-comeback.html.

[24] Lewis Henry Morgan, *Ancient Society; Or, Researches in the Lines of Human Progress from Savagery, through Barbarism to Civilization* (New York: H. Holt, 1877).

[25] Steven Pinker, *Enlightenment Now: The Case for Reason, Science, Humanism, and Progress* (New York: Viking, 2018), 11.

[26] For a counter-view, consider Daniel R. Griswold (@danielrgriswold), "What Christianity is about—much to the horror of the Enlightenment—is that world history really did reach its climax, not when Thomas Jefferson wrote the American Constitution, or Voltaire or Rousseau wrote what they were writing, but when Jesus of Nazareth died & rose again," Twitter, September 30, 2019, 8:46 a.m., https://twitter.com/dannonhill/status/1178667425635733509.

[27] Matthew W. Slaboch, *A Road to Nowhere: The Idea of Progress and Its Critics* (Philadelphia: University of Pennsylvania Press, 2018), 111.

[28] This awesome turn of phrase comes from Peter J. Bowler, *A History of the Future: Prophets of Progress from H.G. Wells to Isaac Asimov* (Cambridge: Cambridge University Press, 2017).

[29] "Best Family Vacations," *U.S. News and World Report*, https://travel.usnews.com/rankings/best-family-vacations/.

[30] Jena Pugh, "5 Oldest Walt Disney Rides That Are Still Around Today," Best of Orlando, May 16, 2016, https://www.bestoforlando.com/articles/5-oldest-walt-disney-world-rides-still-around-today/.

[31] Joseph Tirella, *Tomorrow-Land: The 1964-65 World's Fair and the Transformation of America* (Guilford, CT: Lyons Press, 2014), 3.

[32] Tirella, *Tomorrow-Land*, 48.

[33] Isaacson, *The Innovators*, 33. While there is no agreed-upon inventor of the modern computer, Isaacson attempts to give credit to Charles Babbage, an English mathematician whose prototype "Difference Engine" aimed to replace human tasks with machines.

[34] Peter Jennings and Todd Brewster, *The Century* (New York: Doubleday, 1998), 108.

[35] Jennings and Brewster, *The Century*, 110.

[36] Bowler, *A History of the Future*, 3.

[37] Paul McCartney and John Lennon, "Getting Better," Sgt. Pepper's Lonely Hearts Club Band, recorded March 9, 1967, Parlophone EMI, 33 ⅓ rpm. Notably,

in the background of the recording, John Lennon responds, "It can't get no worse."

[38] The statistical evidence supporting progress is impressive. Swedish liberal historian Johan Norberg notes that, since 1820, the risk of living in poverty has been reduced from 94 percent to less than 11 percent. For the first time, poverty is not growing just because population is growing. Because of this reduction, the number of people in extreme poverty is now slightly less than it was in 1820. Then it was around 1 billion, while today it is 700 million. If this does not sound like progress, note that, in 1820, the world had only around 60 million people who did not live in extreme poverty. Today more than 6.5 billion people do not live in extreme poverty. Harvard humanist Stephen Pinker notes that, over the last twenty-five years, the rate of death due to cancer has fallen about a percentage point every year, saving millions of lives (Johan Norberg, *Progress: Ten Reasons to Look Forward to the Future* [London: Oneworld, 2017], 78).

[39] Brad S. Gregory, *The Unintended Reformation: How a Religious Revolution Secularized Society* (Cambridge, MA: Harvard University Press, 2012), 10.

CHAPTER 2

[1] Walidah Imarisha, *Angels with Dirty Faces: Three Stories of Crime, Prison, and Redemption* (Oakland, CA: AK Press, 2016), 141. The 2002 film Gangs of New York, directed by Martin Scorsese, offers an excellent depiction of this time.

[2] Christopher H. Evans, *The Kingdom Is Always But Coming: A Life of Walter Rauschenbusch* (Waco, TX: Baylor University Press, 2010), 61.

[3] Imarisha, *Angels with Dirty Faces*.

[4] Evans, *The Kingdom Is Always But Coming*, 57.

[5] Robert T. Handy, *"Walter Rauschenbusch,"* in *Ten Makers of Modern Protestant Thought,* ed. George L. Hunt (New York: Association Press, 1958), 32.

[6] Evans, *The Kingdom Is Always But Coming*, 63.

[7] Evans, *The Kingdom Is Always But Coming*, 68.

[8] Interestingly, the same combination of piety and reform characterized another great theologian of the church, John Wesley, giving credence to the idea that all Christian innovation is ex materia, not ex nihilo; it is not a radically new invention but a renewing of the same ancient ideas in new time and space.

[9] Tom Miller, "The 1889 2nd German Baptist Church—407 West 43rd Street," Daytonian in Manhattan (blog), February 2, 2012, http://daytoninmanhattan.blogspot.com/2012/02/1889-2nd-german-baptist-church-407-west.html.

[10] Evans, *The Kingdom Is Always But Coming*, 75.

[11] Evans, *The Kingdom Is Always But Coming*, 79. Later theologians such as H. Richard Niebuhr attacked the naturalistic, liberal theology of Rauschenbusch and others for sin, suffering, and divine judgment, and reducing Christ to a WWJD model for ethical behavior.

[12] Evans, *The Kingdom Is Always But Coming*, 123.

[13] Evans, *The Kingdom Is Always But Coming*, 89.

[14] Evans, *The Kingdom Is Always But Coming*, 107.

[15] Evans, *The Kingdom Is Always But Coming*, 115.

[16] Handy, "Walter Rauschenbusch," 31.

[17] Historian Robert Handy names him, along with Jonathan Edwards and Harold Bushnell, as the three great American theologians. See Handy, "Walter Rauschenbusch." Historian Leonard Sweet adds Reinhold Niebuhr, who was Handy's contemporary. Notably, all four were pastors. Leonard Sweet (lecture, Portland Seminary, George Fox University (Portland, OR: September 11, 2017).

[18] Walter Rauschenbusch, *A Theology for the Social Gospel* (Nashville: Abingdon Press, 1917), 1.

[19] Christopher Lasch, "Religious Contributions to Social Movements: Walter Rauschenbusch, the Social Gospel, and Its Critics." *Journal of Religious Ethics* 18, no. 1 (Spring 1990): 7–25, http://onlinelibrary.wiley.com/journal/10.1111/(ISSN)1467-9795.

[20] Charles Lincoln Van Doren, *A History of Knowledge: Past, Present, and Future* (New York: Ballantine Books, 1993), 203.

[21] René Descartes, Discourse on the Method of Rightly Conducting the Reason, and Seeking Truth in the Sciences (1637), part 4, http://www.gutenberg.org/files/59/59-h/59-h.htm.

[22] While understood as antonyms, doubt and faith do not necessarily negate each other. Rather, doubt may be a basis for faith, such as with the centurion who exclaimed to Jesus, "I believe; help my unbelief!" (Mark 9:24).

[23] Diarmaid MacCulloch, *Christianity: The First Three Thousand Years, 1st American ed.* (New York Viking, 2010), 775.

[24] The difference between verification and truth is worth an entirely separate book. In his seminal work, *Personal Knowledge*, philosopher of science Michael Polanyi writes that it is scientifically impossible to achieve the stated purpose of science to establish complete, empirically verified control over experience because of the necessity of extrapolating the probable to the certain. He uses the example of a bunch of white balls in a sack. If you add a few black balls, and then happen to draw one out, you still believe it is mostly full of white balls: "Now suppose that we had ourselves placed the balls, 95 percent of them white and 5 percent of them black, into the sack, and then having shaken them up, we drew out a black ball. We should be very surprised yet remain unshaken in our belief that the bag contained the balls we had put into it." In other words, scientific knowledge is always probable knowledge. Since we cannot do experiments forever, we must eventually conclude with a high degree of probability that our answer is correct. We start succumbing to a form of confirmation bias and verify only what we believe is probably true. Continued

experiments amount to an infinity rule in mathematics. We can get close but can never know with complete certainty. Polanyi writes, "all truth is but the external pole of belief, and to destroy all belief would be to deny all truth. . . . Objectivism has totally falsified our conception of truth, by exalting what we can know and prove, while covering up with ambiguous utterances all that we know and cannot prove, even though the latter knowledge underlies, and must ultimately set its seal to, all that we can prove" (Michael Polanyi, *Personal Knowledge: Towards a Post-Critical Philosophy* [Chicago: University of Chicago Press, 1958], 22, 301). This is not to say that there is no such thing as truth, as some have concluded; rather, that our personal perspective is both limited and inextricably intertwined with a full understanding of truth. Our ability to see a final answer is limited to our view of the problem.

[25] See, for example, American philosopher John Fiske's "cosmic evolution" in *Outlines of Cosmic Philosophy* (Cambridge: Riverside Press, 1902).

[26] Walter Rauschenbusch, *Christianity and the Social Crisis* (New York: MacMillan, 1913), 45.

[27] Walter Rauschenbusch, *A Theology for the Social Gospel* (1917), 194.

[28] Handy, "Walter Rauschenbusch," 37.

[29] Rauschenbusch, *Theology for the Social Gospel*, 198.

[30] Rauschenbusch, *Theology for the Social Gospel*, 91.

[31] Rauschenbusch, *Christianity and the Social Crisis*, xiii.

[32] Rauschenbusch, *Christianity and the Social Crisis*, xii.

[33] Rauschenbusch, *Christianity and the Social Crisis*, 187–88.

[34] Rauschenbusch, *Christianity and the Social Crisis*, xi.

[35] Philip P. Wiener, ed. "Ancients and Moderns in the Eighteenth Century," Dictionary of the History of Ideas, vol. 5 (New York: Charles Scribner's Sons, 1968), 69.

[36] Michael Gerson, "The Last Temptation," *The Atlantic*, April 2018, https://www.theatlantic.com/magazine/archive/2018/04/the-last-temptation/.

[37] Richard Stearns, *Unfinished: Believing Is Only the Beginning* (Nashville: Thomas Nelson, 2013), 37. Contrast Stearn's title with the words of Jesus, who said, "It is finished" (John 19:30).

[38] James Davison Hunter, *To Change the World: The Irony, Tragedy, and Possibility of Christianity in the Late Modern World* (New York: Oxford University Press, 2010), 12.

[39] Andy Crouch, *Culture Making: Recovering Our Creative Calling* (Downers Grove, IL: IVP Books, 2013), 200.

[40] James Fallows, "Is This the Worst Year in Modern American History?," *The Atlantic*, May 31, 2020, https://www.theatlantic.com/ideas/archive/2020/05/1968-and-2020-lessons-from-americas-worst-year-so-far/612415/.

[41] Leonard I. Sweet, *Me and We: God's New Social Gospel* (Nashville: Abingdon Press, 2014), loc. 170, Kindle.

[42] Alan Kreider, *The Patient Ferment of the Early Church: The Improbable Rise of Christianity in the Roman Empire* (Grand Rapids, MI: Baker Academic, 2016), 275.

[43] Kreider, *The Patient Ferment*, 277.

[44] Sweet, *Me and We*, loc. 182.

[45] John Emerich Edward Dalberg-Acton, *Historical Essays and Studies* (London: Macmillan, 1907), 504.

CHAPTER 3

[1] Donald McGavran, *The Bridges of God* (Eugene, OR: Wipf and Stock, 1955).

[2] David A. Roozen and C. Kirk Hadaway, eds., *Church and Denominational Growth: What Does (and Does Not) Cause Growth or Decline* (Nashville: Abingdon Press, 1993), 142.

[3] Roozen and Hadaway, *Church and Denominational Growth*, 136.

[4] To read more about this period, see Michael Slaughter, *Out on the Edge: A Wake-Up Call for Church Leaders on the Edge of the Media Reformation* (Nashville: Abingdon Press, 1998) and Len Wilson, *The Wired Church: Making Media Ministry* (Nashville: Abingdon Press, 1999).

[5] Michael Miles, "The Lesson of the Sigmoid Curve," Dumb Little Man (blog), October 7, 2008, https://www.dumblittleman.com/lesson-of-sigmoid-curve/.

[6] Most churches count people aged 0-18, which, if applied to our counts, would have resulted in worship well over four thousand a weekend. Further, because the internet was in its infancy, we did not employ live streaming, multisite, video-venue, or most of the church growth techniques that were to emerge in the years following. All this is to contextualize the remarkable phenomenon of our growth.

[7] I published a list of the fastest-growing, large churches in United Methodism on my blog (2011–2019), partly to see if the phenomenon could happen again. For the most recent report on this study, see Len Wilson, "Top 25 Fastest Growing Large United Methodist Churches, 2019 Edition," *lenwilson.us* (blog), May 28, 2019, http://lenwilson.us/top-25-fastest-growing-large-umc-2019/.

[8] It is worth noting that, among "seeker-sensitive" congregational methodologies, there is not a uniform adherence to quantifiable measurements as indicators of discipleship. In an analysis of the Willow Creek REVEAL study, a Christianity Today editorial notes, "Our ongoing concern about seeker-sensitive churches is not their willingness to change church culture so that it is not a needless stumbling block to the unchurched. We're only troubled when such churches uncritically accept the metrics of marketing culture and let consumer capitalism shape the church's theology" ("What REVEAL Reveals," Christianity Today,

February 27, 2008, https://www.christianitytoday.com/ct/2008/march/11.27.
html).

⁹ Richard Hays describes the cross, Christian community, and the New Creation as
the three defining themes of the New Testament story (Richard B. Hays, *The
Moral Vision of the New Testament: A Contemporary Introduction to New Testament Ethics* [New York: HarperOne, 1996], 20).

¹⁰ Statistical data outlining the decline of Americans participating in congregational
life over the last fifty years is by now extensive and widely documented. For a
brief sampling of statistics on this decline, see Len Wilson, "Rising to Heaven:
The Ideology of Progress and the Semiotics of Church Growth" (DMin thesis, 2020), 396, https://digitalcommons.georgefox.edu/dmin/396. Notably,
church decline is a Western cultural phenomenon: the global church is growing and expects to reach three billion people by 2050.

¹¹ Vasilios N. Makrides, "Orthodox Christianity, Change, Innovation: Contradictions in Terms?" *Innovation in the Orthodox Christian Tradition? The Question
of Change in Greek Orthodox Thought and Practice* (Surrey, UK: Ashgate, 2012),
19–50.

¹² The desire to innovate is certainly not universal. In my experience, younger pastors and church leaders, along with some—mostly evangelical—congregations,
commit to innovation as a regular practice. Most small to medium churches,
though, tend to resist change and are stuck in a kind of complacency born of
fear, preferring the discomfort of a declining stasis over the discomfort of new
growth.

¹³ One study highlighted the strong correlation between stress and uncertainty by
having people play a game involving hidden snakes. (No, thank you.) Knowing bad things may happen creates stress, which causes us to resist change
(Archy O. de Berker, et al., "Computations of uncertainty mediate acute stress
responses in humans," Nature Communications 7, no. 10996 (2016), https://
doi.org/10.1038/ncomms10996.

¹⁴ "Fight versus flight" first appeared in Walter Bradford Cannon, *Bodily Changes
in Pain, Hunger, Fear, and Rage* (New York: Appleton-Century-Crofts, 1915),
211, http://www.archive.org/details/cu31924022542470.

¹⁵ For a great analysis of the ways in which congregations become driven by fear,
see Karen Vannoy and John Flowers, *10 Temptations of Church: Why Churches
Decline and What to Do About It* (Nashville: Abingdon Press, 2012).

¹⁶ Edward J. Larson, *Summer of the Gods: The Scopes Trial and America's Continuing
Debate Over Science and Religion* (New York: Basic Books, 1997), 91.

¹⁷ Larson, *Summer of the Gods,* 14.

¹⁸ For an excellent, concise list of value changes introduced by Constantine, see
Alan Kreider, *The Patient Ferment of the Early Church : The Improbable Rise of
Christianity in the Roman Empire* (Grand Rapids, MI: Baker Academic, 2016),
274–78.

[19] Michael Baughman, Facebook comment, September 23, 2020 10:19 p.m. His use of "kindom" is an extension of the same Christian humanism that assumes that the New Creation is characterized by familial love, or a kinship. You can have a community of kin, but without Christ as king, it isn't Christian.

[20] Again, a core theme of the New Testament is the centrality of the community, according to Hays, *The Moral Vision of the New Testament*, 20.

CHAPTER 4

[1] Mark Ravina, *The Last Samurai: The Life and Battles of Saigō Takamori* (Hoboken, NJ: John Wiley and Sons, 2004), 4.

[2] John Hunter Boyle, *Modern Japan: The American Nexus* (Fort Worth: Harcourt Brace Jovanovich, 1993), 69.

[3] Boyle, *Modern Japan,* 82.

[4] Maria Christensen, "The Meiji Era and the Modernization of Japan," The Samurai Archives, n.d., https://www.samurai-archives.com/tme.html.

[5] Boyle, *Modern Japan,* 69.

[6] Stephen L. Carter, "Destroying a Quote's History in Order to Save It," <u>Bloomberg Opinion</u>, February 9, 2018, https://www.bloomberg.com/opinion/articles/2018-02-09/destroying-a-quote-s-history-in-order-to-save-it.

[7] Sherry Tuckle, "Technology and Human Vulnerability," *Harvard Business Review,* September 2003, https://hbr.org/2003/09/technology-and-human-vulnerability.

[8] Frank A. Thomas, *American Dream 2.0: A Christian Way Out of the Great Recession* (Nashville: Abingdon Press, 2012), xii.

[9] David Brion Davis, "Slavery and the Idea of Progress," *The Journal of Southern Religion* 14 (2012): 9, accessed April 5, 2018, http://jsr.fsu.edu/issues/vol14/davis.pdf.

[10] Davis, "Slavery and the Idea of Progress."

[11] Theodore Parker, *Ten Sermons of Religion* (Boston: Crosby, Nichols and Company, 1853), 84.

[12] Peter Beinart, "The Left and the Right Have Abandoned American Exceptionalism," *The Atlantic,* July 4, 2018, https://www.theatlantic.com/ideas/archive/2018/07/the-left-and-the-right-have-abandoned-american-exceptionalism/564425/.

[13] Leon Trotsky, "Towards Capitalism or Towards Socialism?," *The Labour Monthly* 7, no. 11 (November 1925): 659–66. https://www.marxists.org/archive/trotsky/1925/11/towards.htm.

[14] Ross Douthat, *The Decadent Society: How We Became the Victims of Our Own Success* (New York: Avid Reader Press, 2020), 90–91.

[15] One political analyst makes the argument that our current sclerosis is precisely because of the rise of mobile technology and social media networks (Martin Gurri, *The Revolt of the Public and the Crisis of Authority in the New Millennium* [San Francisco: Stripe Press, 2018]).

[16] Kenneth J. Collins and Jason E. Vickers, eds., *The Sermons of John Wesley: A Collection for the Christian Journey* (Nashville: Abingdon Press, 2013), 537.

[17] Diarmaid MacCulloch, *Christianity: The First Three Thousand Years, 1st American ed.* (New York: Viking, 2010), 790.

[18] MacCullough, *Christianity,* 791.

[19] *Computer Business Review* lists the iPhone as one of the top five, along with Facebook, Skype, Bluetooth, and IBM Watson. I would have made it a top-two list (Tom Ball, "Top 5 Technological Advances of the 21st Century," <u>Computer Business Review</u>, February 8, 2018, accessed April 21, 2018, https://www.cbronline.com/list/top-5-technological-advances-21st-century.

[20] Nielsen's Mobile Insights Survey, "Mobile Kids: The Parent, The Child, and The Smartphone," *NielsenIQ,* February 28, 2017, accessed April 21, 2018, http://www.nielsen.com/us/en/insights/news/2017/mobile-kids--the-parent-the-child-and-the-smartphone.html.

[21] Eric Andrew-Gee, "Your smartphone is making you stupid, antisocial and unhealthy. So why can't you put it down?" *The Globe and Mail,* January 6, 2018, https://www.theglobeandmail.com/technology/your-smartphone-is-making-you-stupid/article37511900/.

[22] Naomi Schaefer Riley, "America's Real Digital Divide," *New York Times*, February 11, 2018, https://www.nytimes.com/2018/02/11/opinion/america-digital-divide.html.

[23] James C. Scott, *Seeing Like a State: How Certain Schemes to Improve the Human Condition Have Failed* (New Haven, CT: Yale University Press), 6.

[24] Scott, *Seeing Like a State,* 310.

[25] Scott, *Seeing Like a State,* 603.

[26] Robert Wright, "Why Pure Reason Won't End American Tribalism," *Wired*, April 9, 2018, accessed April 22, 2018, https://www.wired.com/story/why-pure-reason-wont-end-american-tribalism/.

[27] John Gray, *Straw Dogs: Thoughts on Humans and Other Animals* (New York: Farrar, Straus, and Giroux, 2007), 15.

[28] Juliana Jaramillo-Echeverri, Adolfo Meisel-Roca, and María Ramírez-Giraldo, "More than 100 Years of Improvements in Living Standards: The Case of Colombia," *Cliometrica* 13, no. 3 (2019): 323.

29 World Health Organization, "The World Health Report 2007: A Safer Future: Global Public Health Security in the 21st Century" (Geneva: World Health, 2007), https://www.who.int/whr/2007/whr07_en.pdf.

30 Kara Harris, "Fact check: Did Bill Gates predict the coronavirus in 2015?" USAToday.com, March 22, 2020, https://www.usatoday.com/story/news/factcheck/2020/03/22/coronavirus-fact-check-did-bill-gates-predict-outbreak-2015/2890900001/.

31 Ronald Wright, *A Short History of Progress* (New York: Carroll & Graf, 2004), 4.

CHAPTER 5

1 US Congress, Senate, Congressional Tribute to Dr. Norman E. Borlaug Act Of 2006. 109th Congress, 2006. Public Law 109–395. https://www.govinfo.gov/content/pkg/PLAW-109publ395/html/PLAW-109publ395.htm.

2 Mark Stuertz, "Green Giant," *Dallas Observer,* December 5, 2002, https://www.dallasobserver.com/news/green-giant-6389547.

3 Steve Rabey, "Borlaug: Not by bread alone," *GetReligion,* September 15, 2009, https://www.getreligion.org/getreligion/2009/09/norman-borlaug-not-by-bread-alone.

4 Dina Spector, "The US Capitol Just Honored Norman Borlaug, The Man Who Saved A Billion Lives," *Business Insider,* March 25, 2014, https://www.businessinsider.com/who-is-norman-borlaug-2014-3.

5 Penn Jillette and Teller, "Eat This!" *Penn and Teller: Bullshit* (Showtime Networks), release date April 4, 2003.

6 Justin Gillis, "Norman Borlaug, Plant Scientist Who Fought Famine, Dies at 95," *New York Times,* September 13, 2009, https://www.nytimes.com/2009/09/14/business/energy-environment/14borlaug.html.

7 Gregg Easterbrook, "Forgotten Benefactor of Humanity," *The Atlantic,* January 1997, https://www.theatlantic.com/magazine/archive/1997/01/forgotten-benefactor-of-humanity/306101/.

8 Max Roser, Hannah Ritchie, and Esteban Ortiz-Ospina, "World Population Growth," *Our World in Data,* May 2019, https://ourworldindata.org/world-population-growth.

9 Paul Ehrlich, *The Population Bomb* (New York: Ballantine, 1968), 39.

10 Norman Borlaug, "The Green Revolution, Peace, and Humanity," December 11, 1970, https://www.nobelprize.org/prizes/peace/1970/borlaug/lecture/.

11 Liuan Huska, "Christians Invented Health Insurance. Can They Make Something Better?" *Christianity Today,* October 20, 2020, https://www.christianitytoday.com/ct/2020/november/health-care-insurance-reform-medical-system.html.

¹² L. Gregory Jones, *Christian Social Innovation: Renewing Wesleyan Witness* (Nashville: Abingdon Press, 2016), 20.

¹³ Leonard Sweet, "Absolute Relative," <u>Napkin Scribbles: A Podcast by Leonard Sweet</u>, March 7, 2019, https://anchor.fm/napkinscribbles/episodes/Absolute-Relative-e2sggs.

¹⁴ Scott Cormode, "Innovation That Honors Tradition: The Meaning of Christian Innovation," *Journal of Religious Leadership* 14, no. 2 (Fall 2015): 82.

¹⁵ Geerhardus Vos, *The Teaching of Jesus Concerning the Kingdom of God and the Church* (New York: American Tract Society, 1903), 159.

¹⁶ Vos, *The Teaching of Jesus Concerning the Kingdom,* 143–44.

¹⁷ Vos, *The Teaching of Jesus Concerning the Kingdom,* 158.

CHAPTER 6

¹ Joshua Hammer, "Thou Shalt Not Underestimate Florence Nightingale," *Smithsonian,* March 2020, 32.

² Bernard Cohen, "Florence Nightingale," *Scientific American* 250, no. 3 (March 1984): 130–31.

³ William Howard Russell, "The Crimea," *The Times,* October 12, 1854, https://www.thetimes.co.uk/archive/article/1854-10-12/7/3.html.

⁴ Cohen, "Florence Nightingale," 128.

⁵ Cohen, "Florence Nightingale," 129.

⁶ Cohen, "Florence Nightingale," 129.

⁷ Hammer, "Thou Shalt Not Underestimate Florence Nightingale," 33.

⁸ US President Lyndon Baines Johnson introduced the "Great Society" as an ambitious set of social reforms in 1964 (*Public Papers of the Presidents of the United States: Lyndon B. Johnson, 1963-64,* vol. 1, entry 357 [Washington, D. C.: Government Printing Office, 1965), 704–7]).

⁹ Victor Dias, "St. Augustine on the Structure and Meaning of History" (master's thesis, Concordia University, 1996), 94.

¹⁰ <u>Rudy</u>, directed by David Anspaugh (TriStar Pictures, 1993), https://www.amazon.com/Rudy-Sean-Astin/dp/B00171R00O/.

¹¹ Miroslav Volf, "Work, Spirit, and New Creation," *Evangelical Review of Theology* 41, no. 1 (January 2017): 67.

¹² Volf, "Work, Spirit, and New Creation," 67.

¹³ Howard A. Snyder, *The Community of the King* (Downers Grove, IL: InterVarsity Press, 2010), 114.

¹⁴ Volf, "Work, Spirit, and New Creation," 74.

15 See Arthur Jones, *Solid Souls* (Plano, TX: Invite Press, 2021).

16 Frederick Beuchner, *Wishful Thinking: A Theological ABC* (New York: Harper and Row, 1973), 95.

17 Brian D. Cawley and Peter J. Snyder, "People as Workers in the Image of God: Opportunities to Promote Flourishing," *The Journal of Markets & Morality* 18, no. 1 (2015): 163–87.

18 Iain McGilchrist, *The Master and His Emissary: The Divided Brain and the Making of the Western World* (New Haven: Yale University Press, 2009), 199.

19 Etienne Gilson, *The Spirit of Medieval Philosophy* (New York: Charles Scribner and Sons, 1936), 96.

20 Leonard Sweet, *Me and We: God's New Social Gospel* (Nashville: Abingdon Press, 2014), loc. 3025, Kindle.

21 Volf, "Work, Spirit, and New Creation," 102.

22 Timothy K. Jones, *Workday Prayers: On-the-Job Meditations for Tending Your Soul* (Chicago: Loyola Press, 2000), xvii.

23 Michael Rosen and Helen Oxenbury, *We're Going on a Bear Hunt* (Avon, MA: Margaret K. McElderry Books, 2003).

24 L. Gregory Jones, *Christian Social Innovation: Renewing Wesleyan Witness* (Nashville: Abingdon Press, 2016), 20.

CHAPTER 7

1 Chip Heath and Dan Heath, *The Power of Moments: Why Certain Experiences Have Extraordinary Impact* (London: Bantam Press, 2017), 7.

2 James Walvin, *The Zong: A Massacre, The Law and the End of Slavery* (New Haven: Yale University Press, 2011), 96.

3 Ian Bernard, "The Zong Massacre (1781)," Black Past, October 11, 2011, https://www.blackpast.org/global-african-history/zong-massacre-1781/.

4 Walvin, *The Zong*, 97.

5 Jeremy Krikler, "The Zong and the Lord Chief Justice," *History Workshop Journal*, 64, no 1 (2007): 29–47, https://doi.org/10.1093/hwj/dbm035.

6 Irv Brendlinger, "John Wesley and Slavery: Myth and Reality" (2006). *Faculty Publications-College of Christian Studies.* Paper 116. http://digitalcommons.georgefox.edu/ccs/116

7 Walvin, *The Zong*, 107.

8 Daniel B. Wallace, "Granville Sharp: A Model of Evangelical Scholarship and Social Activism," *Journal of the Evangelical Theological Society* 41, no. 4 (1998): 591–613.

[9] Michelle Faubert, "Granville Sharp's Manuscript Letter to the Admiralty on the Zong Massacre: A New Discovery in the British Library," *Slavery & Abolition* 38, no. 1 (January 2, 2017): 178–95, https://doi.org/10.1080/014403 9X.2016.1206285.

[10] Faubert, "Granville Sharp's Manuscript Letter," 178–95.

[11] This statement is not meant to suggest that organizations and people in positions of power cannot innovate. Powerful companies innovate all the time. Rather, it is a statement about need and motivation. Power enables choice; lack of it creates need and motivation.

[12] Guy Kawasaki, "The Art of Innovation" (lecture, Catalyst 2015, Atlanta October 9, 2015).

[13] For a period, forces of stasis were a favorite villain of middle-aged Boomers justifying why they had not yet changed the world, such as the film Tucker, which tells the story of an automotive innovator who fought the big three American car corporations.

[14] Eric Metaxas, *7 Men and the Secret of Their Greatness* (Nashville: Thomas Nelson, 2013), 37.

[15] Metaxas, *7 Men,* 35.

[16] US Congress, Congressional Record, 2007, 110th Cong., 1st sess. vol. 153, pt. 8, 10835–10839.

[17] Metaxas, *7 Men,* 42.

[18] Robert Isaac Wilberforce and Samuel Wilberforce, *The Life of William Wilberforce* (London: John Murray, 1843), 98.

[19] Wilberforce and Wilberforce, *The Life of William Wilberforce,* 98.

[20] Wilberforce and Wilberforce, *The Life of William Wilberforce,* 149.

[21] Richard Gathro, "William Wilberforce and His Circle of Friends," Knowing and Doing, C. S. Lewis Institute, 2001), 1. https://www.cslewisinstitute.org/web-fm_send/471.

[22] Olaudah Equiano, The Interesting Narrative of the Life of Olaudah Equiano, Or Gustavus Vassa, The African, Written by Himself (Project Gutenberg), http://www.gutenberg.org/ebooks/15399.

[23] Willie James Jennings, *The Christian Imagination: Theology and the Origins of Race* (New Haven, CT: Yale University Press, 2010), 188.

[24] John Coffey, "Evangelicals, Slavery & the Slave Trade: From Whitefield to Wilberforce," *Anvil* 24, no. 2 (2007), 101.

[25] Jennings, *The Christian Imagination,* 189.

[26] Coffey, "Evangelicals, Slavery & the Slave Trade," 109.

[27] John Telford, *The Letters of the Rev. John Wesley, Volume 8* (London: Epworth Press, 1931).

[28] Simon Burton-Jones, "What Can We Learn from William Wilberforce?" The Clewer Institute, September 26, 2018, https://www.theclewerinitiative.org/news/2018/9/26/guest-post-what-can-we-learn-from-william-wilberforce.

[29] Burton-Jones, "What Can We Learn?"

[30] Jennings, *The Christian Imagination*, 4.

[31] Jennings, *The Christian Imagination*, 7.

[32] Some argue that this is changing because of the rise of social media, which for the first time gives voice to the "down and out" (See Martin Gurri, *The Revolt of the Public and the Crisis of Authority in the New Millennium* [San Francisco: Stripe Press, 2018]). But the counter to this argument is that, while the "down and out" may have a larger megaphone, their biggest tool remains a compelling story to change the convictions of those who control the levers of power.

[33] C. S. Lewis, *The Last Battle* (New York: Collier Books, 1956), 158.

[34] Sam McFarland, "Abolition! Granville Sharp's Campaign to End Slavery," *International Journal of Leadership and Change*, 7, no. 1 (2019), https://digitalcommons.wku.edu/ijlc/vol7/iss1/5.

CHAPTER 8

[1] D. Bryan Rhodes (@dbryanrhodes), Twitter, May 17, 2020, 4:40 am, https://twitter.com/DBryanRhodes/status/1261954769561804800.

[2] Leonard Sweet and Frank Viola, *Jesus Speaks: Learning to Recognize and Respond to the Lord's Voice* (Nashville: W Publishing, 2016), 64.

[3] Sweet and Viola, *Jesus Speaks*, 28.

[4] C. H. Spurgeon, *Spurgeon's Gems: Being Brilliant Passages from the Discourses of Charles Haddon Spurgeon* (New York: Sheldon, Blakeman & Company, 1859), 155.

[5] Neil Baldwin, *Edison: Inventing the Century* (New York : Hyperion, 1995), 62.

[6] Ernó Rubik, *Cubed: The Puzzle of Us All* (New York: Flatiron Books, 2020), 21.

CHAPTER 9

[1] LeRoy Jones, "The Abernathy Boys," Heritage of the Great Plains/Heritage of Kansas (1957–Present) 43 no. 2, Emporia State University (December 6, 2012), https://dspacep01.emporia.edu/bitstream/handle/123456789/2214/Jones%20Vol%2043%20Num%202.pdf?sequence=1.

[2] Martha Deeringer, "The Astonishing Ride of the Abernathy Boys," *Texas Coop Power* (January 2018), https://www.texascooppower.com/texas-stories/history/the-astonishing-ride-of-the-abernathy-boys.

[3] Jones, "The Abernathy Boys."

[4] Deeringer, "The Astonishing Ride."

[5] Jones, "The Abernathy Boys."

[6] "Abernathy Boys Put Ban on Kissing," *New York Times*, June 12, 1910, https://www.nytimes.com/1910/06/12/archives/abernathy-boys-put-ban-on-kissing-fearless-youngsters-who-have.html.

[7] Jones "The Abernathy Boys."

[8] Nassim Nicholas Taleb, *Antifragile: Things That Gain from Disorder* (New York: Random House, 2012), 5.

[9] Malcolm Gladwell, "Blowup," *The New Yorker*, January 15, 1996, https://www.newyorker.com/magazine/1996/01/22/blowup-2.

[10] Ben Smith, "Inside the Revolts Erupting in America's Big Newsrooms," *New York Times*, June 7, 2020, https://www.nytimes.com/2020/06/07/business/media/new-york-times-washington-post-protests.html.

[11] David Romer, "Do Firms Maximize? Evidence from Professional Football" (University of California, Berkeley, July 2005), https://eml.berkeley.edu/~dromer/papers/PAPER_NFL_JULY05_FORWEB_CORRECTED.pdf.

[12] Adam Himmelsbach, "Punting Less Can Be Rewarding, but Coaches Aren't Risking Jobs on It," *New York Times*, August 18, 2012, https://www.nytimes.com/2012/08/19/sports/football/calculating-footballs-risk-of-not-punting-on-fourth-down.html.

[13] Brian Burke, "A New Study on Fourth Downs: Go For It," *New York Times*, September 17, 2009. http://fifthdown.blogs.nytimes.com/2009/09/17/a-new-study-on-fourth-downs-go-for-it/.

[14] Wayne Gard, "Fence Cutting," Handbook of Texas Online, http://www.tshaonline.org/handbook/online/articles/auf01.

[15] Sacha J. Pidot et al., "Increasing Tolerance of Hospital Enterococcus Faecium to Handwash Alcohols," *Science Translational Medicine* 10, no. 452 (August 1, 2018): 6115, http://doi.org/10.1126/scitranslmed.aar6115.

[16] Taleb, *Antifragile,* 8.

[17] Media-driven fear is well-documented. For an interesting take, see Michael Crichton's last published work of fiction, which is a thinly veiled diatribe against a media-driven state of fear (Michael Crichton, *State of Fear* [New York: Harper, 2009]).

[18] Popularized by Lenore Skenazy in *Free-Range Kids: Giving Our Children the Freedom We Had Without Going Nuts with Worry* (San Francisco: Jossey-Bass, 2009).

[19] Pip Coburn, *The Change Function: Why Some Technologies Take Off and Others Crash and Burn* (New York: Penguin, 2006), 8.

[20] This is partly an indictment of my generational cohort, but also demographic reality, as there are simply a lot fewer Gen Xers than either Boomers or Millennials.

[21] Taleb, *Antifragile,* 91 (parenthesis original).

[22] Natalie Fratto, "Screw Emotional Intelligence—Here's the Key to the Future of Work," Fast Company, January 29, 2018, https://www.fastcompany.com/40522394/screw-emotional-intelligence-heres-the-real-key-to-the-future-of-work.

[23] Walter Isaacson, *The Innovators: How a Group of Hackers, Geniuses, and Geeks Created the Digital Revolution* (New York: Simon and Schuster, 2014), 4.

[24] I outline the decline of the church and the adoption of corporate models of ministry, to little avail, in chapters 1–2 of my dissertation (Len Wilson, "Rising to Heaven: The Ideology of Progress and the Semiotics of Church Growth" (DMin, 2020), 396. https://digitalcommons.georgefox.edu/dmin/396.

[25] Isaacson, *The Innovators,* 80.

[26] Reay Tannahill, *Food in History* (New York: Three Rivers Press, 1995), 53.

CHAPTER 10

[1] Richard Snow, *Disney's Land: Walt Disney and the Invention of the Amusement Park That Changed the World* (New York: Scribner, 2019), 285.

[2] Neal Gabler, *Walt Disney: The Triumph of the American Imagination* (New York: Vintage, 2007), 283.

[3] Gabler, *Walt Disney,* 484.

[4] "Walt's first vision of Disneyland," Walt's Apartment, accessed August 21, 2020, https://www.waltsapartment.com/walts-first-vision-of-disneyland/.

[5] "Dreaming of Disneyland: How Walt arrived at his idea of a theme park," The Walt Disney Family Museum, archived from the original on May 18, 2006. http://disney.go.com/disneyatoz/familymuseum/exhibits/articles/dreamingdisneyland/index.html.

[6] Gabler, *Walt Disney,* 484.

[7] "Tivoli (Copenhagen)," wikipedia.org, accessed August 21, 2020. https://en.wikipedia.org/wiki/Tivoli_(Copenhagen).

[8] "Dreaming of Disneyland."

[9] Richard Snow, "The History of Disneyland: How Walt Disney Created the 'Happiest Place on Earth'," *History Extra,* March 24, 2020, https://www.historyextra.com/period/20th-century/history-disneyland-when-open-how-built-walt-disney/.

[10] Walter Isaacson, *The Innovators: How a Group of Hackers, Geniuses, and Geeks Created the Digital Revolution* (New York: Simon and Schuster, 2014), 82.

[11] Casey Cep, "The Real Nature of Thomas Edison's Genius," *New Yorker,* October 21, 2019, https://www.newyorker.com/magazine/2019/10/28/the-real-nature-of-thomas-edisons-genius.

12 Popular historian and storyteller Erik Larson describes Marconi's eccentric innovation style in *Thunderstruck* (New York: Broadway Books, 2006).

13 George Day, "Is It Real? Can We Win? Is It Worth Doing?: Managing Risk and Reward in an Innovation Portfolio," *Harvard Business Review*, December 2007, https://hbr.org/2007/12/is-it-real-can-we-win-is-it-worth-doing-managing-risk-and-reward-in-an-innovation-portfolio.

14 Day, "Is It Real?"

15 Day, "Is It Real?"

16 For an excellent study of Orville and Wilbur Wright and the dynamics of innovation fueled by Christian faith, see David McCullough, *The Wright Brothers* (New York: Simon and Schuster, 2015).

17 Geoffery Bertram, Robert Feilden, and Sir William Rede Hawthorne, "Sir Frank Whittle, O. M., K. B. E. 1 June 1907–9 August 1996," Biographical Memoirs of Fellows of the Royal Society 44: 435–52. https://doi:10.1098/rsbm.1998.0028.

18 Will McRaney, "Church Planting as a Growth Strategy in the Face of Church Decline," *Journal for Baptist Theology and Ministry* 1, no. 2 (Fall 2003): 69–93.

19 Harrison Price, "Walt's Revolution! By the Numbers," Stanford Graduate School of Business, May 2004, https://web.archive.org/web/20120117120900/http://www.gsb.stanford.edu/news/bmag/sbsm0405/feature_alumnibks_price.shtml.

20 Price, "Walt's Revolution!" notes that this industry drove Disney's entire career.

21 List comes from TripAdvisor.com and Nataly Keomoungkhoun, "What happened to D-FW's theme parks? Curious Texas straps in to investigate," *Dallas Morning News*, August 19, 2020, https://www.dallasnews.com/news/curious-texas/2020/08/19/whats-the-history-of-d-fws-theme-parks-curious-texas-goes-for-a-ride/.

22 I remember being wowed by "Abraham Lincoln" and "Amelia Earhart" waiting on my table at a time-machine themed restaurant in Austin, Texas, in the 1980s. By the late 1990s, "eatertainment" chain theme restaurants were all the rage—or, as Mark Stuertz noted, "all the puke" (Mark Stuertz, "Theme Puke," *Dallas Observer*, January 13, 2000, https://www.dallasobserver.com/restaurants/theme-puke-6396484.

23 Choose Your Own Adventure was a set of books aimed at children raised on immersive storytelling experience of the sort spawned by the interactivity of Disneyland. At the end of each short segment in the book, the reader is invited to choose one of two developments and go to the appropriate page to continue the plot.

24 Paul Graham, "Why Smart People Have Bad Ideas," paulgraham.com, April 2005, http://paulgraham.com/bronze.html.

25 Graham, "Why Smart People Have Bad Ideas."

CHAPTER 11

[1] Mary Wollstonecraft Shelley, *Frankenstein, or the Modern Prometheus* (Revised Edition, 1831), chap. 3, https://en.wikisource.org/wiki/Frankenstein,_or_the_Modern_Prometheus_(Revised_Edition,_1831).

[2] Martin T. Willis, "Edison as Time Traveler: H. G. Wells's Inspiration for His First Scientific Character," *Science Fiction Studies* 26, no. 2 (July 1999): 284–94, https://www.jstor.org/stable/4240787.

[3] Bert Alan Spector, "Carlyle, Freud, and the Great Man Theory More Fully Considered," *Leadership* 12, no. 2 (April 2016): 250–60, https://doi.org/10.1177/1742715015571392.

[4] Leonard Sweet, *So Beautiful: Divine Design for Life and the Church* (Colorado Springs: David C. Cook, 2009), 130-31.

[5] Casey Cep, "The Real Nature of Thomas Edison's Genius," *New Yorker*, October 21, 2019. https://www.newyorker.com/magazine/2019/10/28/the-real-nature-of-thomas-edisons-genius.

[6] Neil Baldwin, *Edison: Inventing the Century* (New York: Hyperion, 1995), 102.

[7] Linda A. Hill, *Collective Genius: The Art and Practice of Leading Innovation* (Boston: Harvard Business Review Press, 2014), 2-3.

[8] Hill, *Collective Genius,* 39.

[9] Stanley McChrystal, *Team of Teams: New Rules of Engagement for a Complex World* (New York: Penguin, 2015), 93.

[10] Elizabeth Gilbert, "Your Elusive Creative Genius," TED talk, February 2009, https://www.ted.com/talks/elizabeth_gilbert_your_elusive_creative_genius.

CHAPTER 12

[1] Lyndsie Bourgon, "A Brief History of Smokey Bear, the Forest Service's Legendary Mascot," *Smithsonian*, July–August 2019, https://www.smithsonianmag.com/history/brief-history-smokey-bear-180972549/.

[2] Bourgon, "A Brief History of Smokey Bear."

[3] Jack Trout, "Peter Drucker on Marketing," *Forbes*, July 3, 2006, https://www.forbes.com/2006/06/30/jack-trout-on-marketing-cx_jt_0703drucker.html.

[4] Nat Ives, "Average Tenure of CMOs Falls Again," *Wall Street Journal*, May 27, 2020, https://www.wsj.com/articles/average-tenure-of-cmos-falls-again-11590573600.

[5] See Leonard Sweet and Michael Adam Beck, *Contextual Intelligence: Unlock the Ancient Secret to Mission on the Front Lines* (HigherLife Development Services, 2021).

[6] Mark Stuertz, "Green Giant," *Dallas Observer*, December 5, 2002. https://www.dallasobserver.com/news/green-giant-6389547.

7 "Borlaug and the University of Minnesota," University of Minnesota, March 10, 2005, https://web.archive.org/web/20050310043736/http://www.coafes.umn.edu/Borlaug_and_the_University_of_Minnesota.html.

8 Stuertz, "Green Giant."

9 Justin Gillis, "Norman Borlaug, Plant Scientist Who Fought Famine, Dies at 95," *New York Times*, September 13, 2009. https://www.nytimes.com/2009/09/14/business/energy-environment/14borlaug.html.

10 Stuertz, "Green Giant."

11 Lester R. Brown, "Nobel Peace Prize: Developer of High-Yield Wheat Receives Award," *Science 170, no. 3957 (Oct. 30, 1970): 518-19.* http://doi.org/10.1126/science.170.3957.518.

12 Stuertz, "Green Giant."

13 Francesca E. Duncan et al., "The Zinc Spark Is an Inorganic Signature of Human Egg Activation," *Scientific Reports* 6, no. 1 (April 26, 2016): 24737, https://doi.org/10.1038/srep24737.

14 Evie Nagy, "How You Know If Your Dumb Idea Will Change the World," *Fast Company*, August 29, 2014, http://www.fastcompany.com/3035032/agendas/how-to-know-if-your-dumb-idea-will-change-the-world.

15 Julie Zhuo, "The Pit of Discomfiture: Or, Where Creatives Fall into Despair," *The Year of the Looking Glass, Medium*, February 18, 2014, https://medium.com/the-year-of-the-looking-glass/the-pit-of-discomfiture-d90ba0eb1974.

16 Robert Cooper, *Successful Production Innovation* (Product Development Institute, 2012).

17 Kaihan Krippendorff, "A Brief History of Innovation . . . And Its Next Evolution," May 9, 2017, https://kaihan.net/brief-history-innovation-next-evolution/.

18 Walter Isaacson, *The Innovators: How a Group of Hackers, Geniuses, and Geeks Created the Digital Revolution* (New York: Simon and Schuster, 2014).

19 Francesca Gino and Gary P. Pisano, "Why Leaders Don't Learn from Success," *Harvard Business Review*, April 2011, https://hbr.org/2011/04/why-leaders-dont-learn-from-success.

20 Steven Krupp, "Busting Leadership Myths in an Uncertain World," Heidrick & Struggles, October 3, 2016, https://www.heidrick.com/Knowledge-Center/Publication/Busting-leadership-myths-in-an-uncertain-world.

21 Leonard Sweet, *So Beautiful: Divine Design for Life and the Church* (Colorado Springs: David C. Cook, 2009), 162.

22 Henri Nouwen, *Bread for the Journey* (New York: HarperCollins, 1997), 11.

CHAPTER 13

1 Paul Collins, *Banvard's Folly: Thirteen Tales of People Who Didn't Change the World* (New York: Picador, 2001), 110.

[2] For example, the apostle Paul exhorts his readers to drink wine instead of water as a balm for stomach ailments (see 1 Timothy 5:23). This verse has served as a counter to the temperance movement.

[3] Sharon Salinger, *Taverns and Drinking in Early America* (Baltimore: Johns Hopkins University Press, 2002), 1.

[4] Salinger, *Taverns and Drinking,* 2.

[5] Collins, *Banvard's Folly,* 110.

[6] Josephine Latham Swayne, ed., *The Story of Concord Told by Concord Writers* (Boston: E. F. Worcester Press, 1906), 160.

[7] Swayne, *The Story of Concord.*

[8] Collins, *Banvard's Folly,* 117.

[9] Collins, *Banvard's Folly,* 121.

[10] William Chazanof, *Welch's Grape Juice: From Corporation to Co-operative* (Syracuse, NY: Syracuse University Press, 1977), 7.

[11] Chazanof, *Welch's Grape Juice,* 8.

[12] Chazanof, *Welch's Grape Juice,* 9.

[13] ChurchPOP, "POPNews: St. Peter's Basilica Renamed 'Tiber Creek Community Church'," September 17, 2014, http://www.churchpop.com/2014/09/17/st-peters-basilica-renamed-tiber-creek-community-church/.

[14] See Kerry Walters and Robin Jarrell, *Blessed Peacemakers: 365 Extraordinary People Who Changed the World* (Portland, OR: Wipf and Stock, 2013).

[15] Scott Cormode, "Innovation that Honors Tradition: The Meaning of Christian Innovation," *Journal of Christian Leadership* 14, no. 2 (Fall 2015), https://arl-jrl.org/wp-content/uploads/2019/01/Cormode-Innovation-that-Honors-Tradition.pdf.

COMING SOON

The End: The Present Age and the Age to Come
by Leonard Sweet and Len Wilson

ARE WE LIVING THROUGH THE BEGINNING OF THE END?

The End has indeed begun. But it is not a special effects explosion. Instead, this book introduces Jesus' most important word in describing the end: the Greek word *telos*. Telos has many meanings. Telos is the melody, harmony, and rhythm of human history. Telos is the presence of God, transcendence in immanence. Telos is the plot, purpose, and completion of the story. The End is the kingdom of God, and the kingdom is here and now.

Getting The End wrong leads to poor decisions with dead-end consequences. Six false endings are playing out in global culture today, which result in tragedy and despair. The common problem is the lie that truth is a proposition. Truth is in fact a person: Jesus. When the kingdom is under Jesus' authority, it is timeless, timely, and the fullness of time. The kingdom is material and real. It gives us hope. It gives us joy. It gives us peace. The kingdom gives us Jubilee.

A lot has been written about the kingdom of God, but nothing like this. If you want to know what happens in The End, and how telos helps us live in God's kingdom and in the stream of the Spirit, read what may be the most important book of our time.

Watch salishsea.press or inviteresources.com for updates.